The Capital Market in China:
A 60-Year Review

The Capital Market in China: A 60-Year Review

Volume 1

Cao Erjie

Enrich Professional Publishing

Singapore • Hong Kong • Beijing • Honolulu

Published by

Enrich Professional Publishing (S) Private Limited
16L, Enterprise Road,
Singapore 627660
Website: www.enrichprofessional.com
A Member of Enrich Culture Group Limited

Hong Kong Head Office:
2/F, Rays Industrial Building, 71 Hung To Road, Kwun Tong, Kowloon, Hong Kong, China

China Office:
Rm 309, Building A, Central Valley, 16 Hai Dian Zhong Jie, Haidian District, Beijing, China

United States Office:
PO Box 30812, Honolulu, HI 96820, USA

Translated by Barbara Cao

Edited by Barbara Cao and Glenn Griffith

ISBN (Hardback) 978-1-62320-002-2

Enrich Professional Publishing is an independent globally-minded publisher focusing on the economic and financial developments that have revolutionized new China. We aim to serve the needs of advanced degree students, researchers, and business professionals who are looking for authoritative, accurate, and engaging information on China.

Printed in Hong Kong with woodfree paper from Japan

Contents

Preface

Despite the facts that there was a 40-year period when China avoided the word "capital," and despite the fact that the U.S. subprime mortgage crisis has evolved into a global financial tsunami, I still choose to name the book "Capital is A Good Thing" [This is the translation of the original Chinese book title.—Ed.], and it will inevitably cause some dispute. In my view, I am judging the contribution of capital to the world and the innovation process of the capital formation mechanism. Although the capital form repeatedly brings disaster to the world, as Marx and Engel said early in the *Communist Manifesto* it was the "bourgeoisie, during its rule of scarcely 100 years, [which] has created more massive and more colossal productive forces than have all preceding generations together." As they further explained: "The inexhaustible productive powers of modern industry" is "the first condition of the emancipation of Labour." A series of questions need to be asked: How is capital formed? How should we look at the efficiency and the expansion of capital? How should we understand capital operation and capital culture? How should we perceive the ratio between investment and consumption? How would we speed up financial reform and direct excessive capital to the capital market? How could we view the global financial crisis? How would we gather financial strength and actively cope with financial crisis and superpower games in the financial area? How would we recognize, be alert to, and prevent a variety of fears towards capitalism? How should the revolutionary party turn workers into men of property? How would we shape a good mechanism which could promote the innovation of the capital formation mechanism and the sustained expansion of capital (namely, capitalization)? and many other similar questions.

This book was inspired by an article on core capital written by Xia Xiaojun in 2006. Initially, I had just published "To broaden the room for the innovation of capital formation mechanism" in *Financial Times* and *China Construction Bank Post*. But later I deeply felt that the capital formation mechanism is broad in content and one or two articles are not enough to get the idea across. My life experiences made me feel the need to conduct an in-depth discussion and therefore the desire to write a monograph sprouted up. The first draft of this book was finished in 2007 but the content was repeatedly revised up until 2011, so the publication of this book missed the 30th anniversary of China's reform and opening up and the 60th anniversary of the founding of the People's Republic of China. The 60-year socialist construction was a long and bumpy road. In the first 40 years, we gulped down the concept of capital without thought, mentioned the concept in a vague sense, and avoided using the word "capital." In the next 20 years, we suddenly became clear-minded that capital is a good thing. This should be the best commemoration for the 30th anniversary of China's reform and opening up and the 60th anniversary of the founding of the People's Republic of China.

Marx is great. Although Marx opposed capitalism and capital, he devoted his whole life to making thorough research on all aspects of capital and its law of motion and contradictions. At last, he focused on share capital and found that it may be "the transitional forms from the capitalist mode of production to the associated one" and may also be "the most perfected form" which turns into communism.

Later Marxists, especially those who were in power in some countries, lacked the truth-seeking spirit of the founders of Marxism who had the courage to study the capital movements through the capitalist mode of production. Those Marxists held paranoid and arrogant attitudes which were incompatible with the ruling proletariat, displayed condescension, and despised capital for fear of being contaminated by capitalist bacteria. They were against and avoided talking about capital, so in their economic construction there was an absence of capital culture. Consequently, later Marxists possessed neither general knowledge of capital movements nor the wisdom to cope with the problems.

Deng Xiaoping is great. He bravely proposed that "if socialism wants to gain advantages comparable to capitalism, it must boldly absorb and draw upon all achievements of civilization created by human society, absorb and learn from the nations around the world, including the developed capitalist countries, all the advanced mode of operation and management methods that reflect the laws governing the modern socialist production." These words become the beacon lighting up our way to build a socialist society with Chinese characteristics.

In the 100 years after Marx's death, the capitalist mode of production underwent new developments and the capital formation mechanism experienced constant innovation. The rapid development of science and technology since World War II pushed forward the progress of productive forces and enabled capitalism to get away from Lenin's prediction that it was "decadent" and "dying." The rulers of the capitalist countries, especially the leaders of democratic socialist parties peacefully rising to power via parliamentary election, borrowed the socialist country's practice of focusing on staff welfare and the public interest. By doing so, they eased the class contradictions, found a way out of the dilemma of being "decadent" and "dying" and pushed the capitalist economy and finance into a new phase of prosperity. They also invested in human resources during the economic development, and namely increased the spending on the investment in the capacity and quality of humans. It exerts more and more an important influence on economic development and therefore middle- and high-income groups greatly increase in the present society and a huge middle class emerges, which Marx failed to foresee.

To follow a road to socialism with Chinese characteristics, to engage in the socialist market economy, and to build a harmonious society putting human fundamentals first, we must manage capital, promote the innovation of the capital formation mechanism, and respond to the call of the CPC Central Committee of "enlarging the proportion of the middle-income group" in order to open a broader path for the economic construction of the socialist society.

I devoted all my life to financial practice and research. After more than 60 years engaged in investment I now review the experiences and research of investment, either investment, loan, replacement of appropriation by loans, asset depreciation and renovation, finance lease, shareholding reform and listing of a company, capital and bond financing in capital market, enterprise asset restricting, corporate merger and acquisition, bankruptcy and debt-equity swap of an enterprise, or investment funds, asset securitization, financial derivatives market, etc., as the innovations of capital formation under different conditions which become the means of capital expansion. From the experience of investment management practice, I understand the nature of capital expansion, and therefore, I would elaborate on various economic issues encountered since the founding of the new China, from the angle of the capital formation mechanism. Those issues include: 1. During the planned economy period, the vicious circle of "production putting pressure on capital construction, capital construction diverting pressure to the finance department, the finance department placing fiscal pressure on the Central bank, and the bank issuing more money" resulting from the pursuit of a high target of the State Planning Commission, the lateral transfer of collective funds by local governments, the bad practice of "pushing capital construction to increase production, then driving overhaul, and finally raising the total costs" and the misappropriation and abuse of loans by enterprises, and the increase of financial excess by expanding the capital through the "small financing loan" by the local governments; 2. After the reform and opening up policy was implemented, the contract operation of the local departments and enterprises, the "fund-raising boom" and "bond boom" of local governments, foundations and financial institutions run by local governments, counterfeited inter-bank lending and circumventing of credit ceiling, replacement of appropriation by loans, fiscal credit and debt-equity swap, red chip stocks, Zibo Securities Trading Automated Quotations System and Chengdu The Red Temple Market for the exchange of private company shares, etc. Some of those are innovations while others are illegal measures. The review of the 60-year history of capital innovation indicates that there is but one step from innovation to violation and from truth to absurdity. The financial administrative authority should keep a clear mind, size up the situation and make the best use of the circumstances. It should be able to straighten out the productive relations based on the institutional reform, stimulate, protect, and control the incentive of all capital and pave the way for innovation of the capital formation mechanism. It should try its best to transform all the idle social wealth into wealth-producing capital and open up the way for the development of the productive forces of socialism, instead of being something indifferent to the needs of the people or which punishes innovative cadres or is easily thrown off course by a slight setback.

In the last 30 years, the socialist market economy of China continued rapid growth with an annual growth rate of more than 9.7% and only half way to the comprehensive industrialization and urbanization. In the future, the remaining works will definitely drive the sustained high-speed growth of Chinese economy, and I think this process will continue for another two or three decades with the expected average growth rate of 7% to 8%. In the last 30 years, we searched all over the world for capital in order to build a prosperous real economy. In the next 30 years, we will spare no efforts to innovate the capital formation mechanism and not only make the real economy bigger and stronger but also devote ourselves to the development of the capital market and the virtual economy, the financialization of the economy, and the control over economic financialization. We could transfer our huge savings at the right price against the backdrop of the global trade imbalance, but must make sure a better return in the financialization of the economy.

At present, the economic and financial globalizations develop very rapidly and the financial development is far faster than the economic development. In the recent 10 years, especially in the five years prior to the global financial crisis, the global real economy increased at a growth rate of 5%, while the finance at a growth rate of 20% to 30% and financial derivative products at a growth rate of 70% to 80%. The over-issuance of the U.S. dollars by the U. S. monetary authority resulted in the depreciation of the dollar, and low-interest dollars spread all over. It gave rise to global excess liquidity and the rapid surge of financial assets, and the scale of and risks born by the financial market were far larger than the promotion and adjustment functions of the financial market to the real economy. But in the end, the virtual economy must serve the real economy because the real quality of life of mankind is decided by the real economy, that is GDP growth, rather than virtual assets. Our current problem is that the excessive development of financial derivatives and the virtual economy is divorced from the real economy and thus losing the foundation.

The current global financial crisis is an unprecedented serious financial crisis. Soros attributed this most serious financial crisis to the market fundamentalism which believes in the self-balancing of the financial market mechanism. Soros' words are very educational. The practical problem is that the prevention, control and management of financial risks fall behind the expansion of the scale of the virtual economy, and financial supervision and global financial coordination lag far behind the development of the real financial market and the virtual economy. But with the deepening understanding of the objective laws of capital movements, we can finally control and manage capital for the benefit of mankind.

Economic and financial globalizations are both a change and a challenge for a rising power like China and force one to keep up with the pace of the globalizations. In the face of the global economic financialization, the lower speed of our nation's economic financialization will result in us being controlled by others and we may also miss a golden opportunity for development in the global economic adjustment. We must learn to swim by swimming. On the one hand, we should develop the virtual economy and the capital market and accelerate the financialization of the economy in order to integrate with the global economy and finance and also benefit from this process. On the other hand, we should learn how to prevent, control, and manage risks in the financial fluctuations, and make the financial market and virtual economy serve, rather than damage, the real economy. Let the economy and finances serve the purpose of improving the quality of life in China's peaceful rise, especially achieving the prosperity of the people, and commit to the appeal of the Central Committee of the Communist Party of China in "expanding the proportion of middle-income group" to turn the workers into men of property.

Cao Erjie

August 2011

Introduction:
The Value of Capital

What is capital? In general, capital is an accumulation of money, but not all money is capital. According to Marx's definition, only when money functions in production and circulation and brings the added value of surplus value (namely, profits) on the basis of modern production methods, can money truly become capital. Until then, money as capital possesses the use value of producing surplus value (profits). In one word, money can turn into capital only when money is able to produce profits.

Capital Is the Prerequisite for Economic Growth and the Prosperity of the People

Capital, like labor, is a prerequisite of economic growth. The development of the economy in any country cannot be done without capital accumulation. The rise of a superpower especially requires capital. The function of capital in a capitalist society is to exploit surplus value and produce profits while in a socialist society it is to complete the accumulation of surplus labor time. In a developing country where labor resources are abundant, capital becomes even scarcer. Undoubtedly, without labor, the machines purchased by capital are just heaps of metal, whereas without the capital necessary for purchasing machines, labor will have nothing to do. The more underdeveloped a country is, the more excessive the labor resources and the scarcer the capital and, therefore, the country has to tolerate exploitation to introduce capital for economic development.

Even in a capitalist country, views on exploitation should be divided into two. Apart from the exploitation of surplus value, capital serves another important function, that is, to accumulate surplus labor time when the surplus value (profits) is again transformed into capital and starts capital accumulation. So, Marx thought that "the surplus labor time, which, even without the existence of capital, must constantly be performed by society, in order to have at its disposal, so to speak, a fund for development."[1] But under a socialist society with public ownership, capital is purified into a development fund essential for sustaining and expanding the development of social production in order to complete the accumulation of surplus labor time by society. As Engels has put it, accumulation is "the most important progressive function of society."[2]

China has long avoided discussing capital during its socialist construction. The 15th National Party Congress of the Communist Party of China (CPC) in 1997, for the first time, confirmed that socialist enterprises should, taking capital as a link, enlarge the function of capital, and improve the operational efficiency, in order to brush away the misunderstanding over capital caused by socialism. The 16th National Party Congress of the CPC in 2002 proposed that "we should establish the principle that labor, capital, technology, managerial expertise and other production factors participate in the distribution of income in accordance with their respective contributions, thereby improving the system under which distribution according to work is dominant and a variety of modes of distribution coexist."[3] The report explicitly regarded "capital" as a kind of production factor which participates in the distribution of income in accordance with its contribution. The Third Plenary Session of the 16th Central Committee of the CPC in 2003 stated that we should "vigorously develop the mixed ownership economy participated in by state-owned capital, collective capital, and nonpublic capital, etc., realize the diversity of investors and make the joint-stock system the principal form of the realization of public ownership." The 17th National Party Congress of the CPC in 2007 made it clear that "we will adhere to and improve the system whereby distribution according to work remains the predominant mode and coexists with various other modes. We will improve the distribution system to allow factors of production such as labor, capital, technology and managerial expertise to have a rightful share according to their respective contribution." A higher requirement made by the 17th National Party Congress was that "conditions will be created to enable more citizens to have property income."[4]

It should be said that capital is the prerequisite for a society to feed its population and achieve prosperity. So, today, 60 years after the reform and opening up and 30 years after the founding of new China, we must justifiably declare that capital is good, and economic growth and the prosperity of people require the constant expansion of capital. Here, what matters is not how much capital has been attracted but a good mechanism of capitalization which promotes the innovation of the capital formation mechanism and the continuous expansion of capital.

It is useless to say that as society employs capital to develop its economy, there is a need to prevent the negative effects of capital. First, restrictions on capital should be made in the form of laws to prevent the distribution of income between labor and capital from overly tilting towards capital, especially to prevent the collusion between power and money which would result in a tense relationship between labor and capital and profits eroding wages. Society should place people first, earnestly safeguard the interests of the vast majority of workers, and construct harmonious labor relations. Second, sufficient attention should be paid to macro-control and policy guidance while we emphasize the fundamental role of the market in allocating resources in order to prevent blind expansion of capital in the market competition and the waste caused by blind investment and the rash launching of new projects.

Capital Operation: Pursuit of Efficiency and Expansion

Marx stated that "[Production] expands annually for two reasons; first because the capital invested in production is continually growing; second because the capital is constantly used more productively."[5]

Profit-seeking is the nature of capital. Enterprises constantly demand technological innovation, management improvement, amelioration of labor relations, shorter production cycle, less time-to-market, and faster capital turnover. In a capital market, there is no lack of enterprises undertaking capital operation and optimizing resource allocation in order to use capital more sufficiently and efficiently.

In this regard, Marx's *Das Kapital* paid attention to the following aspects:

First, how did capitalists transfer depreciation funds for compensation into accumulation funds?

Second, capitalists managed to expand the control over their own capital to others' capital by way of credit.

Third, banks turned deposits into interest-bearing capital, so that all the spare capital could fully function. Banks "act as middlemen between the actual lender and the borrower of money-capital...The other side of the credit system — the management of interest-bearing capital, or money-capital, develops alongside this money-dealing as a special function of the money-dealers...Borrowing and lending money becomes their particular business."[6]

Fourthly, with the scientific and technological progress and the development of the socialization of production, industrial enterprises need to increase the size of minimum capital based on the requirements of technological economy and economies of scale. Joint-stock investment, beyond the personal financial power of a capitalist, adapts to the socialization of production by means of centralizing social capital. It gives "an impetus never before suspected to the concentration of capital."[7]

Fifthly, the rise of the capital market induced the emergence of stocks, bonds, bank bills, treasury notes, and other valuable instruments, which Marx termed as "fictitious capital." Marx also named the formation of fictitious capital as "capitalization" and believed that the value of fictitious capital was a derivative of the expected yield of real capital in the future.

Over a century after the death of Marx, the capital market in developed countries has undergone substantial progress. The expansion of enterprises impels industrial capital to go beyond its own accumulation and undertake capital and business expansion. Therefore, when capital increases, IPOs, and mergers and acquisitions frequently occurred, capitalization brings about capital operation in the capital market. Capital operation is a kind of economic behavior which relates to market financing and the capital expansion of enterprises. That is to say, only when an enterprise turns its asset with expected returns into securities and undertakes certain financing activities (i.e., cashing those bills and other securities via financial instruments) in the capital market, could the enterprise make use of social capital or capitalization to expand its business and capital as well as to realize annexation. This is what we call capital operation. It is true that capital operation could not turn a stone into gold, but it indeed develops the asset with expected returns into capital.

During the economic reform of China, there is a desperate shortage of capital. Until the opening of the capital market in the 1990s, parts of the assets with future returns were able to be, via financial instruments and by means of certificates of title or pledge, capitalized and converted into cash before finally being developed into capital. As a result, in the past 20 years, capital in China grew larger and larger and brought about greater economic growth.

The Construction of Capital Culture Has a Long Way To Go

Capital movement involves a wide range of aspects, including: Production, circulation, capital compensation, fund raising, reshuffling of an enterprise, industrial integration, bankruptcy reorganization, and asset securitization. There is an inherent law underlying capital movement and development, which composes a rich culture of capital. If China wants to develop its economy, it has to learn how to deal with capital, and must construct capital culture in its market, legal system, regulation, and corporate governance. The essence of capital culture building is to establish the idea of protecting investment and investors. It is not only an institutional arrangement and code of conduct, but a social consciousness, moral guideline, or social responsibility. It would form a habit of mutual trust, understanding, and agreement. After repeatedly being implemented in the market behaviors of the whole society, it will become a conventional and unconscious spirit. The capital culture building has to solve the following questions.

First, the organizational form of capital. No matter if it is a limited partnership or joint-stock, and at an advanced or lower level, the key is to emphasize limited liability, and coordinate managers and investors to fully motivate both parties.

In the past, we encouraged the joint-stock system and believed that the limited partnership was a low-level organization form of property, less standard than the shareholding system. Its legal status was not admitted until much later. Limited partnership finds its origins in the commenda agreements in the 16 century. At that time, sailing the globe could lead to fortunes, but to build a fleet required an enormous sum of money and churches were forbidden from lending money for seafaring. Against such a backdrop, commenda agreements bypassed the ban and formed a limited partnership by letting everybody contribute what they had. Following this practice, many famous funds and investment banks in the U.S. implemented limited partnerships. The reason was simple: This can fully motivate administrators. Administrators devote their wisdom and talent and become decision-makers and operators, shouldering unlimited liability, while investors make use of administrators' wits to make a profit and are liable only to the extent of their investments.

Later, the joint-stock system simplified capital, rights, and liabilities in shares. The investors purchase the shares just like they buy commodities, and their liabilities are limited to their invested capital, called limited liability. On the other hand, the actually functioning administrators are transformed into "a mere manager, administrator of other people's capital."[8] This point is very important because it composes the very basic idea of capital culture to protect investment and the investor.

Second, capital of an enterprise should discriminate between self-owned capital and borrowed capital, and handle correctly the relationship between debt and equity.

This implies a capital culture as well as a culture of credit. The logic is simple: You have to own equity before others would lend you some money. For one thing, you must respect equity and reward shareholders with returns on investment. For another, you must honor credit and repay debt with interests. The lesson from state-owned enterprises which sank into excessive debts in the middle of the 1990s due to the transformation of fiscal grants in capital construction into repayable loans should be borne in mind. Therefore, an enterprise cannot run without its own capital or reverse the relationship between debt and equity.

Third, the value of a company is by no means its asset but a future profit-generating ability of the asset.

It is often said that the capital market is where assets can be exchanged for capital. However, this view is incorrect. Because the capital initially invested in an enterprise, including self-own capital and borrowed capital, has been solidified in fixed assets such as plant and machinery equipment, and no one can directly take the houses, machinery equipment, and other fixed assets to capital market for financing, let alone bargain over them. Furthermore, only the asset able to create future profits can be traded for capital in the capital market. The asset without future profitability cannot be exchanged for capital in the market. Last but not the least, even though the asset can make profits in the future, there is still a development process before it becomes tradable in the market. The asset should be restructured to transform the company into a joint-stock one before the company is qualified for listing. Only when the asset turns into exchangeable and possessable stocks with clear property rights (i.e., certificate of title), would the asset be eligible for circulating and be exchanged with capital in the market.

Fourth, emphasis should be laid on capital returns and recovery.

Capital is the operation fund for building a company and forming an all-the-year-round stable turnover. It only needs to flow back to the company in the form of depreciation during a long-term operation of commodity reproduction within the duration of the company, instead of repaying the money to its investors. But during the capital operation and turnover, value-addedness or return should be generated. The return that investors demand is one higher than the loan interest, which is one of the important parts of capital culture. The underlying reason is that capital is a scarce resource, more costly than bank loans. Loans have a repayment agreement and are generally able to be paid back, while capital invested in enterprises has to run the risk of receiving no repayment due to market competition and business failure.

But, the operations of equity funds and venture capital have paid particular attention to capital recovery. Because equity funds realize the reproduction of equity investment through purchasing shares in the case of a company starting up or restructuring its asset, and then selling the successfully founded or reorganized enterprise. This kind of equity funds, from injecting capital for a business start-up or reorganization to recoup the investment after the company is listed, operates the capital all along by ruling out risks amid high risks and enhancing the capital efficiency; therefore to open the growth enterprise market (GEM) is very important. This will create a road for venture capital to be gotten back through the company going public. For quite a long period of time, we have blamed commercial banks for sending out loans to high-tech enterprises and small- and medium-sized enterprises

(SME), but made no efforts to set up GEM. You can lead a horse to water, but you cannot make it drink. This is a result of the lack of capital culture.

Fifth, to realize "money begets money" by enterprise investment, we should make allowances for opportunity cost, marginal benefit, and sunk cost.

The idea of "money begets money" is inherent in the concept of capital culture. During the first 30 years of new China, school education, including class struggle in its curriculum, made an inappropriate connection between compound interest and usury by the landlord Huang Shiren in the story of *The White Haired Girl* in the textbooks. For a long time, schools did not clarify compound interest, and banks did not calculate compound interest, so citizens lacked financial awareness and equated the idea of "money begets money" with exploitation. But enterprise investments under the market economy meant to transfer currency into capital, and equip the currency with profit-making ability. Therefore, investment decision-makers must commit to realize "money begetting money" and balance among opportunity cost, marginal benefit, and sunk cost.

1. We should take into consideration opportunity cost, namely, when you decide to pursue a certain investment, you have to forgo the cost of an alternative. The Chinese philosopher Mencius once said: "Fish is what I desire, and so are bear's paws. If I cannot have them both, I would choose the latter and forsake the former." Mencius was so shrewd that he would rather forsake little fish than give up a hard-to-get bear's paw. This reflects the Chinese ancient idea towards opportunity cost.

There is a Chinese proverb that says "pick up a sesame seed only to lose a watermelon." In this case, the discarded watermelon is the opportunity cost of getting sesame. But Chinese do not use the term "opportunity cost," they have formed a concept of losses and gains instead. This concept believes that the results of each choice cannot go beyond the three possibilities: Gains outweigh losses; gains and losses balance each other; losses outweigh gains. This concept is the core of opportunity cost and the common practice for Chinese people to weigh pros and cons in their daily life. When people play Chinese chess, this loss-and-gain-concept is even indispensable. The strategies of "better lose the saddle than the horse" and "give up a rook to save the king" are the plainest reflection of the idea of opportunity cost which helps one to avoid being pennywise and pound foolish.

2. We should be concerned with marginal benefits. In industrial production, it is wiser to increase production by improving existing production capability and overcoming the bottlenecks in production than building new factories. In transportation service, to broaden a narrow bridge can help expand

transportation capacity. In enterprise decision-making, applying the same strategy used above, we can achieve marginal productivity by investing in scarce resources; we can expand a company's strength and greatly enhance its competitiveness by merging another enterprise rather than establishing a new one.

The planned economy implemented for a long time in China was accustomed to apply "base-plus-growth" method9 to plan an equal-proportion growth of investment. The government, therefore, cannot concentrate capital on broadening narrow bridges and overcoming bottlenecks but spread the money in a large range of long-term projects. In this way, we not only lost the largest marginal benefit which could be otherwise attainable, but also waste time and money in ineffective sectors and projects. According to the statistics of the ministry of electric power in 1986, the 15-year power shortage resulted in a loss of 1,500 billion in national income. This marginal benefit was able to be obtained with just a little investment in electric power and that is a pathetic lesson of forsaking marginal benefit.

3. Sunk cost should be taken into consideration. There are no more than two ways, and one is to save the paid sunk cost. For example, if we convert the uses of stopped and suspended projects of an enterprise, additional capital of just 20%–30% to the total could revitalize the paid sunk cost of 70%–80% and thus we would maximize marginal benefit of the additional investment. The other way is to make use of others' sunk cost, including purchasing the discontinued and uncompleted projects of other companies and even acquiring and integrating a whole enterprise.

In short, during the transformation to the socialist market economy, capital culture is indispensable. There is a long way to go to construct capital culture, learn to respect the rights and interests of investors and sponsors, and place the protection of investors above all else.

Investment Scale Should Adapt to National Power

Capital has its value and we must determine investment scale of each period based on the changes of national power in different stages.

In the early socialist economic construction of China, "to tighten our belts for construction" incurred the 30-year painful experience of accumulation (investment) crowding out consumption. The problem lies in that capital injection, namely investment, will experience a long process which has only input but no output. Therefore, Chen Yun suggested repeatedly that investment scale should comply with national power and the relationship between consumption and construction should be properly dealt with.[10] After the reform and opening up in 1978, a series of measures, such as suppressing accumulation but accelerating consumption during the sixth five-year plan, improving the economic environment and rectifying the economic order in 1989, and financial macro-control in 1993, devoted to restraining investment and making the investment scale adapt to the national power during the period of inadequate food and clothing.

But it did not suggest that capital (investment) is not good and the control over investment scale, especially over investment percentage, should be made a constant policy. Another experience we got after the reform and opening up is that due to the construction during the three five-year plans (sixth, seventh, and eighth), national power of China has substantially increased. China entered into a period of building a moderately prosperous society, urban residents overcame the problem of inadequate food and clothing, and middle- and high-income people which grew in number had the wish and capability to upgrade their consumption structure. In 1995, when drafting the ninth five-year plan, the government still demanded to limit investment rate within 30%, following the policies implemented during the period of inadequate food and clothing. The inappropriate investment control between 1996 and 1997, combined with the financial crisis in Southeast Asia, led to deflation, shrinking investment, and stagnant consumption in 1998. In 1998–2004, the Chinese government had to implement a proactive fiscal policy and a prudent monetary policy. On the one hand, national bonds were issued to raise money for additional investment in infrastructure and to boost investment; on the other hand, consumer credit, together with consumption loans, housing mortgage loans, car mortgage loans, etc., was started to stimulate domestic demand. After the seven-year expansion of investment and stimulation of consumption demand, the economy finally picked up in 2004 and walked out of deflation. At last, the average rate of investment during the ninth five-year plan was 35.7%, between 2001 and 2004 the rate reached up even to 36%–40%, and between 1998 and 2004, the rate was 39.2%. It was the growth of investment that boosted the growth of the economy. This indicated that when national power increased substantially, in order to realize the upgrade of resident consumption structure, the investment scale during the stage of building a moderately prosperous society should fit the increased national power. This is what we have not gotten accustomed to. Whether it can fit or not is still a sign for whether an economy can develop and become stable. The key is to have enough investment to satisfy the upgrade of consumption structure and foster the consumption capability of future added urban citizens, rather than to reduce investment to encourage consumption since China has passed the period of fighting for adequate food and clothing. Now, the mistake of construction crowding out consumption no longer exists, but if investment fails to satisfy the upgrade of consumption structure and provide consumption facilities or ignore developing future spending power, it will result in a greater mistake.

The growth in national power during the building of a moderately prosperous society was because the policy of "encouraging some people to become rich first" has raised the income of urban residents. The increase of middle- and high-income population requires more investment for the upgrading of consumption structure of citizens. At this point, it is related to not only how to accelerate the investments in public utilities, education, employment, social security and medical and health services, but also how to speed up the institutional reform of housing, health care and education. The employees' expenditure on health care, education, and housing, which was, based on a low standard, invested by enterprises and public institutions or through collective consumption, should be diverted to private investment, personal investment (such as housing) or personal consumption. In this way, various demands and enthusiasms of the originally restrained personal investment and consumption could be released. But, neither should they be overemphasized at the expense of the other. At present, China's central government emphasizes putting people first and improving people's livelihoods, which requires accelerating affordable housing projects, and increases the construction of low-rent housing, in order to meet the housing consumption requirement of the low-income population. The government also demands to strengthen the construction of public service system, including education, employment, social security, and health care. It is precisely for the purpose of upgrading citizen's consumption that investment should be properly increased to enlarge the consumption in the above-mentioned aspects.

Housing construction is the most useful livelihood project to revitalize consumption, and it occupies a major part in upgrading citizen's consumption. After reform and opening up, the total floor space of residential buildings in urban areas increased from 2 billion square meters to 11.9 billion between 1990 and 2007. Among them, there was a large number of residential housing projects which were built as a response to the target of "getting out of the housing plight" before the housing reform from the early 1980s to 1998, in addition to the housing built in the cities of the old industrial base areas in the 1950s and the makeshift houses erected during the ten-year Cultural Revolution. This large amount of residential housing is the main body of the present housing reform. According to the estimation of Chen Huai (2009), it equaled approximately half of the existing housing resources. However, buildings constructed at that time can no longer meet the needs of people to improve their living conditions, in terms of either housing layout or dwelling size. These residences have to be rebuilt in the next 15 to 20 years. The statement that "among the residents who have purchased a public house, 80% want to buy a new house to expand their living space" (Zheng Xinli, 2003) is true. To upgrade housing consumption demands not only enabling low-income workers to be able to live in low-rent housing and replace their "pigeonholes" of welfare housing with larger dwellings, but also ameliorating the living conditions of the middle-income population. From 2008 to the end of 2010, the government decided to carry out affordable housing projects and construct or transform 13 million sets of affordable houses or shanty towns, with the accumulative investment over RMB1,300 billion. It can be expected that there will be a lot of differences in the housing market in China.

Maintain Relatively High Investment Rate, Speed Up Urbanization

Since 2006, the investment rate has surpassed 50% for five years in a row and the rate even exceeded 67% between 2009 and 2010. Some worried and pointed out that the investment-consumption ratio in developed countries is 2:8 and in developing countries is 3:7, but in China the consumption rate is less than 60%. With only a simple contrast, they came to the conclusion that investment in China is excessive and the investment rate is too high. Actually it is a groundless fear. It is true that the high investment rate of China in the recent years relates not only to the upgrade of consumption structure, but also a special factor that China's government has issued a "RMB4 trillion stimulus package" to cope with the financial crisis. Nonetheless, a more rudimentary cause is that during the 60-year construction of China, there has been a huge gap between urbanization and industrialization under the condition of a dual economy. The massive supply resulting from over-industrialization cannot be consumed because urbanization lags behind and is unable to create corresponding effective consumption. A lot of people blame China for its high investment rate, and especially in the recent five years the rate surpassed 50% with two years even over 67%. This trend is really difficult to sustain. The question is how to accelerate consumption, adjust the relationship between investment and consumption, and change the situation of the excessively high investment rate. To rely on the little income of Chinese farmers and migrant workers to change the mode of economic growth and revitalize consumption is just empty talk. The top priority is to speed up urbanization and realize the dual expansion of city in land and population. This requires accelerating the construction of urban infrastructure as well as investing more in residential communities, public facilities, medical services, and education services, in order to direct the surplus rural labor of several hundred million people to cities and towns to participate in the non-agricultural economy, and at the same time satisfy their consumption needs in employment and living. In a word, we should count on urbanization to foster future consumption capability.

Firstly, to speed up urbanization. For one thing, several hundred million surplus laborers should be relocated to cities and towns. In 1978–2008, the proportion of the urban population of China was raised from 17.92% to 45.7% with only 607 million in the urban population including migrant workers. It is estimated that by 2020, assuming that the total population is 1.5 billion, people living in cities and towns will reach 850 million, taking up only 55% of the total. At present, there are 480 million people in the labor force in rural areas but the actual need for agricultural production is just 170 million. That is to say, 300 million surplus laborers demand another 300 million employment opportunities. Moreover, those laborers should be transformed into the urban population having registered urban residences unlike the migrant workers who cannot settle down in cities, and thus remain unable to truly become a spending force of the city.

For another, cities and towns would be expanded. In 1990–2007, China's urban built-up area grew from 12,900 square kilometers to 35,500, with an expansion rate of 175% over more than 10 years. The key to the urban expansion is to transform rural house sites into lands for urbanization through the process of creating towns in country areas. According to the calculation of Wang Jian (2009), China now has 250 million family households and supposing each occupies 200 square meters, the total rural house sites amount to 75 million *mu* (50 billion square meters). If the urbanization rate is 85%, maintaining 50 million rural households is enough and 80% of rural house sites would be available for the purpose of urbanization, nearly 60 million *mu* (40 billion square meters). This figure is more than two times as large as the areas of farmland that the government plans to occupy for construction in the next 10 years (namely, 23 million *mu* ≈ 15 billion square meters). In conclusion, investment in accelerating urbanization should go first, before rural labor surplus will settle down in cities and towns, turn into newly added urban dwellers of non-agricultural economy, and finally become a source of urban consumption.

Secondly, we should rely on building a new socialist countryside and undertake scale operation of agriculture in order to increase peasants' incomes. At present, there is a policy mismatch. The rural-urban separated household registration system gave rise to the situation that 160 million farmers-turned-workers worked in cities but cannot be registered there. Migrant workers lived in the poor areas of cities while saving money to build in their home villages new houses which they have no chance of residing in. Moreover, the migrant workers still occupied an uncultivated farmland which created a dilapidated village and caused desolation and the loss of arable land. Aging rural population, farmers engaged in sideline business, an increasing number of left-behind children together with the above mentioned problems restrict the scale development of agriculture, enlarge the urban-rural income gap and cause frequent occurrence of mass disturbances. It has been reported by *Ban Yue Tan* (半月談, "Semi-month Talk") in February 2011 that by the end of 2010, the total amount of arable land in China was less than 1.826 billion *mu* (1.217 trillion square meters), close to the warning line of 1.80 billion *mu* (1.20 trillion square meters). More importantly, the idle rural land has surpassed 100 million *mu* (66.67 trillion square meters), 1/18 of total national arable land. Therefore, to realize full reform of the century-long small-farm economy and build a strong professional team capable of scientific farming and intensive cultivation, the Chinese government has to allow more flexibility over rural land, free farmers from the traditional household registration system and land system, and transfer surplus rural labor to work in cities. This should be a premise for developing a new socialist countryside, implementing scale operation of agriculture, and substantially improving farmers' income.

Thirdly, China must push forward urbanization and reform the urban industry. Due to the fact that village and township enterprises (VTEs) which occupy a big share in China's GDP and possess an added value of 28.5%, are dispersedly distributed, urban industry must be remolded to facilitate centralized treatment of industrial pollutants and create a favorable external market environment. It will in turn reduce the costs in labor flow, technology and information acquisition, storage and legal service. Additionally, centralized urban industry could benefit more from efficient financial service, compared to those dispersed in rural areas.

The heavy and chemical industrialization and urbanization are in the ascendant and China's industrial structure requires upgrading. At the same time, transnational capital of manufacturing business of developed countries flows toward China, so there is a strong demand for investment. The twelfth five-year plan of China proposed that we should revitalize the old industrial base of the northeast, develop the west, encourage the rise of the central, form metropolitan areas, and drive the growth of the regional economy. These demand the Chinese government to reshape the agglomeration layout of regional economy, speed up the construction of domestic transport infrastructure, and lead the transfer of parts of industrial enterprises to central and western regions. Besides, it is imperative to solve the problems of environmental pollution, climate change, and water crisis occurring in many cities. By doing so, investment will definitely increase. In general, only with rapid urbanization, can we create huge long-term demand in China. If in the next 20 years, we can lift the urbanization rate to 75% and have 400 million members of the urban population, there will be a need to increase housing and public facilities for city expansion, as well as to build a modern urban system capable of supporting several hundred million more people in the population. It is sure that there will be a huge demand for investment. After all, it is only possible to completely crack the problems of the growing income gap, three rural issues, and poverty, when the government can successfully transfer rural labor and population to cities, realize urban expansion, and increase employment.

It has long been a controversial topic as to whether the investment rate in China is high or not. Judging from China's actual situation, what matters is not the total volume of investment but its efficiency and quality. In my opinion, investments in high-polluting and high-energy consuming industries, politics-driven investment by which the local government constructs industrial parks in a blind way, and investments in vanity projects should be largely cut down. On the other hand, investments of objective demands should be supported as long as they are beneficial to improving people's livelihoods, upgrading the consumption structure, increasing job opportunities and future consumption capability, and building a harmonious society. In a nutshell, in order to enhance the real spending power of farmers, high investment rate is out of absolute necessity. Large investment at least would result in a great number of fixed assets, which is better than the export business to the U.S. in exchange for treasury bonds with a risk of depreciation.

Now, it is important to note that an insufficient source of capital for local government and excessive debts would incur bank risk and debt crisis. In addition, several ineffective investment projects could also bring about low production efficiency of an enterprise and thus cause systematic crisis of debt. The risk of local financing platform loans in 2010 triggered hot discussion among many parties, and consequently, the China Banking Regulatory Commission (CBRC) even got involved to raise risk weight in calculating capital adequacy ratio as a necessary preventative measure. In consideration of China's present industrialization and urbanization, it is of a great possibility that the high investment rate (40%–50%) will last for the next 20 years. The government must dedicate itself to reforming the economic development mode, revolutionizing the present government-led investment, and allowing private capital to play its role. At the same time, investment scale should be kept within controls to prevent impairing domestic demand and fairness; however, to resolve the risks of high investment rate will ultimately depend on the increase of investment efficiency.

It needs to be specially mentioned that to determine whether an investment is high or not, not only investment rate but also return on capital should be taken into consideration. For a long period of time, we tended to believe that the return on capital of China's enterprises is low and the investment is large in size, high in speed but low in efficiency. In 2006, Song Guoqing from Peking University calculated that since 1999, the return on investment of China was on the rise, from 6% of 1999 to over 18% of 2006, showing an unprecedented development trend. This discovery was called by Zhao Xiao[11] as a "subversive understanding." Meanwhile, Qian Yingyi, Bai Chongen, and Xie Changtai published an article "The Return to Capital in China" in the *Brookings Papers on Economic Activity* in 2006.[12] It calculated the return on capital in China based on two calibers of fixed capital formation and got the results of 18%–27% and 8%–12%, respectively. Using the latter caliber, they found that the return to capital in developed countries between 2000 and 2003 was between 7% and 13%, which indicated that the rate in China is no less than those developed countries. Obviously, the high rate of return on investment is a reason for global capital to steadily flow towards China.

Maintain Reasonable Social Financing Scale and Direct Surplus Capital to Capital Markets

One of the outstanding problems faced by China's economy is excessive money supply, also known as "excess liquidity," in the financial community.

The root of the problem is that the capital market has developed slowly in China. For a long time, following the mindset of a planned economy, the financial authority of China has placed indirect finance at a leading position for more than 20 years. The financial authority preferred to let banks dominate everything but only assessed their annual credit growth target, for fear that enormous sums of money would flow out of the controllable pond of banks and jump into the unruly ocean of direct finance. Consequently, it resulted in a deformed pattern of "excessive large banks but an extremely small capital market." To solve the excess liquidity, the central bank of China proposed enlarging the size of direct financing in 1996 and suggested for many years to strictly control the monetary and credit aggregates. In fact, however, lots of loans were issued by banks every year. The key lies in the incomplete capital market which is unable to increase the proportion of direct finance. Between 2001 and 2008, bank loans have always accounted for around 80% of the total financing of the non-financial sector while stocks and corporate bonds only took 20% (19.5% in 2009). The substantial growth in the proportion of stocks and corporate bonds, as reported by the financial media in 2010, is just a possibility of breaking through 30%.

In recent years, direct finance has undergone radical reforms. The SMEs Market and GEM were opened in Shenzhen successively and the futures market and stock index futures were launched as well. In addition, the government initiated in succession the pilot projects of asset-backed security based on bank loans, and margin trading and short selling of brokerages. Especially in 2005 and 2008, the central bank of China started to issue short-term financing bonds and medium-term notes, respectively, and in 2007 corporate bonds of listed companies were permitted to be traded. Meanwhile, in the financial market, financial innovation activities were increasingly active and there was a tendency to circumvent the control over credit scale. The innovation of financing tools, such as entrusted loans, off-balance sheet (OBS) transactions, and structured products accelerated the financial disintermediation in China. The data of China's central bank showed that in 2010 the entrusted loans amounted to RMB1.13 trillion and the banker's acceptances which was an OBS transaction containing bank's credit rose up to RMB2.33 trillion, up 60% and 400%, respectively, compared to 2009. There were still other financing channels, mainly including loans from small-loan companies or loan companies and industry fund investment. In 2010, new loans of small loan companies alone were recorded at RMB102.2 billion, an increase of 33.4% over the previous year, equivalent to the annual growth of a small- and medium-sized joint-stock commercial bank. But there was a deficiency in the statistics of newly-emerged financial institutions and tools released by the central bank. The statistical framework of the central bank gave insufficient attention to the financial tools which recently showed up, such as financial derivatives of OBS business, structured products, and contingent assets and liabilities, but just stuck to the balance sheet of commercial banks (Zhang Tao, 2010). The New problem is that commercial banks generally bypass the credit ceiling through OBS transactions, and thus to simply evaluate new RMB-dominated loans by the central bank can hardly reflect the aggregate financing of the real economy.

In the face of financial disintermediation, the working conference of China's central bank in 2011 for the first time gave up proposing a new target of annual credit growth; instead it suggested maintaining a reasonable social financial scale, which was immediately confirmed by the State Council in January 18 of the same year. Later in the *Report on the Work of Government* (March 2011), the government of China clearly stated that to "keep financing from all sources at an appropriate level" and "increase the proportion of direct financing." In February 2011, a dramatic change was that after collecting various data, the central bank disclosed a ratio between bank credit and non-credit financing in 2010, which had already reached 56:44. Sheng Songcheng, director of the Financial Survey and Statistics Department of the People's Bank of China, wrote an article in the website of China's central bank and said that from 2002 to 2010, the total financing volume increased from RMB2 trillion to RMB14.27 trillion with an annual average growth of 27.8%, 9.4% higher than that of total RMB loans. The aggregate social financing in 2010 occupied 35.9% of total GDP, increasing 12.9 percentage points compared to 2002. According to statistics, among the RMB14.27 trillion of total social financing in 2010, new bank loans took up RMB7.95 trillion, decreasing to 56% from 92% in 2002, while the proportion of direct financing rose markedly with corporate bonds and stocks increasing 6.8 and 1.1 percentage points, respectively.[13] This implies that the monetary policies of China have suddenly shifted its focus from new bank loans to social financing scale. According to the definition by the central bank, total social financing is a sum of total loans in RMB and foreign currency, entrusted loans, trust loans, banker's acceptances, corporate bonds, non-financial corporate bonds, compensation from insurance companies, investment property of insurance companies, among others.

Undeniably, China is slow in expanding direct financing in some ways. For example, the asset-backed securities account for over 20% of the bond market in Western countries with a mature market. In contrast, China only started several pilot projects on asset-backed securities which have worked intermittently. From 2005 to 2008, there were only 19 records of credit asset-backed securities issued in the inter-bank bond market, with a total amount on offer being RMB66.8 billion, disproportionate to RMB19 trillion bond market of the same period.

The financial reforms should be targeted at speeding up the development of capital market, expanding direct financing, diverting bank deposits and loans to the capital market, and broadening the environment and space for capital formation mechanism. I strongly agree with the notion of "keep[ing] financing from all sources at an appropriate level" and it is better to have a quantitative target. In 2006, I proposed that we could conceive that within 10 to 15 years, under the government's great efforts, loans of the bill market will equal bank loans, investment funds will correspond to personal savings of bank, bond market will have a same size with the stock market, and asset-backed securities will take up 1/4 or 1/3 of the total bonds; at the same time, there will be considerable financial derivatives to ensure a favorable hedging mechanism of the capital market. This may be an ideal financial pattern beneficial to building diversified capital formation mechanisms.

The development of various types of financial markets cannot be accomplished overnight, and the government needs to build up a set of fair and impartial institutional structures accommodating the securitization market as well as a corresponding talent pool while accumulating experiences and lessons. The capital market should be expanded, the financial market should be developed in a comprehensive way and equipped with abundant financial products, and larger liquidity demand should be created. Only in this way, can the money of banks be directed to the capital market and the problem of excess liquidity be solved in a wider scope through developing a virtual economy.

To Understand the Global Financial Crisis through Economic Globalization

Capital is good, the undesirable expansion of capital during the rapid development of the capitalist economy, however, brings about crises and disasters. The Sterling Crisis in 1990s, the Mexican Pesos crisis, financial crisis in Southeast Asia, the decade-long recession of Japan, and especially the global financial tsunami evoked by the Wall Street collapse since 2007 are the best proofs.

To examine the global financial crisis triggered by the U.S. subprime mortgage crisis requires a view of economic globalization.

First of all, this crisis was a result of an inappropriate response to domestic and international economic and trade imbalance by the U.S.

In economic globalization, the U.S. constantly cut down the production of material products by first transferring capital to the financial market and then relocating the manufacturing industry to developing countries. In this way, not only the surplus agricultural population in the developing countries got employed, but also a large number of high-quality products manufactured in those countries were exported at a lower price as substitutes for the U.S. products. As a result, there was a long-term trade surplus and an accumulation of considerable foreign exchange funds in those manufacturing countries. A fragile international economic structure was thus formed: The developed countries featured a lower savings rate but a higher consumption rate while the emerging market countries featured a higher savings rate but a lower consumption rate. The problem is that when assessing a country in terms of its economy and finance, its speed of economic development, its trade surplus and deficit, its amount of foreign exchange reserves, and its transfer of industries, we still adhere to the perspective of a single sovereign state in the age of globalization. The developed countries including the U.S., despite embarking on economic globalization, failed to make preparations for the possible complicated changes brought along with the economic globalization regarding the formulating and practicing of economic and financial policies. Following the theories of trade and monetary policy adopted when the globalization was not very well developed, those countries stuck to the habit of assessing domestic and foreign economies and finance from an angle of an individual sovereign state and even made wrong economic responses out of their own national interests or the benefit of the ruling party. In addition, they may also force late-developing countries to appreciate the currency, put restrictions on exporting high-tech products as in cold war times, limit the mergers and acquisitions of American enterprises by foreign investors, and implement trade protectionism in imports and exports in order to increase trade frictions. Taking the 2007 financial crisis as an example, the inexpensive goods from emerging market countries brought about low commodity prices in the U.S., however its economic and financial authorities failed to understand the interdependent relationships between the trend of global commodity prices and its domestic financial market under the new condition of globalization, and the U.S. habitually attributed the low prices to its increase of labor productivity and clear macroeconomic policies. When the I.T. bubble burst in 2000 and the September 11 terrorist attack happened in 2001, to avoid economic crisis, the Federal Reserve lowered interest rates and depreciated the dollar to maintain a long-term loose monetary policy instead of taking measures to strengthen infrastructure and market supervision. This led to excess liquidity and the excessive subprime mortgage industry inflated into a property bubble. Finally, the over-innovated finance and improper financial supervision, together with the over-expansion of the housing credit market and financial derivatives market blew the bubble up and made this subprime mortgage debacle spread into a global financial crisis.

Secondly, this crisis in the U.S. was an outcome of financial imbalance which was caused by the American culture of consumption on debt, the economic environment of long-term low interest rates and high consumption, and the instable asset-dependent economy that overly relied on property income.[14]

With the decreased production of material products in the U.S., the actual growth of industrial workers' nominal income allowing for inflation was very slow in the past 20 years. At present, Americans annually spend nearly USD9 trillion, 20% higher than Europeans, three times as much as Japanese, and nine times as much as Chinese. Nevertheless, since 1985 till now, the savings surplus of Americans has not changed much. The most significant change is that the consumption of the U.S. citizens is supported by property incomes rather than wage incomes, which was named as an asset-dependent economy by Stephen S. Roach. Now, property income accounts for 40% among the disposable income of the U.S. citizens and over 90% of American households owns stocks or investment funds. The wealth of the American people mainly accumulates through the asset appreciation of stocks and residential property. Within just five years from 1996 to 2000, the income from the premiums in the capital market amounted to USD11 trillion. The home ownership rate of Americans was 64% in 1995 and rose up to 69% in 2006, and the rapid growth of property income covered up the weakness of pay rises. Under the support of cheap credit, household debt accounted for 133% of the disposable personal income, and the income-based savings turned into a negative in the latter half of 2007. This series of reasons collectively contributed to the dependence of the income growth of the U.S. residents on wealth effect, debt-fueled consumption, and the earnings of two-parents working families. People, therefore, have had little reason to save out of their current incomes as they traditionally did. Five years prior to the financial crisis, the U.S. net national savings was only 1.4% of the gross national income (GNI) in general, and thus the government has to import overseas savings surplus. The huge current account deficits of America absorbed around 75% of global savings surplus. American banks have to raise funds from sources other than savings. They have no choice but to rely on asset securitization and selling financial derivatives to take in the funds from all over the world, which constituted the purchasing and spending power of the U.S. But the problem lies in the instability of property income. In fine weather, everything goes smoothly but once there is a financial crisis, asset bubbles will burst. The Federal Reserve's data showed that the U.S. household net worth was USD51.5 trillion in the end of 2008, USD11.2 trillion less (a drop of 18%) than the previous year. Among it, the housing price depreciated USD2.7 trillion and all kinds of investment in the stock market shrank over USD8 trillion. Consequently, the loan default rate rose up and foreign funds stayed away from

American financial derivatives. The banks in the U.S. could hardly raise any funds in the market and faced liquidity problems, which led to the bankruptcy or closure of banks.

Third, the 2007 financial crisis was not just one of subprime mortgage and financial derivatives, but also an outcome of over-innovation of the financial institutions' blind pursuit of profits and insufficient regulation by financial authorities. The fundamental cause, however, is the latter one. First of all, the banks issued subprime housing mortgage loans to borrowers with poor credit, and the modern credit scoring system and automated underwriting system made the issue of loans overly reliant on computer models. The lenders intended to earn high returns by finding out high-risk innovative financial products based on default rates and quantitative models. In the next place, financial innovation went beyond limits. Asset securitization has turned housing and car mortgage loans and all kinds of consumption loans into mortgage-backed securities (MBS) and asset-backed securities (ABS), based on which financial instruments, such as multi-layer and multi-level collateralized debt obligation (CDO) and credit default swap (CDS) as a hedge against the risks of CDO, were invented. Most of them were traded over-the-counter (OTC) and became what Buffet had termed "financial weapons of mass destruction." The biggest problem remained the regulatory loopholes which resulted from regulatory philosophy lagging behind the business model of financial institutions. Lastly, high leverage ratio indulged speculation and uncontrolled risks. In the U.S., the capital leverage ratio was generally 11:1. The excessive speculation of investment banks were reflected in its high leverage ratio of 28:1 or even 33:1. The recent emerged derivative market with an asset of over USD600 trillion was satirized by some as a new kind of borrowing and leverage culture being formed around the world. This cannot be separated from the inadequate financial supervision by the American government.

Fourth, this new round of financial crisis was closely related to the fiscal crisis triggered by long-term tax cuts, the treasury's overdraft at the Fed for wanton engagement in military aggression, and the manipulation of the currency by the U.S. government. Monetarists emphasized tax cuts, and from 1985 until now the tax revenue-to-GDP ratio fell from 27% to 17% in the U.S., 7 to 8 percentage points lower than that of Europe and Japan. The U.S. treasury security was USD5.7 trillion in size a decade ago, USD7.7 trillion in 2005, and USD12 trillion at the end of 2009, and it surmounted the statutory debt ceiling of USD14.294 trillion on May 16, 2011, greater than the GDP of 2010. Such a huge amount of outstanding national debt is not merely a financial problem but a fiscal one. The U.S. Congress

Joint Economic Committee released a report which said that until the end of 2008, the U.S. government had spent USD1.6 trillion on the wars of Afghanistan and Iraq. Meanwhile, according to a report named "Costs of War" made by Brown University, the wars were estimated to have cost USD3.7-4.4 trillion, far beyond the total budget proposed by the Congress and the federal government. Due to the fact that fiscal surplus was turned into huge fiscal deficit during the Bush era, the Obama administration has to continue debt financing. However, America, by taking advantage of the world currency (i.e., the U.S. dollar), let the dollars depreciate to make the low-yielding dollars spread unchecked around the world. By doing this, the U.S. government not only shifted the financial crisis to the world, but also plundered the whole world with seigniorage. Now, the Euro intends to replace the U.S. dollar, and Russia and Iran refuse to use the dollar. China and many other countries have agreed on expanding the scale of local currency settlement. G20 nations also have held meetings on the reform of the international monetary system. All these examples showed the dissatisfaction from various countries in the world with America's manipulation of currency. Of course, this issue cannot be settled with one or two international meetings. Additionally, America will by no means give up the hegemony easily and a hard push would probably turn the economic crisis into a military crisis. *Currency Wars* by Song Hongbing published in 2007 linked the world economy, politics, and many dramatic historical events with the financial and military wars which occurred in the last 200 years. Some criticized this book as being completely erroneous, but many of its cases are true examples of Western countries playing the bully by means of monetary hegemony. This book is really thought-provoking and raises alarms for all of us. After all, the United States holds a huge war machine, and the world must prevent the risks, or even a currency war, brought by the expansion of the financial crisis.

Fifth, this was a crisis of finance seriously breaking away from the real economy when capitalism developed into a new stage of financial capitalism. In 1999, America abolished the six-decade long severe regulation on the mixed operation of the finance industry and further promoted the financialization of the economy. The developed countries successively pursued high yields from the capital market and developed the financial derivatives market, which led to the over-development of the financial sector and the disengagement between the fictitious economy and the real economy. Take as an example the huge international hot money quickly flowing in international financial markets. The daily turnover in global foreign exchange markets was approximately USD1.4 trillion in 2001, but the number surpassed

USD3 trillion in 2007. The daily volume of foreign exchange doubled within six years and the annual trading volume of foreign exchange markets was dozens of times that of global GDP. As the American columnist, Richard C. Longworth, pointed out in his book Global Squeeze: The Coming Crisis for First-World Nations that "two weeks' worth of these dollar transfers fund the movement of all goods and services; The other 50 weeks consist of speculation, pure and simple." This hot money sought investment opportunities around the world to pursue profit maximization, which displayed both huge charm and destructive power and aroused the upsurges of international oil and food prices. When the existing transaction channel cannot meet the demand of the hot money, financial derivatives were pushed to undergo innovations, and thus the financial derivatives on the basis of high-leverage and high-risk subprime mortgages were invented.

Economic globalization has promoted the lopsided development of the financial sector. For one thing, many financial institutions have become "too big to fall." In the pricing of debt and stock, such a status endowed those institutions with a special competitive edge running counter to the law of the market (Greenspan, 2009). For another, financial globalization boosted asset securitization and financial innovation and a shadow banking market parallel to the existing banking system was formed. Ba Shusong wrote an article and said that this market was very huge and the estimation of the financial asset of those institutions was more than four times the global GDP. The result was that financial assets showed a typical inverted pyramid structure: In general, the traditional money (M1 and M2) only occupied 1%, broad money 9%, and financial bonds 10%, while financial derivatives accounted for 80% of the financial market. Driven by the high leverage, the financial sector was overextended and the profits of the global financial sector even made up over 40% of the entire U.S. corporate earnings. The problem was also reflected in that shadow banking operates through counterparties privately negotiating and trading one-on-one in the OTC market. Those financial derivatives are considered OBS items by the regulatory institutions of various countries and are loosely imposed by regulations. As a result, the traditional regulatory means, such as the capital adequacy ratio, cannot fully supervise the derivative market and this creates a huge gap in regulation, which further pushes forward asset securitization and financial innovation.

In 2006, the global GDP was USD48.2 trillion, the total market capitalization worldwide was USD50.8 trillion, the total global assets of financial institutions were USD190.4 trillion, and the total market value of derivatives in the world was USD485.7 trillion. They were, respectively, the same as, four times, and ten times of the global GDP. From 2009 to 2010, the nominal values of global derivatives were severally USD630 trillion, USD743.5 trillion, USD637 trillion, and USD618 trillion (slightly falling after the financial crisis), and this accounted for 11.8 times, 12.57 times, 10.9 times, and 10.13 times the respective year's global GDP. During this period of time, international financial capital underwent the fastest explosive growth in human history. Financial innovations totally broke away from the basic economic aspects of production-demand and supply, and were more involved with the financial service demands which were increasingly divorced from reality. Financial innovations entered into a development stage of self-creating financial service demands far away from the real economy.

The global financial crisis was enlightening. American President Barack Obama expressed the idea that what we have learnt from this financial crisis was that "21st-century markets could not be properly regulated with 20th-century regulations."[15] He said that to prevent a similar crisis from happening again, the U.S. must completely renovate the current financial regulatory system. "Wall Street will remain a big, important part of our economy, just as it was in the '70s and the '80s," he added. "It just won't be half of our economy...We don't want every single college grad with mathematical aptitude to become a derivatives trader."[16] The global financial crisis indicated that capital has a dual nature. The undesirable expansion of and the inadequate supervision towards capital in the capitalist countries would bring about crises and disasters to the whole world. As long as we can learn lessons from this crisis, properly handle the relationship between savings and consumption, financial innovation and financial regulation, as well as the fictitious economy and the real economy, we are able to find out solutions to the crisis. Capital movement has its laws and if we could make the best use of the laws, we could utilize capital to create wealth for the prosperity of the people and the rise of the country.

Financial Regulations Should Not Be Relaxed

The most profound lesson of the latest global financial crisis stemming from America has taught us is that financial regulation should never be relaxed.

Financial regulation comes into being because of the uncertainty of finance. Not only are the benefits and costs related to the time allocation of financial resources uncertain, but the risks that each financial instrument will bring are also uncertain. In fact, finance is an on-going process of solving old contradictions while creating new contradictions and risks. The invention of every financial instrument including currency has brought along some uncertainties (namely, risks) while facilitating people's economic life, and thus there is a need for a new financial instrument to evade risks. The new financial tools will solve the original contradiction but at the same time produce new uncertainties, and therefore more new financial tools are needed to be found or invented. It is right under such a condition that various financial instruments and the related markets are occurring in our economic life, such as indirect financing of bank deposits and loans, direct financing of stocks and bonds, security markets, mutual funds, asset-backed securities (securitization of assets), financial futures, futures markets, as well as a variety of financial derivatives markets. Financial products which emerge one after another in this way constantly accumulate risks and crisis in the growing financial markets and will incur losses and disasters to savers and investors. Financial supervision is the guideline and regulation that governments have summed up in their attempts to cope with the financial crisis and protect the interests of investors. Governments are responsible for the supervision towards the operation of financial institutions and products, risk disclosure, information disclosure, and investor protection. Moreover, the high leverage, high correlation, and high asymmetry of modern financial markets and institutions render new features to the generation and transmission of risks in the modern financial system and increase the flexibility of financial regulation. Consequently, financial supervision is directly related to the property, interests, and lives of people, and the stability of finance will directly impact national economic security and social stability.

As a nation owning the most developed financial markets and most active financial innovation activities, America has been boasting that its financial regulatory system was the most complete. It should be said that America's banking industry has enjoyed for 30 years a comparatively stable development since the Great Depression of the 1930s when the monetary system was reformed, a series of strict regulatory acts were imposed, and separate operation and supervision of banking, securities, insurance and trust industries were established. However, in the 1980s and 1990s, the U.S. government began to relax its financial regulations in order to enhance the international competitiveness of its financial industry. As a result, the financial institutions gradually expanded their business scope and various innovated financial products and derivatives markets developed vigorously. Until November 1999 when the *Financial Services Modernization Act* was passed, the boundary in business among banks, securities organizations, insurance companies and other financial institutions were completely eliminated to allow mixed operation, and universal banking was again permitted to be set up. But this act ran too far in releasing financial control and the lax regulations have continued for the next 60 years.

Part of the problem is that when Alan Greenspan served as Chairman of the Federal Reserve from August 1987 to January 2006, he constantly proposed extremely loose control over financial innovations and strongly opposed intensifying government regulation on finance. In 1998 when the notional value of derivatives contracts outstanding at U.S. commercial banks grew 30%, Greenspan noted that this "growth underscored the need for such financial instruments in 'unbundling' financial risks around the world." He believed that "by far the most significant event in finance in the past decade has been the extraordinary development and expansion of financial derivatives; the greater use of OTC derivatives doubtless reflects the attractiveness of customized over standardized products."[17] By 1998, the development of OTC derivatives incurred the Long Term Capital Management crisis. In 1999, the U.S. Commodity Futures Trading Commission (CFTC) advocated a tighter regulation on the OTC derivatives market, a move opposed by both Mr. Greenspan and U.S. Treasury Secretary Robert Rubin. Greenspan even stated that "the fact that the OTC markets function quite effectively" without CFTC oversight "provides a strong argument for development of a less burdensome regime for exchange-traded financial derivatives."[18] In May 2005, Greenspan made the famous assertion that the market was often a more effective regulator than the government.

In addition, government oversight has loopholes. The philosophy of America's financial supervision is based on the business model of financial institutions and overlooks some necessary links between direct and indirect finance. For example, the business pattern of traditional banks is "issuance, holding and recovery" of financial products, and therefore, financial institutions will actively manage risks. With the development of asset-backed security, banks target the selling and transfer of loans and risks to purchasers as soon as possible and this business pattern gradually changes into "loan issuance, sale of securitized debt, and risk diversification" (Ba Shusong described it as "issuance and sale, and issuance and diversification"). Consequently, banks give up the basic principle of actively managing risks, which is the premise of Greenspan's self-monitoring of financial institutions. Greenspan always believed that "the enlightened self-interest of owners and managers of financial institutions would lead them to maintain a sufficient buffer against insolvency by actively monitoring their firms' capital and risk positions."[19] ThIs is right because of the management idea lagging behind the business mode of financial institutions that loopholes in supervision have emerged.

Besides, America always thinks that a relaxed system is needed for the development of hedge funds and thus leaves a blank in regulation. Many countries, including the G7, repeatedly advocated the tighter oversight of hedge funds but only met with objection from the U.S. To make it worse, the profit-seeking nature of capital has encouraged the greed of financial institutions and their management to risk moral hazard in pursuit of financial manipulation and high salaries or bonuses.

The U.S. subprime mortgage crisis of 2007 was triggered by the dramatic growth of the unregulated OTC derivatives which became the "financial weapons of mass destruction," a term popularized by Buffet, and the crisis finally evolved into a global financial tsunami. The acquisition of Bear Stearns by J.P. Morgan on March 15, 2008 was the first domino. A series of tragedies happened half a year later: The American government took over Fannie May, Freddie Mac, and AIG; Lehman Brothers went bankrupt; Bank of America acquired the 94-year-old Merrill Lynch; and Goldman Sachs and Morgan Stanley were transformed into traditional banks. Unfortunately, the top five investment banks in Wall Street all failed.

In the face of the facts, Greenspan admitted part of the mistake in the Congressional hearings on October 23, 2008. He said that until 2005 the Fed was still ignorant of the size of the subprime mortgage market, and financial institutions did not do their best to protect the interests of their shareholders as he had expected. He conceded for the first time a flaw in his market philosophy of unfettered free markets. He said distressfully that "that is precisely the reason I was shocked, because I have been going for 40 years or more with very considerable evidence it was working exceptionally well."[20] On March 27, 2009, He published an article in the *Financial Times* and admitted that "the risk-management structure cracked" and "all the sophisticated mathematics and computer wizardry essentially rested on one central premise: That the enlightened self-interest of owners and managers of financial institutions would lead them to maintain a sufficient buffer against insolvency by actively monitoring their firms' capital and risk positions. For generations, that premise appeared incontestable but, in the summer of 2007, it failed." Moreover, "even with the breakdown of self-regulation, the financial system would have held together had the second bulwark against crisis — our regulatory system — functioned effectively. But, under crisis pressure, it too failed."[21]

In short, finance has uncertainties (i.e. risks), and the risks are unpredictable. At present, countries around the world lack experience in the oversight of finance, especially of those complicated financial derivatives, and financial supervision always falls behind the development of the market. A lesson from this global financial crisis is that oversight of finance should be strengthened. We should bear in mind the following experience.

1. Finance serves the real economy. Compared with the real economy, the scale of finance should basically be stable. When its size expands rapidly and surpasses that of the real economy, the regulatory department must be alert to latent dangers.
2. Encourage should be given to financial innovation but with a limit. Innovation at the initial stage may be allowed to "play edge ball" and make new attempts when the existing policies are not clearly prohibited, but the subsequent promotion of the innovation must be under supervision and new regulations should be formed.
3. There should be a limit over the size of financial institutions and governments can neither let the institutions be too big to fail nor allow the institutions to break the market rules in the pricing of debt and equity to exercise monopoly and manipulation.
4. Loans can be securitized and made into asset-backed securities for sale and credit risk management mechanism (such as provision for bad debts) should also be transferred along with the loans. There should be a corresponding risk management mechanism for the asset-backed securities.
5. The development of financial derivatives has to make sure that risks are controllable. Financial innovation should be allowed under the condition of a lower leverage. What Liu Mingkang said was right: "We must resolutely oppose highly leveraged financial innovations."[22]

Be Alert to and Prevent Various Fears towards Capital

China is at the primary stage of socialism, and should treat with caution the policies of developing capitalism during the transition from a planned economy to a socialist market economic system.

The objective of new China is to build a socialist country. In the war of national liberation, Mao Zedong once accurately defined the new democratic revolution in China as a bourgeois democratic revolution, but the leader was the Communist Party instead of bourgeois parties and the goal of the revolution was not capitalism, but socialism. At the new democratic stage when the new China was just founded, Mao Zedong continued advocating redemption of capitalism and allowing a limited space for the development of capitalism. China, however, implemented a centralized planned economy in pursuit of socialism with an ownership by the whole, after China entered into large-scale economic construction in 1953, especially after Stalin put forward the theory of product economy, and the three-anti and five-anti campaigns[23] were carried out to oppose the bourgeoisie, and Mao Zedong suggested the "General Line" for the transitional period of "one industrialization, three transformations."[24] Later on, the government was eager to eliminate capitalism and speed up the transition to socialism by carrying out the Great Leap Forward and the People's Communes campaigns in 1958, launching the Cultural Revolution, fully implementing the public-private partnership, even putting an end to the capitalist redemption on the basis of a fixed rate of interest,[25] and abolishing self-employment and farmers' private plots to cut off tails of capitalism. Judging from the actual development of productive force, China was still a backward developing country at that time and its economy was on the verge of collapse due to the decade-long calamity of the Cultural Revolution. As a result, after announcing the policy of reforming and opening up in the Third Plenary Session of the Eleventh Central Committee of the Communist Party of China (CPC) in November 1978, the party has to face the reality and admitted the facts that China was still in the primary stage of socialism, and the development of the private economy to a certain degree would promote production, build an active market, and expand employment, which would better meet the needs of people in many aspects of life and was a necessary and beneficial supplement to a state-owned economy. This action was to correct the mistake of being eager to transform into socialism and the government did not restore the name of "new democratic revolution," instead it used a new term of "primary stage of socialism." For one thing, this name clarified the objective of the socialist revolution under the leadership of the CPC; for another, since China was at the primary stage of socialism, it was justifiable for the country to recognize the necessity for developing a certain degree of the private economy, namely capitalism, which was a significant and indispensable step to greatly enhance socialist productivity. During the 16th CPC National Congress in 2002, a greater breakthrough was that the party further identified that "individual, private and other non-public economies that exist within the limits prescribed by law are major components of the socialist market economy," and the party also clearly stated that "we must unswervingly support, encourage and guide the development of the non-public sector of the economy," which was given equal importance with the policy of "unswervingly consolidating and developing the public sector of the economy."

It was the first time that the government justified individual, private, and other non-public economies in the form of political policy. This policy was reiterated at the 17th CPC National Congress and even written into the constitution. The new constitution identified the new social class including private entrepreneurs, as builders of China's socialist cause.

China is still at the primary stage of socialism, and therefore when formulating policies towards the capitalist economy, the government needs to be vigilant and prevent a variety of fears towards capitalism. Examples of such fears are as follows:

1. For fear of exploitation, China avoided talking about capital and even dared not freely introduce capital and develop the private economy. After China's reform and opening up, even though the 12th Central Committee of the CPC in 1982 had recognized private economy as a necessary and beneficial part of the socialist economy and being subject to the socialist economy, individual and private enterprises were always attached to a government department in the name of a state-run or collective-run enterprise and endured repeated "exploitations" in order to realize development. With regard to introducing foreign investment, at first the country was merely content with making loans from banks of capitalist countries, issuing bonds overseas, and engaging in compensation trade. Until very lately, the government began to dabble in joint ventures, and not until 1990s did the Chinese enterprises have the courage to issue shares and get listed abroad. This was in fact a fear of being contaminated by capitalism.

2. The fear for capital circulation caused all kinds of blockages in circulation. The government bond was resumed in 1980, but its circulation was not allowed. Until 1987, the circulation of governments bonds was finally piloted. The Chinese government initiated stock market pilots in 1990, but for fear of drainage of state assets, it only allowed circulation of additional issuance of new shares to the public and secondary offering of state-owned shares could merely be transferred via negotiation. Consequently, it gave rise to abnormal price growth of outstanding shares and real depreciation of the non-tradable state-owned shares for a long time and this in turn caused equity division, a chronic disease which successive security market supervisors would hardly risk to treat. The welfare-oriented distribution of the public housing system was reformed in 1998 but there is still a concern for the loss of state assets. Just as equity division would block full circulation in the stock market, the fact that public housings are under the ownership of the central, school, and military

authorities together with some explicit and implicit policies, retarded the circulation of old houses, which is a primary cause for the unsmooth trade in the secondhand housing market.

3. Egalitarianism. One example was the avoidance of compound interest after the founding of new China. Following that, it was the four decade-long "iron rice bowl" policy in China's state-owned companies, and then egalitarianism sacrificed efficiency by distributing the wages of three to five people. Later, convertible bonds were going to be piloted in the stock market among listed companies. But, the words of a senior leader — "timely help was more favorable than additional bonus" — altered the original plan and made the bonds to be issued by non-listed companies, which placed the pilot in an awkward position to become a laughing stock.

4. The government was worried about all kinds of financial means in the capitalist market economy lest it was contaminated by "capitalist bacteria," and gave up easily with a slight risk. For a long period, China had much concern over usury and thus dared not open up to non-government credit. Later on, the Law of Negotiable Instruments of China refused to use commercial paper and employed bank acceptance to cover all the business. Corporate bonds were permitted to be issued only if the company had some engineering projects, which denied the financing function of the bonds.

5. The government was overly cautious about and always on guard over capitalism. Since the reform and opening up in China, once the private economy had developed a little bit, there would always be a variety of leftist thoughts to question the nature of the economy, whether it was capitalist or socialist, and public or private. Some people have been worried that a new bourgeois has risen in China and if the proportion of the private sector exceeds the public to a certain degree, it will seriously impact the nature of China's economy and even national security.

6. Some people would rather be leftist than rightist and provoke controversy at every turn. They even do not allow others to try what they dare not to do. When the former chairman of China Strategic Holdings, Oei Hong Leong, acquired several beer and tire enterprises in China and got them listed overseas for financing, some people accused him of making something from nothing and stirred up a debate over the "China Strategic storm."Chen Guang, the former municipal party secretary of Zhucheng City, Shandong Province, carried out a reform of 288 enterprises above the county level and sold small-

sized companies among them. Some people satirized him as "Sold-out Chen," "a vanguard of privatization," "wastrel," and "bellwether for the restoration of capitalism." Some central departments also warned him by saying that "you cannot solve all the problems by selling up and you could hardly get rid of the ideological constraints."

7. Pay lip service to revolution. China's government talked about making a strategic adjustment in the distribution of the state-owned economy when implementing privatization, while in practice, it protected just the state-owned property and took no account of encouraging the private economy to step in to take the state's place in the ownership of business. In the past few years, not a small number of privately-controlled companies ran into equity disputes, and it was often the case that private capital was in an inferior position. When state-controlled companies were driven into a corner under the old system, they had to seek help from private capital. Once they were out of trouble, however, those companies would force the private economy to step down on the excuse of prohibiting the loss of state assets. Meanwhile, the government seldom took the initiative to regulate privatization or protect the active participation of private capital to ensure that the state asset was willing to withdraw from the ownership of business while the private capital could come in as a replacement and enjoy development free from the discrimination and disruption from force of habit.

8. In the face of the weakness of privatization, the government denied the entire practice rather than solved the problems with care. In 2004, Professor Larry Lang from the Chinese University of Hong Kong criticized some large state-controlled enterprises, including Haier and Kelon, for the loss of state assets in the reform of state-owned enterprises, and many people echoed his opinion and cited several extreme cases to question the direction of the reform.

9. During the equity trading in privatization, transactions of corporate control were avoided from being mentioned. In fact, a capital market of any country can never be called mature if no corporate control is traded and transferred. Only with the flow of corporate control, can resources be really optimized, and assets restructured, the industry structured, and synergy effects be truly realized. Being state-controlled is not always the story, trading of corporate control cannot be avoided and must be tackled in either private capital absorption or management buy-outs (MBO) during the strategic adjustment in the distribution of state-owned economy and the reduction of state-owned stocks.

Turn Workers into Men of Property

Capital is useful. It is a prerequisite for a society to feed and enrich its people. The revolutionary party upheld the slogan of "Workers of all lands, Unite!" to lead the proletariats to power at the revolutionary stage, and after the party came into power, it had the responsibility to turn workers into men of property.

First, the party should raise the income of workers, upgrade low-income group to middle-income, and constantly enlarge the proportion of middle earners. After the reform and opening up, Deng Xiaoping repeatedly criticized the "poor socialism" and "poor communism" clamored for by the Gang of Four. He said that "there is no such thing as socialism and communism with poverty."[26] "We have been making revolution for several decades and have been building socialism for more than three. Nevertheless, by 1978 the average monthly salary for our workers was still only 45 yuan, and most of our rural areas were still mired in poverty. Can this be called the superiority of socialism?"[27] "According to Marxism, communist society is a society in which there is overwhelming material abundance...How can we apply this principle [that is, from each according to his ability, to each according to his needs] without highly developed productive forces and vast material wealth?"[28] "To apply this second principle [the above principle] will require great material abundance: How could a poor society afford to operate on the principle of 'to each according to his needs'? How could a communist society be poor? ...Poverty is not socialism, and development that is too slow is not socialism either."[29]

Second, to allow workers to use their earned income as capital to make investments in production and participate in profit distribution by subscribing stocks, and thereby to allow all the members of society to do the same by making use of their savings. Since China is a developing country with lower social productive forces and is still at the primary stage of socialism, it has to mobilize all the positive factors and constantly encourage workers and members of society to make investment of all the temporarily spare money in socialist construction in order to achieve a rapid growth of socialist economy, highly developed productive forces, and vast material wealth.

Third, to allow intellectual workers to take their technological knowledge, managerial skills, and other factors of production as human capital to gain profits the way material capital does, and establish a sound system of distribution according to contributions, which is very necessary. First of all, to permit technology investment is not only an acknowledgement of technology as complex labor, but also recognition of the primary productive forces of science and technology being able to be invested like material capital. In this way, science and technology personnel would share profits according to their contribution of technology investment and become men of property. Next, to include payment motivation and shareholding in distribution to managers is recognition of managers being capable of enjoying property rights through their excellent management work. The logic is obvious. If you want to abolish the policy of the "iron rice bowl" in labor, you ought to also abolish it in management, and good and bad management should be differentiated. The logical way, therefore, is that regarding management as a kind of capital to share the fruits of profit maximization (including meager profit and loss), when managers organize and operate corporate capital.

Fourth, the government should create conditions for increasing property income of the masses. Interest on deposit belongs to property income so does dividends and bonuses from investment by deposit. Housing is a property and thus the income through renting or transferring surplus houses is also a yield of this nature. Other kinds of property income include: Share premium from buying stocks, income received from the transfer of land-use rights, royalties from patents and know-how, etc. The key is that the government should create more conditions for more people to own property income.

In conclusion, the revolutionary party of socialism should shoulder the responsibility to turn workers into men of property, which would be a significant and profound power for breaking away from the shackles of thoughts. The government should have the courage to stick to the ideas: "Poverty is not socialism, and development that is too slow is not socialism either;" the objective of proletarians to call for "Workers of all lands, Unite!" is by no means to continue being have-nots; and by doing so, "the proletarians have nothing to lose but their chains; they have a world to win."[30] For this reason, the government has to first lift workers from poverty, create better living and consumption conditions, and turn men of no property into middle-income earners and owners of their own earned income. Meanwhile, to develop too slowly is not socialism. A socialist country must mobilize all the positive factors and create conditions to enable more citizens to have property income. The government must constantly encourage workers and other members of society to put all the factors of production including labor, capital, skills and management, into production and circulation, and to participate in distribution according to their contributions. All the citizens should get engaged in the lifelong pursuit of socialist construction and ensure a rapid grow of socialist economy.

To turn workers into men of property is not a socialist utopia, but a reality for socialism with Chinese characteristics. We should be more far-sighted. If all the workers of the society become men of property and the society as a whole has only propertied men of middle- and high-income, then the government and the citizens should consider how to deal with the investment in property, how to manage their property income, and how to govern this brand-new all-haves society. These will be new questions for political economists to tackle in all seriousness.

1

Chapter

How Capital Is Formed: The Mechanism of Capital Formation and the History of Capital Expansion and Innovation

Prologue: 60 Years on the Wheel of Fortune

When I visited Japan during the mid-1980s and lunched with Ito Masanori, the vice president of Nomura Securities, we had a conversation on currency and the economy.

It was the best Chinese restaurant in Tokyo, and Ito said with pride, "Mr. Cao, I am treating you to the world's most expensive Chinese cuisine!" He was not wrong, as that was the most expensive Chinese restaurant in Japan, and the Japanese yen was then appreciating. This led to a conversation on currency and economy. It was the heyday of the Japanese and West German economies, and the Japanese yen and Deutsche mark were strong, rising currencies.

Ito said, "The world economy is like 60 years on the Wheel of Fortune. It was the century of the British pound before World War I. But after the war, the 'empire on which the sun never sets' went into decline. Since World War II, it was the age of the U.S. dollar. Now, Japan and West Germany enjoy the benefits of defeated nations, with rapidly growing economies and non-participation in the arms race. Japan bought the Rockefeller Center and Columbia Pictures, infuriating the Americans; and Japan published a book titled *The Japan That Can Say No*. If done well, even if it may not be a century of the Japanese yen and Deutsche mark, at least we can be on equal ground with the U.S. dollar!" Perhaps realizing his words might be inappropriate in front of a Chinese guest, Ito quickly laughed. "I must have drunk too much!" Then he followed up: "Maybe the twenty-first century will be the century of the Renminbi!" I replied, "Thank you for your auspicious words. I hope that China can have a rapid economic growth like Japan!"

Mr. Ito is my good friend and it is unfortunate that he passed away many years ago. Yet none of us foresaw that Japan would fall into a 10-year-long recession after the Southeast Asian economic crisis, and, in the twenty-first century, China's economic growth would rank second in the world following the 2008 global financial crisis, and the Reminbi would rise strongly! Of course, the Reminbi is still not a world currency, but as the *2008 Development Report on Developing Countries* states: Growth is not everything, but it is the basis of everything. I want to stress that currency is not capital, but capital is, in part, the manifestation of currency. In the end, the Reminbi will make the most important leap towards becoming a world currency!

Now, let us discuss the mechanism of capital formation and its innovation.

The Initial Forms of Capital: Own Capital and Credit

Capital is in part the manifestation of money but not all money is capital. Money is only transformed to capital under the foundation of modern production when it has functions in production and circulation, and can bring about value-addedness (i.e. profit). Only then will currency have the functional value of generating profit, thus becoming capital.

Similarly, not all bank deposit is capital. Only when banks accumulate a certain amount of deposits and turn them into loans — that is, transferring the control and the profit-making ability of currency to borrowing companies — does the deposit become capital.

This is called capital formation in economics. Capital formation is the process of a country saving its citizens' net income and investing it to create productivity. The economic development of all countries must rely on capital formation. Savings, investment, and production are the three stages of capital formation.

So how is capital formed?

From the perspective of companies, initial accumulation is the root of capital formation. This includes money legally earned by capitalists and shop owners, and illegally gained through theft, smuggling, and looting. The initial accumulation of quite a few capitalist countries began from looting, such as the enclosure of colonies and the selling of slaves. Of course, this includes the capitalists' exploitation of workers through prolonged working hours and an increased work rate. This continuous capitalization of remaining value, this transformation of profit into more capital for expansion and increased productivity, is the basic method of capital formation.

Own capital is needed for the startup of a company, and refers to the capital originally owned by the company. All companies need to have a certain amount of own capital and it has five main functions:

1. As operating capital during startup and for turnover — this does not need to be repaid during the operation of the company
2. As return, or value-addedness, during business turnover — this should be greater than loan interest, so capital is a scarce resource that is far more valuable that the interest of bank loans;
3. As debt capacity — companies can use capital as mortgages, to bear debts, or as a guarantee for legal responsibility;

4. As a reflection of ownership — owners show their control over capital and invested-companies through how much capital they have contributed; and

5. As bearing the risk of business loss in times of difficulties.

Obviously, it is not enough to rely on a single capital source and self-accumulation. Marx stated that "[Production] expands annually for two reasons; first because the capital invested in production is continually growing; second because the capital is constantly used more productively."[1] Therefore, as production size expands, the size of needed capital will expand, and the pursuit of expansion is logically inevitable.

After production is developed, when the own capital of the company is insufficient for turnover and cannot meet the needs of production development, company owners have to expand capital. The most common way is to make use of available capital in the society through credit. There are two common types of credit. The first is business credit which includes prepayment among companies. It is the receivables and payables resulting from buying on credit and payment by installments. The other is bank credit, such as loans and overdrafts (as stated before, bank loan is the transfer of capital control to borrowing companies for the price of interest). As opposed to own capital, when companies make use of others' capital through credit, it is called "borrowed capital" or "non-owned capital." Own capital and credit are the two basic forms of the initial capital of companies.

Other than own capital, credit is the most common and widespread form of capital expansion in initial capital. Credit creates control rights for an individual — it gives someone absolute control over others' capital within a certain boundary.

There are usually four conditions when companies borrow bank loans: The loan is time-limited; the loan is used with interest; the interest is the price for capital use, and the interest rate is usually dependent on the market's demand and supply of capital as well as the length of the loan; and the principal plus interest have to be paid at maturity.

There is one more limiting condition for bank loans, and that is the evaluation of debt capacity of borrowing companies by the bank. Generally, own capital should not be less than 30%, and this is used to analyze the debt situation of the company, as well as to evaluate credit risk. Similarly, the Basel Agreement stipulates that when commercial banks conduct loan businesses, its core capital should not fall below 8%.

As discussed, there are conditions for money borrowing for both banks and companies. This is determined by the debt capacity of the company's own capital. In other words, if the company has 100 dollars of own capital, it can make use of assets (or debt claim) acquired from this 100 dollars as mortgage (or guarantee of legal liability), and obtain a 70–80 dollars loan. Normally, it will not be able to obtain a loan of more than 100 dollars since it will exceed the limit of debt capacity of the company's own capital.

It is the capitalists' own capital and the resulting accumulation, as well as the control of others' capital through the use of credit that form the foundation of the capital formation mechanism. However, the expansion of capital does not stop here. With the continual expansion of production, and when own capital and borrowed capital cannot satisfy the needs of capital expansion, there will be a need for innovation of the capital formation mechanism. In turn, under the basis of credit, partnerships and joint-stock companies are formed in addition to sole proprietorship. However, this is not an expansion of borrowed capital, but an expansion of own capital through the use of social capital. With expanded own capital, debt capacity is also expanded, and borrowed capital is increased.

On an additional note, Marx has highly rated the innovation of capital formation mechanisms by banks in *Das Kapital*. The credit and bank systems place "all the available and even potential capital of society that is not already actively employed at the disposal of the industrial and commercial capitalists so that neither the lenders nor users of this capital are its real owners or producers." Marx even thinks that such a system even "does away with the private character of capital and thus contains in itself, but only in itself, the abolition of capital itself. By means of the banking system the distribution of capital as a special business, a social function, is taken out of the hands of the private capitalists and usurers." Of course, Marx continues with a warning, that "at the same time, banking and credit thus become the most potent means of driving capitalist production beyond its own limits, and one of the most effective vehicles of crises and swindle."[2]

The Innovation, Development, and Changes in the Capital Formation Mechanism

There is no end to capital expansion. In the study of the innovation of the capital formation mechanism, it can be seen that since the Industrial Revolution and the rise of mass production, many innovations appeared in the last 200 years. This section will discuss some of the main new mechanisms of capital formation, beginning with a brief summary of its development.

With the development of capitalism, the Industrial Revolution, and the rise of mass production, the limits of individual ownership and single sourced capital have been broken. The joint-stock company evolves from sole proprietorship and partnership. The innovation of this system is the creation of a way to centralize the use of social capital despite a spread of ownership. It is a form of mass capital adapting to mass production.

It should also be noted that the Soviet Union abolished capitalism in the 1917 October Revolution, becoming the first country to adopt a planned economy where capital is centralized to build state-owned companies. This use of capital resulted in rapid industrialization and the adoption of mass production and it raised the national power of the Soviet Union, and supported its victory against fascist invasion in World War II. After the war, this mode of capital formation through state-owned capital became an example for socialist countries such as China and the nations of Eastern Europe. This sequence of events also helps one to understand the intervention of Western powers.

Later, in the rapid development of capitalism, overproduction resulted in a shrink in investment, which in turn led to economic crises such as the Great Depression in 1929. The Keynesian theory of government intervention was raised, and President Roosevelt realized the idea with his policies. The experience of the Soviet Union provides a source of reference, where government investment fills the missing link of capital formation, under the shrinking of private investment. After this, nationalization went overboard, and a wave of privatization occurred during the Reagan-Thatcher period. Private capital again replaced government capital in the capital formation mechanism.

When technology begins to develop rapidly, a low depreciation rate cannot compensate, in terms of capital, the loss incurred from the increased replacement rate of technology and facilities. As a result, the Western countries created the concept of accelerated depreciation to gain capital advances, and thus invented a new form of capital formation mechanism. When writing *Das Kapital*, Marx discovered that the sinking fund (i.e., the fund for wear and tear of the fixed capital) is, at the same time, a fund for accumulation that can be expanded and used in reproduction. He discussed the issue with Engels.[3]

Accelerated depreciation has allowed this recovery of the sinking fund into production to be fully developed. After World War II, rental of facilities appeared under the inducement of accelerated depreciation. This uses facilities as a type of loan capital on the foundation of credit, and does away with the bank as the intermediary, creating another innovation in the capital formation mechanism.

The development of science and technology requires a large amount of advanced capital invested in research, followed by a suitable way to recover the invested capital through technology transfer. This in turn gives rise to commercial fees in technology transfer, including one-off licensing fee and royalties from total production, which are ways of getting returns on investment. Such fees in technology transfer are actually recovery of the intangible asset of invested capital, and are similar to the recovery of depreciation and accelerated depreciation of tangible assets.

Next will be the reform of bankruptcy law. It involves the restructuring of the insolvent companies and the transformation of the creditor's rights to equity, allowing the creditor to control and renew the company. This transformation of debt into ownership is another innovation in the capital formation mechanism.

Equity and debt financing in the capital market are good mechanisms that can increase core social capital. Initial public offerings (IPO) and refinancing can directly expand the own capital of a company. On the other hand, debt financing is a direct financing of the debtor to the creditor that replaces bank credit. As opposed to bank loans, it is a type of quasi-core capital that has a corresponding time-limit and risk. Equity and debt financing in the capital market are innovations in the capital formation mechanism as they make use of assets that will have profit-making ability in the future without the bank as an intermediary. The exchange of securities such as stocks, bonds, and bills (or fictitious capital in Marx's words) for capital in the market, can lead to an expansion of capital. Marx termed this formation of fictitious capital as capitalization, which is a derivative of the expected yield of real capital in the future. However, this new mechanism of financing can directly create capital in the capital market, and expand the real capital. Thus, people in the capital market call this mockingly "misappropriation".

After the 1970s, innovations in the capital formation mechanism are mainly related to the rapid development of new and advanced technology. A relatively independent financial system, comprised mainly of venture capital firms and submarkets, has been formed to support the ventures of scientists. Venture capital firms undertake high risk to provide capital for scientists with no mortgages, guarantee, and capital to support their inventions and innovations. A submarket is a market with lower listing requirements that allows companies to list, finance, and expand their capital based solely on their growth potential and expected yield. It also provides an exit path for venture capital.

In later developments of the capital market, mergers and acquisitions, as well as financial and debt restructuring, are introduced. Leveraged buyouts, through the raising of subprime credit and bonds, make use of social capital to expand the corporation itself, instead of to expand its development. Such mergers are usually planned, organized, and operated by investment banks, and this is a reformation of the capital formation mechanism. Through mergers, liquidity is increased, assets are optimized, and industrial structure is adjusted. Restructuring results in businesses complementing each other. It results in corporate synergy, raising the overall value of capital.

The securitization of assets occurs because direct financing has bypassed the financial intermediary, thus hurting the deposit and loan businesses of banks. Short-term deposits and long-term loans have increased the risk of banks, and to solve this problem, a major innovation in the capital formation mechanism is created. It allows banks to covert excess assets into cash and creates a new investment tool for investors. On the foundation of such asset-backed securities, investment banks developed various new derivatives, such as collateralized debt obligations and credit default swaps that caused the 2007–2012 global financial crisis.

Mutual funds have reformed the capital formation mechanism entirely. This changed the inherent weakness of financial institutions (such as banks) where the maturity dates and risks of assets and debts were not synchronized, resulting in a situation where the institutions have to bear most of the risk. In the formation and operation processes of mutual funds, the concentration of investments, the choice of investees, the management and manager of funds, have all been commoditized and marketized. Mutual funds can put together and provide a large amount of assets flexibly, meeting both the investor's needs for personalized service and the needs of companies for a huge amount of capital during mass production. In the development of mutual funds, the manager has to adjust the holdings of different stocks and securities continuously to maximize profit. This forces corporate operators to work with the aim of profit maximization, or face the punishment of being sold by funds, resulting in a takeover or merger of the company.

In conclusion, the need for capital expansion is the main driving force behind the capital formation mechanism innovation. There are five main requirements as listed below:

1. To break through the limitation of a single capital source and self-accumulation, and gather capital from the society and other sources through the use of credit.
2. To break through the limitation imposed by financial intermediaries, and gather capital from the society and other sources.
3. For banks to resolve the conflict of uneven deposits and loans, as well as to create liquidity and gather social capital with new methods. From the perspective of banks, they have accumulated social capital in the form of deposits with their

credit, and then use them for business loans. However, the maturity dates and risk of deposits and loans may not be synchronized. Banks have to maintain a certain level of liquidity to ensure that there will be loans reaching maturity to pay up possible withdrawal of deposits. There will be a risk of bank failure if the bank becomes too illiquid due to uneven deposits and loans.

4. Investors require a diverse choice of financial products and investment methods other than making bank deposits. As capital, money must be used in the production process, and this is a limitation. Under current financial conditions, there is a need for excess capital to breakthrough this limitation, so that investors can invest, adjust their portfolios, and exit their investment flexibly.
5. In the capital market, investors with a huge amount of excess capital are separated from investors who require huge amounts of production capital. Investors have to find suitable and reliable investees who can provide an ideal return without excessive risk. A new investment industry is therefore created to meet this need. Investment bankers, fund companies, and asset management companies have taken up the role of finding outlets for excess capital, and the role of finding a capital source for investees with urgent needs. They have thus reformed the capital formation mechanism and satisfied the needs of both parties.

The Development of the Capital Market and Fictitious Capital after the Collapse of the Bretton Woods System

The capital formation mechanism is related to monetary systems. Before World War II, most countries in the world adopted the gold standard. After World War II and until the 1970s, the Bretton Woods system was formed under the lead of the United States, where the currency issuance of various countries was pegged to the U.S. dollar, while the U.S. dollar was pegged to gold. Therefore, before the 1970s, the formation of capital of countries was closely related to material production. Even the capital market was developed based on the stocks and debt financing of production institutes. After the collapse of the Bretton Woods system in the 1970s, currencies of countries unpegged with the U.S. dollar. Currency is like a wild horse after its removal from material production and it can result in the rapid development of the capital market and fictitious capital.

As a result, two major changes occurred in the world economy since the 1970s.

First, a huge fictitious economy has been formed in addition to the real economy. The capital market has helped create various derivatives such as asset-backed securities, stock index futures, government bond futures, foreign exchange swaps, and interest rate swaps. In 2000, the global GDP was under USD30 trillion, but the total fictitious economy was worth over USD160 trillion. Of this, stock prices and premium bonds were worth USD65 trillion, while over-the-counter trading of derivatives reached USD95 trillion. In 2004, the total fictitious economy was worth USD248.2 trillion, which was six times that of the global GDP of USD40.8 trillion. In 2006, the global GDP was USD48.2 trillion, the global total market price of stocks was USD50.8 trillion, the global total assets of financial institutions were USD190.4 trillion, and the global total market value of derivatives was USD485.7 trillion. They were, respectively, 105%, 395%, and more than 10 times of the global GDP. The development of derivatives has rapidly increased in recent years. In 2007, the global total notional amount of derivatives was USD630 trillion, which was 11.81 times that of the global GDP that year. In 2008, it was USD743.5 trillion, and this was 12.57 times that of the global GDP. In 2009 and 2010, it was USD637 trillion and USD618 trillion, respectively, and this was 10.9 and 10.1 times that of the global GDP.

Second, developing together with the fictitious economy and economic globalization, there has been a huge amount of fluid capital removed from material production. In 2007, before the global financial crisis, the global daily volume of foreign currency transactions exceeded USD3 trillion, which has doubled in the six years since then. In 2010, the global daily volume of foreign currency transactions reached USD4 trillion. The global annual volume of foreign currency transactions is dozens of times that of the global GDP.

These two characteristics are interrelated. The fictitious economy provided a new platform for the global concentration and circulation of fluid capital. As it absorbs fluid capital, it in turn creates new needs for fluid capital. Therefore, after the 1970s, the social capital formation mechanism is more related to the development of the fictitious economy and fluid capital.

In the last 30 years, these two major changes have created an essential financial ecology and a large room for various innovations in the capital formation mechanism.

The Characteristics of the Capital Formation Mechanism Innovation in Western Countries

There are five main characteristics of the capital formation mechanism innovation of Western countries with a market economy.

1. It is dominated by profit-oriented private investments, and complemented by state-intervention, when necessary, to strengthen the basic market function of resources allocation. Private investment is emphasized in competitive industries, while government investment is emphasized in infrastructure building, public goods and services, and non-profit industries. When private investment shrinks, government investment is strengthened, while privatization is encouraged at suitable times to replace government investment with private investment. When there is a shortage of capital during industrial renewal, the government encourages accelerated depreciation and the rental of facilities through tax exemption and deduction.
2. Financial reform is deepened. Capital market and direct financing is developed outside of financial intermediaries, and various financial innovations are encouraged. New financial products and derivatives are developed to provide new investment opportunities and hedging mechanisms for excess capital. There is also an emphasis on the balance of investment return and risk. Wealth is distributed among investors, capital is financed from investors, while at the same time, risk is distributed among investors to diversify risk.
3. The investment banking industry is developed in addition to the banking industry, becoming a main driving force behind the capital formation mechanism innovation. Investment banks form a finance and investment industry that specializes in capital utilization, assets management (including fund management), corporate mergers and acquisitions, and corporate restructuring. In situations of overcapacity, excess capital and a decreased average profit rate occur, and investment bankers can find growth companies and investment return opportunities among various companies that are not making profits. It also creates opportunities for investment returns through planning and organizing corporate mergers and acquisitions, as well as financial innovation. It has made investment, assets management, and capital utilization into a specialized financial service.
4. The fictitious economy is developed in addition to the real economy, creating more room for the expansion of core social capital. Due to various innovations in capital formation mechanisms, the stock, bond, bill, fund, futures, and derivatives markets, as well as the submarket, are all developed to form a huge fictitious economy.
5. The development of the capital market and fictitious economy has driven innovations in capital formation mechanisms. Such innovations, in turn, drive

the specialization of financial industries such as banking, securities, trust, and insurance industries.

Of course, the capital market, derivatives market, and fictitious economy form a doubled-edged sword. They nurture risks as they develop, especially when overspeculation leads to the formation of economic bubbles, such as the stock market bubble or the real estate bubble. During the Great Depression, the stock market and real estate bubbles burst. Risk was overconcentrated in banks, resulting in the widespread failures of banks. The 1997 Asian financial crisis and the "Lost Decade" in Japan were both the results of the real estate bubble burst that led to the failure of banks. After the dot-com bubble burst in the United States in 2000, the NASDAQ Composite index fell from more than 5000 to 2000. Banks were not affected mainly because the capital market and direct financing had dispersed the risk of banks. When the stock market bubble burst, it was the investors who directly felt the effects of risk and loss. However, the global financial crisis, which started from the subprime mortgage crisis in the United States, led to a worldwide panic run centered in the repurchase market involving several trillion U.S. dollars. This created a new form of debt crisis in the financial industry. Wall Street was shaken, while investment banks, commercial banks, and insurance companies suffered heavy losses.

Capital Expansion in China's Age of Planned Economy

In the first 30 years after the establishment of the People's Republic of China, cities carried out a centrally planned economy consisting mainly of state-owned enterprises, while villages carried out a social economy was formed by poor farmers and agricultural laborers. This created a publicly-owned capital formation mechanism. The concept of capital was avoided, while the national plan was emphasized as "law." All wealth was state-owned, all revenue and expenses were centralized in the government accounts, and all credit was centralized in banks, but these factors had not stopped the expansion of capital and capital formation mechanism innovations. It is the inherent nature of capital to expand. It will find any opportunity, even in a highly centralized system, to express itself.

Other than centralized infrastructure building plans, the financial department first issued "small-scale technical loans" and "export product loans" through the China Construction Bank. Then, various "potential development and reform funds" were directly used from the budget, expanding the capital formation mechanism. In the 1970s, Shanghai, Changzhou, as well as Xiangyang (then known as Xiangfan) and Shashi in Hubei, expanded capital with small-scale loans, thus allowing the local governments to overshoot economic targets. This was a clever innovation in the capital formation mechanism.

The State Development Planning Commission induced an expansion of capital too. The commission adopted an objective that emphasized production over infrastructure building and infrastructure over finance. It expanded capital and the formation mechanism when financial needs caused the banks to issue money.

Other ways of capital expansion include the lateral transfer of collective capital by local governments. Companies pushed infrastructure building to increase production, and then drove repair and maintenance, finally raising the total costs. The unreasonable use and transfer of debts also contributed to the expansion of capital.

After the economic reform, the planned economy in China was replaced by a socialist market economy. In the beginning, bank loans replaced government funding as the capital source for infrastructure building, creating a dislocation of equity and debt in the capital formation mechanism. Bank loans were used for society building, and were in turn a mechanism for capital expansion. On the other hand, local governments encouraged "financing fever" and "bonds fever," while local offices organized foundations and local finances. Some banks also engaged in borderline activities such as lending out long-term loans with interbank lending capital, and lending out convoluted loans that involved a third party acting as an agent. These formed the first invested-capital used in building markets, companies, and rural companies so as to create the first capital formation mechanisms under a market economy.

Capital markets were developed later. The regulating authority had frequently prohibited the use of company capital in speculative activities, the use of bank capital in the stock market against regulations, and illegal private financing. However, due to the expanding nature of capital, capital tends to seek any opportunities in the system. Red chips are listed in Hong Kong, while public-initiated markets, such as the Zibo trading market and the Chengdu Hongmiaozi market, appeared. When credit regulation was at the tightest, underground financing appeared in Wenzhou, Zhejiang.

These capital expansion methods may sound questionable, but they show that however tight the administrative regulations, they cannot stop the inherent expanding nature of capital. "A clear pond has no fish" — economy and finance should not be regulated too tightly. Western markets only regulate actions that are specifically prohibited. Actions that are not specified in regulations, that were neither allowed nor prohibited, are treated with flexibility. Such flexibility is very important, and such open-mindedness is the key to China's reform. Many important policies are the evolution results of such flexibility. Looking back at the various breakthroughs in past "forbidden areas" that have occurred since China's reform, it seems that only a thin line separates groundbreaking and rule-breaking, truth and nonsense. The monetary authority has to keep a clear head, be sensitive to changes, be able to optimize production relations through system reform, and be able to induce and utilize capital. They have to encourage innovation in capital formation mechanisms, to transform as much idle social capital as possible into wealth-creating capital, and assist in the development of socialist productivity. In the innovation of capital formation mechanisms, regulators cannot always say no and punish innovative officials. More importantly, there is no reward without risk, and regulators should not throw out the baby with the bath water.

The Role of the Human in Capital Formation Mechanism Innovation

Capital formation mechanism belongs to the field of production relations.

Although the ultimate objective of capital formation mechanism innovation is the expansion of capital, it cannot be separated from human relationships in the formation of capital. That is, it cannot be separated from the relationships among investors, investees, banks, intermediaries, and the investment industry. From a social perspective, to encourage more human resources into developing capital formation mechanisms, and to encourage the transfer of deposits into investments, are the keys to speed up the accumulation and gathering of social capital. These are determining factors in the expansion of core social capital.

Capitalism is profit-oriented, and its objective is to maximize profit. This characteristic leads to capital being used more efficiently, and an annual increase in production, as pointed out by Marx. This nature of profit maximization is the key to attracting more human resources into working on capital formation mechanism innovation.

The way the investment bank manages finance can serve as an example. As stated above, the investment bank specializes in capital utilization, assets management (including fund management), corporate mergers and acquisitions, and corporate restructuring. Since there is a huge amount of excess capital that has a tendency to pursue maximum profit, and investment bankers work with the idea of "reward lures talents," bankers not only created opportunities for excess capital to create great profit, but also created a higher-than-average income for themselves. This helps in the deployment of more talents into innovating capital formation mechanism, developing investment banks into a high-income industry. In the example of helping companies with their IPO or listed companies with refinancing, investment banks are skilled in studying and comparing the opportunity cost and marginal value that capital may bring in future operations. They can thus discover the potential value of the capital, present it through specialized financial service, and realize the value by seizing investment opportunities. At the same time, since investment banks work with large amounts of capital, the related intermediary industry is, as a result, developed simultaneously. This includes accounting, the legal system, and the related supporting services, which together forms a high-income group that drives the development of the entire service industry.

The capital market and fictitious economy are other examples. The market economy has the ability to adjust supply and demand of a product, through changes in market price. One of their major contributions of the capital market and the fictitious economy is that they further push forward this function of the market economy. A huge amount of fictitious capital has been developed, and the fall or rise of their market price allows the public to adapt to differences in expected profit caused by differences in factors such as price, profit, interest rate, and currency exchange rate. This encourages people to be more active in the use of capital, bringing out the ability of the market in discovering value and in optimizing resource allocation. Excess capital is, as a result, channeled into new industries or regions, so that overproduction and underproduction are adjusted, and the regional economy and industrial structure are improved.

2 Chapter

Capital Is Not Only a Product of a Capitalist Society

Prologue: Blind Men and an Elephant

Capital is a sensitive topic that can stimulate a lot of debate.

It reminds me of the story of the blind men and the elephant. Four blind men were told to touch an object and describe what they felt. The first person described a snake; the second, a piece of canvas; the third, a tree trunk; and the forth, a piece of rope. Of course, it was an elephant.

We are probably like the blind men describing the elephant when we discuss capital from our own perspectives. The problem is to reach the concept of an elephant from the surface images of snake, canvas, tree trunk, and rope!

Let us return to the topic.

In the 60 years of socialism in the People's Republic of China, the concept of capital was avoided for 40 years. In these 40 years, capital was confused with money, and own capital was not distinguished from borrowed capital. When we discuss capital formation mechanism innovation, we have to trace the origin of capital, or we will be haunted by this specter of "capital avoidance."

The avoidance of capital in China comes from the inflexible socialist economic theory. Since the socialist revolution had destroyed the capitalist and exploitative systems, it seems logical that capital, which is dependent on the exploitative system, will cease to exist. There are no capitalists in state-owned companies, thus all capital distributed to state-owned companies by the national finance were called "funds." Long after the 1978 economic reform, there is still debate and avoidance within academia on whether companies under socialism need capital like all other companies.

In 1997, the 15th National Congress of the Communist Party of China confirmed, for the first time, that companies under socialism need capital as links. To increase the function of capital and to raise the efficiency of companies and capital become recognized goals. The fog on socialist capital was removed, but debate still persists even after 1997.

We have long been avoiding the topic of capital, thinking that it is a product of the capitalist society, and is only related to how capitalists exploit surplus labor. We think that exploitation does not exist under socialism, so capital that exploits surplus labor does not exist too. These are incorrect concepts. I once published an article "One Two Three: Questions on Capital" in *Investment Studies* No. 2, 1998, to explain this problem. In my opinion, if China were to build a socialist market economic system, the country has to build conglomerates through the market with capital as the link. It has to maximize the function of capital, and raise the efficiency of companies and capital. A correct concept on socialist capital is essential: Like all companies, companies under socialism require capital. This is the natural course of economic operation.

Capital Existed before the Capitalist Society

Capital is not the product of a capitalist society, it exists before the capitalist society, and before labor is commodified.

Currency has become capital with the development of the commodity economy. It is manifested as either commercial capital, or usury capital. It creates growth of wealth through buying cheap, selling expensive, and through high interest from loans. Marx called them "antediluvian forms,"[1] and differentiated them from the capital of economic institutions of modern-day society. At this stage, capital is only related to commodity production and circulation, and labor-power as a commodity is not a condition. The creation of surplus value is unrelated to capital, as profit is not the transformation of surplus value. The profit from capital in a pre-capitalist society is a result of the necessary labor and surplus labor of the merchant.

This shows that capital, commodity, and profit existed before the capitalist society. They are natural products in the development of the commodity economy, and are unrelated to the production and surplus value of the capitalist society. They, however, should be differentiated from the capital, commodity, and profit as defined by modern economics.

Capital Accumulation Is the Most Important Function of the Advancement of Society

Capital, as defined by those in modern economics, is created from money on the capitalist production foundation where labor is commodified. Capital can be "transformed from a given value to a self-expanding, or increasing, value," and "enables the capitalist to extract a certain quantity of unpaid labor, surplus-product and surplus-value from the laborers, and to appropriate it." In this way, capital, "aside from its use-value as money, acquires an additional use-value, namely that of serving as capital. Its use-value then consists precisely in the profit it produces when converted into capital."[2] Marx calls this value of money, which additional use-value can potentially bring a growth larger than the original excess of capital, surplus value.

Engels once said that Marx had two major discoveries. The first is the discovery of historical materialism, which proved that the "history of all hitherto existing society is the history of class struggle."[3] The second is the discovery of the theory of surplus value. It explains the relationship between capital and labor, and revealed how capitalists exploit the surplus value of workers. Marxist economy argues that for money to become capital, labor must be commodified. Marx proved, with various facts, that wages are not equal to the value produced by labor in the production process. The latter is greater than the former, and thus there is surplus value, and exploitation of such. This is an essential concept in understanding capital under a capitalist society.

Long before Marx, many bourgeoisie classical economists had proved the existence of surplus value. This surplus part of value is formed from the unequal pay for labor-produced products. However, as Engels pointed out, their studies stopped there. One of the most influential classical economists, David Ricardo, had on one hand discovered that value is produced by commodity producers through labor, in the labor theory of value. On the other hand, he was limited by the principle of equivalent exchange, thinking that it is only through commodity exchange that the amount received in sales can be greater than the original price in which the product is brought. Yet if commodity exchange can only be an equivalent exchange, how is value growth possible? This conflict left Ricardian theories in a dilemma. If the labor theory of value and the principle of equivalent exchange are adhered to, the existence of surplus value cannot be explained. If surplus value is to be recognized, either the labor theory of value, or the principle of equivalent exchange, or both, is wrong. Marx's theory of surplus value solved this problem. In the words of Engels, Marx "analyzed the transformation of money into capital and demonstrated that this transformation is based on the purchase and sale of labor-power. By substituting labor-power, the value-producing property, for labor he solved with one stroke one of the difficulties which brought about the downfall of the Ricardian school."[4] Marx differentiated the concepts of labor-power and labor. Capitalists buy labor-power from workers, and pay them in equal amount of wages in accordance to the principle of equivalent exchange. However, capitalists buy labor-power for their own use, meaning that they use the labor-power to carry out labor. Since labor-power creates a greater value than wages in the process of labor, surplus value is created, allowing capitalists to exploit this surplus. Marxist philosophy argues that for money to be transformed into capital, labor-power must be commodified, so that capital can exploit surplus products and values without paying any price.

Mao Yushi added a premise for exploitation: It must be an unequal and non-free exchange. Exploitation does not occur in equal and free exchanges, but occurs in exchanges when one of the parties is under control. Wage delay, wage deduction, practices that break labor laws, overtime work without pay or subsidies, and an unsafe working environment are all examples of exploitation. It is not exploitation if there are no such problems. Since the market is free and competitive, exploitation is impossible as the worker will look for a non-exploitative employer.

The concept that exploitation occurs when one of the parties in the exchange is under control, is very important. However, a capitalist economy is by nature led by capital, and capital is always in a dominant position in the production process. Workers only have labor-power, and are always in a disadvantaged position. Although the market is free and competitive, the non-exploitive employer does not exist since there is a surplus of labor. In the early stages of capitalism, capital lacks regulation, while allocation between labor and capital is strongly sided to capital. Even for China, which is in the early stages of socialism, some factories in the north have tense employee-employment relationships, and situations where profit erodes wages are common. Statistics show that the personal income to national income ratio has fallen from 64.10% in 1994 to 57.68% in 2004. Labor remuneration to national income ratio has fallen from 57.09% to 47.15%. This shows a decreasing trend in the amount received by workers in social distribution. In the new *Labor Contract Law* passed in 2007, the minimum wage is adopted. This is the use of the law to intervene in employee-employer conflicts, to protect workers' rights, and to ensure a fairer balance of profits and wages.

The first function of capital is that it exploits the surplus value in the capital-labor exchange. It performs another function, as it simultaneously changes a portion of surplus value back into capital, and brings about accumulation. It is impossible for capitalists to use all surplus value in consumption, and a considerable portion is transformed as capital to be re-used in production. Marx calls this process capital accumulation. In *Das Kapital*, Marx sees accumulation, the transformation of surplus value into capital, and the expansion of production as the same. It is this process that realizes the expansion and production of capital, or in other words, capital growth. Such capital activity allows capital to snowball and brings about capital accumulation. Marx points out in *Theories of Surplus Value*, "This part of the profit consists of "the surplus labor-time, which, even without the existence of capital, must constantly be performed by society, in order to have at its disposal, so to speak, a fund for development, which the very increase of population makes necessary."[5]

There are two layers of meaning in this quote.

Even without capital, society needs funds for development, which are created by surplus labor-time. Marx pointed out this necessity when discussing capitalist production methods and this necessity is even more relevant to socialist societies.

Capital realizes the accumulation of surplus labor-time. Other than the function of exploiting surplus value, capital also helps society accumulate surplus labor-time as it transform surplus value into capital. This accumulation is the most important function of the advancement of society.

Thus, even exploitation should be differentiated. On one hand, it is a shameful function that exploits the surplus labor of workers and help capitalists fulfill profit goals. On the other hand, when capitalists use a portion of profit as capital, they change surplus value back into capital and use it for capital accumulation of production expansion. This portion of exploitation helps society accumulate surplus labor-time, and this accumulation is important for society's advancement. Therefore, even without capital, even without capitalists exploiting the unpaid labor of workers, workers have to "exploit" themselves. That is, to accumulate surplus labor-time with unpaid labor.

On another note, Marx was writing in the early nineteenth century, where capitalism was in its early stages and rapidly developing. There was a mixture of slavery, feudal, and capitalist systems. What we now call "old capitalism" is the primitive, early, barbaric, and anarchic capitalism. Initial accumulation of capital originated from the enclosure movement more than 300 years ago, the colonial slave trade, and the capitalists' exploitation of workers through longer working hours and increased work rates. Marx witnessed the violent means of capitalists in the process of initial capital accumulation, writing "capital comes dripping from head to foot, from every pore, with blood and dirt."[6] This phenomenon was closely related to poor technology, low productivity, and a lack of regulation over capital at the primitive stages of capitalism. Marx and Engels write in *The Communist Manifesto*: "The bourgeoisie, during its rule of scarcely 100 years, has created more massive and more colossal productive forces than have all preceding generations together."[7] Marx also mentions that the unlimited productivity of modern industries is the first condition of the liberation of labor. Zhou Youguang states that "capitalists do not only exploit without producing value. Capitalists worked on the startup, management, and technological aspects of production. Startup is the most difficult step. If we annihilate capitalists, we annihilate talented entrepreneurs. Capitalists are all managers before the appearance of professional management staff. Most state-owned enterprises suffered deficits due to poor management. Capitalists are also the first engineers, before the appearance of professional engineers."[8] Marx too, has recognized the work of capitalists in the aspects of business startup, management, and technology.

Under Socialism, Capital Is a Socialist Element With Merely a Capitalist Name

Now, let us discuss whether capital exists in a socialist society. The "socialist society" here does not mean the primary stage of socialism as now in China where diverse forms of ownership coexist. It refers to the advanced stage of socialism which implements unitary public ownership. Or to put the question in another way, in a socialist society with unitary public ownership, can currency, commodity, enterprise, bank and other factors which have developed within the capitalist mode of production continue to exist independent from capitalism? At this time, can capital as an outcome of the capitalist mode of production get rid of its capitalist nature? Or to be more frank, is capital still related to the exploitation of surplus labor under a socialist society with unitary public ownership? And can capital exist without capitalism?

Before go into the above questions, we will first see some quotes from Karl Marx and Friedrich Engels with a hope to draw some inferences.

First, Marx had inferred from the economic realities of capitalism the distribution of total social product in the communist society in *Critique of the Gotha Program* and before dividing the total social product among the individuals, he made several deductions to establish various funds. These funds include: (1) Compensation funds which is a "cover for replacement of the means of production;" (2) accumulation funds which is used to expand production; (3) "reserve or insurance funds to provide against accidents, dislocations caused by natural calamities, etc." The remains are consumption funds which are "intended to serve as means of consumption."[9] Here, the compensation and accumulation funds are equivalent to the capital in our present society. The former is the original social capital while the latter is the additional capital which resulted from the capitalization of the surplus value, namely, the capital proliferation.

Second, when talking about distribution, Engels in the Socialism section of *Anti-Dühring* regarded accumulation as "the most important progressive function of society" and repeatedly talked that "accumulation is a social necessity," and society was required to secure an accumulation fund "for the maintenance and extension of production."[10]

Third, there was a passage in volume 3 of *Das Kapital* by Marx about the cooperative factories run by the workers of the capitalist society. "The co-operative factories of the labourers themselves represent within the old form the first sprouts of the new, although they naturally reproduce, and must reproduce, everywhere in their actual organization all the shortcomings of the prevailing system. But the antithesis between capital and labour is overcome within them, if at first only by way of making the associated labourers into their own capitalist, i.e., by enabling them to use the means of production for the employment of their own labour."[11]

As we have said in the previous section, the capital of the capitalist society, in addition to the "exploitation of surplus value," possesses another important role which is to accumulate the surplus labor-time. This accumulation is the most important function of the advancement of society. Therefore, in the socialist society with unitary public ownership, as long as the social reproduction does not stop, the transformation of capital to productive capital on the basis of socialized mass production as well as the currency-proliferation movement when currency serves as productive capital (namely, the movement of the accumulation of the surplus labor-time) also will not stop. Nonetheless, in the socialist society with unitary public ownership, once society destroys the shell of the capitalist mode of production, capital is deprived of the function of exploitation and is completely purified into a fund of production and development, necessary for the maintaining and expanding of the social production and development modes. At this time, capital has undergone the socialist baptism, gotten rid of the original capitalist nature, and become a socialist element — a socialist element with merely a capitalist name. The reasons are as follows:

First, within the state-owned economy and public economy under socialism, labor is no longer a commodity. The workers as masters of socialist enterprises are both their own capitalists and their employed labor. Surplus products created by the labor are no longer occupied by the capitalists for free (at this time, capitalists do not exist in the public economy), and instead the surplus is a kind of voluntary labor contributed by the workers for the social accumulation.

Second, socialist society achieves the public ownership of the means of production. Within public economy, capital is no longer a means to rule labor force and exploit surplus value, but continuously creates accumulation during the social reproduction and constantly completes the capitalization of the accumulation in order to form a large social development fund.

Third, in the public economy of socialism, there is no surplus value which results from the capitalists' exploitation of workers, but surplus labor-time and surplus products exist in the social reproduction. This kind of surplus, as Marx said, is the workers "using the means of production for the employment of their own labour." This employment of labor, as a kind of accumulation, represents the most important function of the advancement of society.

The capital mentioned in the above paragraphs is within the context of the public economy of socialism. It is separated from the capitalists, has nothing to do with capitalism and is not exploitative in nature. This capital can be referred to as either "fund" or "capital." I prefer to maintain the name "capital," because there are still capitalist countries and enterprises around the world, and socialist enterprises need to use their capital in a way conforming to all sorts of commercial practices of international capital and as a basis for commercial dialogues with the enterprises of the international capital. To continue using the name of "capital," just as we have kept the original names of commodity, currency, profit and bank, could make it easier to remember the original form. Someone maybe would ask why we could not call it "fund" instead of "capital." To be frank, capital was avoided to be called "capital" in the 40 years after the founding of new China and was called "funds" instead. Unfortunately, this name failed to sort things out but added to the confusion. The first 30 years saw a heavy financial burden caused by the excessive funding, while within the 10 years after the reform and opening up policy, over-indebtedness of enterprises took place.

Further, to make logical reasoning in accordance with the traditional socialist theory, we could say that only when a large-scale socialized planned economy is established and all land, factories, means of production are owned by the society, could all exploitation be possibly eliminated. Logically speaking, the relations of production in the socialist public economy should be perfect. No surplus value resulted from the capitalists' exploitation of workers exists, but the surplus labor-time and surplus products contributed by workers for the social accumulation in the form of voluntary labor. Meanwhile, there is no capital from the exploitation of laborers but production funds of the accumulation of surplus labor-time and surplus products. Nonetheless, although the Soviet Union, China before the reforming and opening up policy, and the eastern European countries have implemented planned economies and socialist public ownership systems, the relations of production of their state-owned economies are still not in harmony. I think there are many reasons for this matter, but the most fundamental ones are:

First, excessive accumulation. There should be a limit to accumulation when distributing the total social product. The socialist country replaced the capitalists and turned the surplus value generated from the capitalists' exploitation of laborers into the nominal accumulation of surplus labor-time and surplus products. These surpluses were all turned over to the state for the priority development of heavy industry and thus there was a great scarcity of consumer goods. The workers were dubbed "masters of the country" but in reality they worked at a low wage. After the jubilation and enthusiasm of the status conversion from workers to the master of society at the early days of the victory of the revolution, in the face of the long-term low-wage "voluntary contribution," workers would recognize this "voluntary contribution" as the synonym of "exploitation" which socialist countries refused to admit. In this case, the "masters" would start to embrace the thoughts of employment, and the "to give remuneration on the basis of work done" would develop into "to do work on the basis of remuneration given" and "to spine the work out." This is a logical punishment of "iron rice bowl" and "reward of egalitarianism." In Western countries, democratic socialist parties have set a standard of minimal wages to restrain the capitalists' exploitation of laborers. In the socialist society, laborers are in power and workers are the masters of the country, but they offer long-term "voluntary contribution" with low wages. How should such enterprises and workers display motivation and vitality?

Second, rigid management and failure in motivating the enthusiasm of enterprises. In the Soviet Union and Eastern European countries, as well as China before the reform and opening up, state-owned enterprises would turn all the profits over to the treasury. The state-owned enterprises have neither capital nor the capitalization of surplus value, and therefore there is no snowballed capital accumulation as in grassroots enterprises. Thus, the state-owned enterprises of the Soviet Union, Eastern European countries, and China are not as good as the Western capitalist enterprises which possess the capability and vitality of self-transformation, self-accumulation, and self-development.

Third, with only top-down arrangements, the enterprises of those socialist countries excluded the market. Consequently, the enterprises lacked the information of supply and demand from the market and lost the flexibility and enthusiasm of independent production arrangement based on the market demand.

Finally, a more fundamental problem is that in the Soviet Union, Eastern European countries, and China before reform and opening up, the productivity of society was low and far beyond the level enough for implementing "socialist public ownership." Therefore, the "planned economy and public ownership" carried out by those countries surpassed the development stage of the history. Moreover, the "planned economy" itself is till controversial and even though in a socialist society under public ownership, moderate accumulation, flexible management, attention to market, and motivation to employers, enterprises and market are indispensable.

The Coexistence of Two Kinds of Capital at the Primary Stage of Socialism

China is now at the primary stage of socialism with diversified forms of ownership, and there are also various forms of capital which can be roughly divided into two categories:

The first is being capitalist by nature. In the primary stage of socialism, there is still a part of the economy of capitalist nature, including foreign-owned enterprises, Sino-foreign joint ventures and domestic private-capital enterprises. That is because the productivity at this primary stage is very low and there is a need to make room for the development of the capitalist economy to a certain degree; therefore, the state recognizes the legitimacy of private capital and its exploitation of a certain degree in the form of law and protects its legal interest. On the other hand, the government protects the legitimate interest of the workers (such as stipulating the standard of minimal wages) and controls the degree of exploitation of capital via tax laws (such as income tax, windfall tax, and inheritance tax). Overall, the capital of the capitalist enterprises in the present society is both a restricted capital and a capital whose development must be protected for the development of social productivity forces.

The other is the capital of a socialist nature. In addition to state-owned enterprises and enterprises under collective ownership which are comprised of government capital and public capital, respectively, there is still a large number of joint-stock companies of a diverse economic composition. This is a share economy, a mixed ownership economy, and, of course, a socialist economy. It should be noted that a large number of shares of the economy are held by the massive number of laborers and the source of the capital is the accumulation of labor income. The nature of the capital should be deemed more as what Marx called the capital of cooperative factory by the workers. In Marx's words: To make "the associated labourers into their own capitalists," and they "use the means of production for the employment of their own labour."

Specially, the *Decision of the Central Committee of the Communist Party of China on Some Issues concerning the Improvement of the Socialist Market Economy* passed by the Third Plenary Session of the Sixteenth Central Committee of the CPC Central Committee in 2003 decided to "vigorously develop the mixed ownership economy participated in by state-owned capital, collective capital, and nonpublic capital, etc., realize the diversity of investors and make the joint-stock system the principal form of realization of public ownership." This decision has inestimable theoretical significance and will play an important role in promoting the joint-stock reform of state-owned enterprises and the development of a mixed ownership economy.

3 Chapter

Joint-Stock System: From Socialized Mass Production to Capital Socialization

Prologue: Financing through the Joint-Stock System by Yantai Power Plant and the Reason Why New York Became a World Financial Center

Let us begin with two stories.

The first story took place in China after the start of the reform and opening up policy.

Shandong Province used to suffer from power shortages while Yantai City, located in the north of the province, contained coal reserves. In 1980, the municipal government of Yantai proposed to the Ministry of Electric Power of China the building of two power plants with an installed capacity of 200,000 kilowatts for each. The first-phase investment required RMB165 million. The ministry, however, did not have such a large sum of money and suggested a joint investment with the local government. Unfortunately, the Yantai government was on a tight budget. At that time, the government came up with the idea of raising funds through issuing shares. The municipal government planned to commission the Yantai City Branch of China Construction Bank (CCB) to float stocks of 110 million to be subscribed to by big electricity consumers and rural communes and production teams. In practice, the Yantai CCB had drafted a financing plan and reported it to the State Planning Commission, the Ministry of Electric Power, and the headquarters of CCB. After several rounds of discussions, the stocks were finally issued in 1981. Li Peng, the then Minister of the Ministry of Electric Power, wrote an inscription for the Yantai government, which read "Financing for a power station, first in the nation." Actually, the so-called "stock" would generate interest together with dividends, and at last the principal would also be paid back. Strictly speaking, it was not a real stock and it was more like a bond. Despite this, the practice was indeed a pioneering work in China.

I do not know whether the shareholding system in the Yantai power plants was successful or not, but the first innovation in capital formation mechanism after the reform and opening up should be attributed to the pilot in the Yantai power plants. This innovation broke away from the restrictions of the planned economy and collected money by introducing a joint-stock system.

The second story happened in the U.S. and was told by a famous Chinese economist, Xu Xiaonian.

The financial industry was developed earlier in London than other cities around the world, and London was the world's first financial center. But why did New York exceed London later on to become the global financial center? It is said that the primary cause was the introduction of the capacity for a limited liability company in the U.S. law which was enacted by the Empire State in the late 19th century. When a company of this nature goes bankruptcy, its investors will only be held liable for the amount invested in the company and not be subject to unlimited responsibility. This is a very effective way to protect the interest of investors, and therefore many people registered their companies in the State of New York and New York became a popular investment destination for investors. In fact, this was the prelude to the rise of New York as the world financial center later. Seeing the financial prosperity in New York, London did the same thing in order to incorporate limited liability into its law.

Socialized Mass Production Requires Capital Socialization

The industrial revolution brought about the socialization of production and the production mode of workshop handicrafts was required to make a breakthrough in order to expand the scale of industrial production and capital. At that time, owing to the introduction of a joint-stock system, the capital formation mechanism realized its first innovation. It was a concrete manifestation of socialized production which called for capital socialization.

In Western countries, stock companies and stocks first emerged in large-scale businesses such as voyage trading and banking industries in the 16th century. Earlier stock companies and stocks were just simple means of fundraising and profit-making through speculation, and had nothing to do with the socialization of production.

In the 16th century, among the ocean steamers which engaged in overseas voyage trading (in fact, colonial plundering) in the old capitalist colonial countries, such as the U.K. and the Netherlands, there appeared shareholding companies to raise capital and spread risks owing to the industry's huge costs. For example, the Muscovy Company (also called the Russian Company) was the first major chartered joint-stock company to be established in the U.K. in 1553, followed by the Levant Company (later, known as the Turkey Company) which was formed in 1581, and then the East India Company in 1600. These companies raised funds from adventurous merchants and dealt with long-voyage trade by way of overseas pillaging. Due to a series of reasons, such as the construction of long-distance ocean steamers which needed a large amount of money, the business was vulnerable to the attacks from aborigines, and large profits were accompanied by high risks. The steamers, at first, collected capital stock before each voyage, and returned the money with dividends when the journey was completed. These companies, however, felt the inconvenience of raising money every time before sailing and gradually transformed into companies of fixed shares, distributing dividends on a regular basis. As a result, a shareholding system came into being. In 1602, the Dutch East India Company was set up by issuing penny stocks as a joint-stock company. Later on, shareholders had the need to cash in their stocks so people conducted private mortgage, discounts, and transfer of shares, which evolved into today's stock transactions. The first stock exchange was established in 1613 in Amsterdam, the Netherlands, and a group of government-backed joint-stock banks showed up in the European and American banking industries in the late 17th century. The joint-stock companies and stocks at this time, however, were simply aimed at raising funds, making profits through speculation, and spreading risks. They, from the very beginning, displayed a feature of using other people's capital to run a risk without a single sign of socialized mass production. The stock companies and security investment did not appear in the industrial sector until the late 18th century.

The delayed development of stock companies and stocks in the capitalist industrial sector, compared to that in other domains, was mainly due to the fact that the productive force of capitalism at that time was not high enough to break through the constraint of individual capital.

In the earlier stage of capitalism, the workshop handicraft industry was in a dominant place and the amount of capital needed for production was not very large thanks to the small size of the workshops. Initially, the asset of a workshop was contributed to by a single capitalist or a few capitalists, and the investors were the capital users with the ownership and management rights of a workshop being tied closely together. Until the 18th century, the British Industrial Revolution drove forward the transition of major industrial sectors from handicraft production to large-scale production with machinery, and social productive forces made a great leap forward. Not only did industrial production expand rapidly, but also basic industries such as transportation, energy, raw materials, and public utilities had the demand to correspondingly scale up their productions and make huge investments in order to push forward socialized mass production. At this point, the investment scale of industrial enterprises was beyond the financial capability of an individual capitalist. Neither could a capitalist government sustain the massive investment in the public works sector. Mechanization and socialized mass production demanded a new kind of capital formation mechanism. Consequently, during the late 18th century and early 19th century, the heavy investment demand from industries involved in waterways, railways, highways, electricity, telegraph, gas, water, docks, and mining caused these industries to undertake equity financing. So the first innovation of a capital formation mechanism could be attributed to the joint-stock system.

The innovation in capital formation adapted to the needs of mechanization and socialization of production, overcame the restriction of an individual capital, and developed from a sole proprietorship and partnership to a joint-stock company collecting funds from the whole society. The joint-stock system, therefore, met the requirements for developing industrial productive forces, made the industries no longer confined to private ownership and individual capital, and created a way to collectively use social capital despite a spreading of ownership. Mass production led to capital socialization, just as what Marx had said in *Das Kapital*: "The world would still be without railways if it had had to wait until accumulation had got a few individual capitals far enough to be adequate for the construction of a railway. Centralization, on the contrary, accomplished this in the twinkling of an eye, by means of joint-stock companies."[1] Marx praised joint-stock companies by stating that "they gave in one word, an impetus never before suspected to the concentration of capital."[2] From then on, enterprises were able to build great social productive forces by centralizing mass capital according to the scale of industrial production, free from the limitation of individual capital.

Another innovation of the joint-stock system in capital formation was limited liability. During the years of workshop handicraft economy, the enterprises' property organization form was transformed from a single proprietorship to a partnership, namely when the capital of an individual capitalist was not sufficient, at least two capitalists would add in their capital to form a partnership. The property, however, was merely the accumulation of capital from two or more capitalists who collectively shared the interest and risks, and it was nothing more than a simple addition of several individual capitalists. For instance, if Mr. Zhang opens a Zhang's Candy Factory and later Mr. Wang invests in the company, the company will become Zhang and Wang's Candy Factory. Of course, the two share the profits and risks of the factory together since both have contributed capital. It has to be noted that this partnership, the same as sole proprietorship, is accompanied by unlimited liabilities. In addition, the growth in the number of partners would give rise to conflicts in plant control, business decision-making, profit distribution, and risk sharing. As a result, partnership was transformed into a limited partnership, that is, everyone contributes whatever he has, either money or labor. The one who invests money is only liable to the value of his investment in the company while the one who invests labor is the decision-maker and manager of the company and will bear unlimited liability. In benefit distribution, the latter, the same as the former, will receive a certain amount of money in accordance with his contribution, usually 20%–25% of the total profits.

A joint-stock system evolves from the partnership with limited liability and makes a complete separation between money contributor and labor contributor. Labor contributor, i.e., "the actually functioning capitalist" transforms "into a mere manager, administrator of other people's capital," whereas money contributor, i.e., "the owner of capital" turns "into a mere owner, a mere money-capitalist."[3] If the limited partnership developing on the basis of workshop handicraft needs a contract to specify each partner's rights, obligations, and responsibilities, a breakthrough made by the joint-stock system based on socialized mass production is to simplify capital, rights and responsibilities into shares, due to the large scale of businesses, huge capital demands, and a great number of investors. In this way, investment resembles the purchase of goods with the only difference being that this time the goods are shares. The obligation of respective investors is clear: An investor's financial liability is limited to the value of his investment, which is called "limited liability," and thus a stock company is usually a "limited liability company."

The joint-stock system must emphasize a limited liability and a shareholder's liability is only limited to his financial contribution. This is very important and constitutes the essence of capital culture — to protect investment and investors.

The Twists and Turns in China's Practice of a Joint-Stock System

China is a socialist country and this calls for the socialization of production. Logically, China should not hesitate to carry out a joint-stock economy, but for various reasons, the practice of the joint-stock system has become a tortuous process. In later sections, we will talk about some sensitive topics related to this.

For a long time, the issues of a joint-stock system, stocks, and the securities markets were the forbidden areas of socialism. At the beginning of 1992 when the former Chinese leader Deng Xiaoping paid a visit to a few southern cities, he pointed out: "Are securities and the stock market good or bad? Do they entail any dangers? Are they peculiar to capitalism? Can socialism make use of them? We allow people to reserve their judgment, but we must try these things out. If, after one or two years of experimentation, they prove feasible, we can expand them. Otherwise, we can put a stop to them and be done with it. We can stop them all at once or gradually, totally, or partially. What is there to be afraid of? So long as we keep this attitude, everything will be all right, and we shall not make any major mistakes. In short, if we want socialism to achieve superiority over capitalism, we should not hesitate to draw on the achievements of all cultures and to learn from other countries, including the developed capitalist countries, all advanced methods of operation and techniques of management that reflect the laws governing modern socialized production."[4] This talk provided the Chinese people with a clear direction for trying out a joint-stock system, securities, and stock markets.

As a matter of fact, new China, in its early economic life, inherited the concepts of joint-stock system, share capital, stocks, securities and securities trading from old China. In the initial period of new China, when the government confiscated bureaucratic capital and built a state-owned economy, the government shares transformed from the confiscated bureaucratic capital were assigned to China's Bank of Communications for collective management. At that time, I was working for the Bank of Communications (predecessor of CCB) and the bank once gathered a group of comrades to set up a department, especially responsible for participating in the broad of directors of joint ventures, regularly inspecting the companies' operation and collecting dividends. People called those joint state-private enterprises "state capitalism," and the government encouraged the private enterprises to implement a joint state-private ownership because it believed this measure would lead to the peaceful transformation of private capitalism to socialism.

We should be clear here that at the early stage of new China when Mao Zedong still advocated the new democratic revolution, he supported the need for a great development of capitalism in China. Mao believed that before China turned to socialist revolution, there must be a long period for private enterprises of democratic management, and China's industrialization must take advantage of the growth of private enterprises and the investment from foreign capitalists. He was also convinced that it was inevitable for new democracy to experience a long period of capitalist private economy. In that period, moreover, to develop joint state-private enterprises (i.e. state capitalism) was a necessary way to lead to the peaceful transition of private capitalism to socialism. Despite the fact that the government's policies allowed and encouraged the joint state-private ownership, people tended to underestimate the value of joint ownership and share capital, and regarded them as makeshift methods for the transition from capitalism to socialism. They thought that the joint ownership will finally be transformed into a unitary ownership by the whole people. By 1952, Mao Zedong saw that industrial working capital accounted for 67.3% and the working capital of commercial-retail sector also reached 40% in China, and thus believed that socialist economic power had achieved an advantageous and leading position. Accordingly, in 1953, the Central Committee of the CPC officially determined the general line of the Party for the transition period: "Basically, to accomplish the industrialization of the country and the socialist transformation of agriculture, handicrafts, and capitalist industry and commerce in 10 to 15 years, or a little longer."[5] Therefore, the "Great Leap Forward" between 1958 and 1960 promoted the joint state-private ownership with eagerness and zest in the hopes of fulfilling the reform of private capital ahead of the schedule and entering socialism in advance. Additionally, the 10-year Cultural Revolution after 1966 more directly forced a way to socialism by announcing the cancellation of capitalist redemption on the basis of a fixed rate of interest.

New China took over the stock exchanges from old China when Shanghai, Tianjin, and Peiping were liberated. At that time, Chen Yun, who was in charge of China's financial works, thought of utilizing and reforming those stock exchanges to make them serve new China. Later, speculative capital in Shanghai took advantage of the modern telecommunications facilities of the Shanghai Stock Exchange to disseminate false information to the whole city, which incurred an inflation of silver dollars and the price tripled within 10 days. Consequently, the Shanghai Military Control Commission punished the speculators and closed the Shanghai Stock Exchange in June 1949. On the contrary, the Tianjin and Beijing Stock Exchanges started business in June 1949 and February 1950 in succession. Not until the "Three-Anti and Five-Anti Campaign" of 1952, did the two suspend operations (in July and October, respectively) due to the reduced number of brokers.

There are two points I want to make clear.

First, in the early stages of new China, people, based on their understandings of new democratic revolution, correctly regarded the joint-stock system as the best form for promoting state capitalism and reforming private capitalism, but they did not make great efforts to develop the system and share capital. On the contrary, under the leftist thinking of being eager to transition to socialism, people always deemed public ownership as the advanced form of state capitalism and thus were longing to step into socialism as early as possible.

Second, at that time, China followed the economic pattern of the Soviet Union, and despite keeping stock exchanges, China did not possess the conditions for the distribution of securities, which was deemed to be a blind alley. Thirty years later, when the Third Plenary Session of the Eleventh CPC Central Committee in 1978 ushered in a new era of reform and opening up, the Chinese government decided to strengthen domestic lateral economic ties, attract foreign investment, and encourage the construction of Sino-foreign joint venture and cooperation projects. This action naturally caused a debate over whether the joint-stock system, share capital, stock and securities markets were socialist or capitalist in nature. The core issue was whether a socialist market economy should engage in joint-stock, share capital, stock and securities markets? To put it more directly, do those things exclusively belong to capitalism? Can socialism make use of them? These questions indicated that there was a large realm unknown to the Chinese people.

To solve the above questions, we need to refer to Marxism.

Marx: Share-Capital as the Most Perfect Form Leading to Communism

We know that as early as a century ago, Marx spoke highly of stock companies by saying that "stock-company business represents the abolition of capitalist private industry by social capital."[6] When Marx studied the capitalist mode of production, he examined various forms of capital in the process of social reproduction, and exposed a contradiction in the capitalist mode of production, which cannot be solved by capitalism itself, namely, the contradiction between the socialization of production and private ownership. Marx investigated not only individual and social capital but also production and circulation capital, fixed and floating capital, variable and constant capital, and industrial and financial capital. At last, he focused on share capital and found that it may be the "final form" and "ultimate positing of capital," and may also be "the most perfect form...leading to communism." And the capitalist stock companies would be "the transitional forms from the capitalist mode of production to the associated one."[7] Unfortunately, latter Marxists failed to give due attention to this important theoretical insight of Marx, so they took an indifferent attitude towards share capital and the joint-stock system in the long-term practice of socialism.

Marx affirmed the positive meanings of share capital and stock enterprises from four aspects.

1. Share capital manifests itself as a kind of social power and product in the form of social capital and enables capital to reach its final form.

Marx commented on stock companies by saying that:

(1) *[The formation of stock companies resulted in] an enormous expansion of the scale of production and of enterprises, that was impossible for individual capitals. At the same time, enterprises that were formerly government enterprises, become public.*

(2) *The capital, which in itself rests on a social mode of production and presupposes a social concentration of means of production and labour-power, is here directly endowed with the form of social capital (capital of directly associated individuals) as distinct from private capital, and its undertakings assume the form of social undertakings as distinct from private undertakings. It is the abolition of capital as private property within the framework of capitalist production itself.*[8]

The socialized concentration of social capital and social undertakings described by Marx is different from the concentration in a general sense. The concentration in the above block quotation — "a social concentration of means of production and labor-power" — still refers to the concentration which originally existed in the general capitalist private capital and private undertakings. On the other hand, social capital and social undertakings under the context of share capital specifically refers to the socialized concentration of individual private capitals. The individual capitals collected for founding a joint-stock company thereby acquire a social nature to become "associated individuals," and are "endowed with the form of social capital." They manifest themselves as social power and products.

We know that the minimal capital requirement for effective production in capitalist industry will increase along with the improvement of productivity. The development of the capitalist mode of production will raise the minimum amount of capital necessary to operate a business under normal conditions. As for the industries which have a longer production cycle and larger scale, such as railways, they require in the long-term a huge amount of advanced capital, and thus there must be abundant capital in the hands of the capitalists. In this case, to solely rely on the capital accumulation of a single capitalist is far from enough and the social concentration of capital must play a complementary role. Credit and competition, therefore, become the most powerful levers of concentration. There are two ways for social concentration: one "by the violent method of annexation" in competition; and the other is on the basis of credit and through "the smoother process of organizing joint-stock companies" to realize "the fusion of a number of capitals already formed or in the process of formation."[9] The social concentration of a joint-stock company achieved through "the fusion of a number of capitals already formed or in process of formation" is an innovation in the capital formation mechanism which is the topic for this book. It guarantees adequate capital for industrial enterprises to expand their production scales and achieves the final form of capital in which "the mode of production based on capital is already developed to its highest stage."[10]

Marx repeatedly praised the social concentration of capital through establishing a joint-stock company. In *Das Kapital*, he commended that centralization, "in the twinkling of an eye, by means of joint-stock companies," accomplished capital growth "enough to be adequate for the construction of a railway." "The masses of capital fused together overnight by centralization reproduce and multiply as the others do, only more rapidly, thereby becoming new and powerful levers in social accumulation."[11] In a letter written from Marx to Nikolai Danielson in April 1879, he praised railways as "couronnement de l'oeuvre," because "they were the basis of immense joint stock companies" and "they gave in one word, an impetus never before suspected to the concentration of capital."[12]

As for share capital which obtains social attributes through the socialization of capital, Marx pointed out that "hence mostly share capital, the form in which capital has worked itself up to its final form, in which it is posited, not only in itself, in its substance, but is posited also in its form, as social power and product."[13]

2. Share capital is the ultimate positing of capital after social capital dissolving private capital.

First is the abolition of private capital by share capital.

In the above block quotation, Marx regarded the social funds collected via stocks by joint-stock companies under the capitalist mode of production as "social capital," and defined "social capital" as "capital of directly associated individuals as distinct from private capital." He also defined joint-stock companies as "social undertakings as distinct from private undertakings."

In other places, Marx referred to "capital of directly associated individuals" as either "associated capitalists"[14] or "collective capitalists,"[15] and both terms emphasize the social attributes obtained through the socialization of capital. As a result, share capital is transformed into social capital and dissolves private capital. Similarly, enterprises established on the basis of "capital of directly associated individuals" gain a social nature. Despite the fact that this kind of capital is first and foremost the private property of capitalists, the enterprises funded by this capital become social undertakings instead of private undertakings.

Second is the abolition of individual capital by share capital.

Marx talked about the abolition of individual capital by competition and share capital in *The Grundrisse* (1857–1858).

> *The influence of individual capitals on one another has the effect precisely that they must conduct themselves as capital; the seemingly independent influence of the individuals, and their chaotic collisions, are precisely the positing of their general law. Market here obtains yet another significance. The influence of capitals as individuals on each other thus becomes precisely their positing as general beings, and the suspension of the seeming independence and independent survival of the individuals. This suspension takes place even more in credit. And the most extreme form to which the suspension proceeds, which is however at the same time the ultimate positing of capital in the form adequate to it — joint-stock capital.*[16]

These words of Marx elaborated to us how competition realizes suspension of independence and independent survival of the individual capital through the interaction among individual capitals, and finally generates joint-stock capital which is "at the same time the ultimate positing of capital in the form adequate to it." The form of share capital or Joint-stock capital, moreover, abolished the "seeming independence and independent survival of the individuals [i.e. individual capital]" and becomes "the most extreme form" of the suspension.

Third is that share capital is "the abolition of capitalist private industry on the basis of the capitalist system itself." Marx believed that stock-company business "destroys private industry as it expands and invades new spheres of production."[17]

We can find explanations of the above words from the supplementary materials contributed by Engels in *Das Kapital*.

In the Chapter 27 of *Das Kapital* Vol.3, Engels listed a number of enterprises which have developed as "new forms of industrial enterprises" like cartels, "representing the second and third degree of stock companies…In every country this [bankruptcy] is taking place through the big industrialists of a certain branch joining in a cartel for the regulation of production. A committee fixes the quantity to be produced by each establishment and is the final authority for distributing the incoming orders." "This [insufficient association in production] led in some branches, where the scale of production permitted, to the concentration of the entire production of that branch of industry in one big joint-stock company under single management."[18] In another chapter, Engels went on, "thereafter, gradual conversion of industry into stock companies" happened, and "one branch after another suffered this fate...Then the trusts, which create gigantic enterprises under common management (such as United Alkali); The ordinary individual firm is more and more only a preliminary stage to bring the business to the point where it is big enough to be 'founded'."[19]

Fourth is the abolition.

When mentioning abolition, Marx said it in four ways: 1. The social capital forming on the basis of joint-stock enterprises and share capital is "the abolition of capital as private property within the framework of capitalist production itself;"[20]

2. Joint-stock system is "the abolition of capitalist private industry on the basis of the capitalist system itself;"[21] 3. "This is the abolition of the capitalist mode of production within the capitalist mode of production itself, and hence a self-dissolving contradiction, which prima facie represents a mere phase of transition to a new form of production;"[22] 4. Through competition, share capital finally achieves "the ultimate positing of capital in the form adequate to it," abolishes "the seeming independence and independent survival of the individuals," and establishes the form of share capital as "the most extreme form" of abolition.[23]

When Marx was reviewing capitalist society, he focused on the abolition of private capital "within the framework of capitalist production itself," which is the essence of studying a society by Marxism. The reason why Marx criticized many vulgar economists is precisely because "the *vulgus* is unable to conceive the forms developed in the lap of capitalist production, separate and free from their antithetical capitalist character."[24]

3. The Joint-stock company is a transitional form from the capitalist mode of production to the associated one.

Marx believed that stock companies are the abolition of capitalist private capital by social capital, and at the same time conducted research based on the contrast between stock companies and cooperative factories. He thought that "the co-operative factories of the laborers themselves represent within the old form the first sprouts of the new;" "but the antithesis between capital and labor is overcome within them, if at first only by way of making the associated laborers into their own capitalists." The laborers "use the means of production for the employment of their own labor." Marx held the idea that the antagonism is resolved negatively in the capitalist mode of production while positively in the associated mode. Marx, however, saw from cooperative factories "how a new mode of production naturally grows out of an old one." So he concluded that "the capitalist stock companies, as much as the co-operative factories, should be considered as transitional forms from the capitalist mode of production to the associated one."[25]

Marx continued discussing the transitional form. He said that "in stock companies, the function is divorced from capital ownership, hence also labor is entirely divorced from the ownership of the means of production and surplus-labor. This result of the ultimate development of capitalist production is a necessary transitional phase towards the reconversion of capital into the property of producers, although no longer as the private property of the individual producers, but rather as the property of associated producers, as outright social property. On the other hand, the stock company is a transition toward the conversion of all functions in the reproduction process which still remain linked with capitalist property, into mere functions of associated producers, into social functions."[26]

What is important here is that Marx called the future producers of communist society "associated producers" when talking about "the property of associated producers" and "mere functions of associated producers." It will be helpful for solving the Sphinx riddle in the reestablishment of individual ownership in the future communist society, if we study this notion together with the conception of giving producers "individual property based on the acquisition of the capitalist era: i.e., on cooperation and the possession in common of the land and of the means of production" in the future society,[27] and the conception of "free individuals." In a community of free individuals, people "carry on their work with the means of production in common," social product is to satisfy the social production and consumption, and "[the] apportionment [of labor time] in accordance with a definite social plan maintains the proper proportion between the different kinds of work to be done and the various wants of the community." "Labor time also serves as a measure of the portion of the common labor borne by each individual, and of his share in the part of the total product destined for individual consumption."[28]

4. Share capital is "the most perfected form" that is "turning into communism"

In a letter from Marx to Engels talking about *Das Kapital*, Marx drafted an outline. In the outline, the words related to capital and share capital were as follows.

> *Capital falls into four sections. a) Capital en general (This is the substance of the first instalment) b) Competition or the interaction of many capitals. c) Credit where capital, as against individual capitals, is shown to be a universal element. d) Share capital as the most perfected form (turning into communism) together with all its contradictions.*[29]

This outline corresponds with the ideas put forward in Chapter 27, Vol. 3 of *Das Kapital* and other works of Marx. However, to regard share capital as "the most perfected form" that is "turning into communism" is the most explicit and best condensation of share capital by Marx. Unfortunately, Marx has not elaborated on why share capital is "the most perfected form" that is "turning into communism" and how share capital could turn into communism and all other contradictions, so that we have to infer from this simple outline and other analysis of Marx on share capital.

It is also the case that Marx pointed out some negative impacts of share capital while admitting its positive role. He warned us that "the conversion to the form of stock still remains ensnared in the trammels of capitalism; hence, instead of overcoming the antithesis between the character of wealth as social and as private wealth, the stock companies merely develop it in a new form."[30] He added that in the capitalist mode of production, the joint-stock system "reproduces a new financial aristocracy, a new variety of parasites in the shape of promoters, speculators, and simply nominal directors; a whole system of swindling and cheating by means of corporation promotion, stock issuance, and stock speculation. It is private production without the control of private property."[31] Obviously, all those negative effects should be overcome when we carry out the joint-stock system in today's world.

It has been one and a half century since Marx wrote those words on share capital. One interesting fact is that capitalist countries did not give up share capital easily just because it would lead to communism, but stepped up the development of the joint-stock system, stocks, and securities markets by following the law of socialized production instead. On the contrary, in socialist society, people repeatedly claimed to develop the socialized production to the highest level; however, for a long period of time, they refused the socialized forms including the joint-stock system, stocks and securities markets which could make the most of social capital. More importantly, when China was at the stage of New Democratic Revolution, the government dared to declare without scruple that we encouraged private capitalist enterprises to implement a public-private partnership and would lead a peaceful transformation of private capitalism to socialism. China used to be so close to Marxism on the issues of joint-stock system and share capital, but moved away from the ideas of Marx when the country was eager to transform itself into a socialist country. Now, when China announces again that it would "make the joint-stock system the principal form of the realization of public ownership," the above detours should be avoided.

Stock System Starts Amid Numerous Ideological Obstacles After Reform and Opening Up

The Third Plenary Session of the Eleventh CPC Central Committee in 1978, which proposed the policy of opening to the outside world and invigorating the domestic economy, encouraged all sectors, local governments, and enterprises to be active in building socialism. Since the construction of socialism needed capital, a great variety of financing methods emerged and the stock system was among those methods.

As mentioned earlier, the State Development Planning Commission approved the issuance of shares by Longkou Power Plant, Yantai City, Shandong Province, to big electricity consumers and rural communes and production teams. This was the first case of a government giving a formal consent to stock issuance.

After this practice, joint-equity investment happened frequently. After a year of research, the State Planning Commission, State Economic and Trade Commission, Ministry of Finance, People's Bank of China, and CCB in October 1982 jointly formulated *Interim Measures for Trial Implementation of Domestic Joint Venture Construction*, in order to promote and guide the healthy development of joint ventures. The *Measures* put forward that joint venture construction projects could be set up, regardless of the restrictions of sectors, locations, and ownerships, between central and local governments, urban and rural areas, the entire society and a group of people, industry and agriculture, industry and commerce, agriculture and commerce, and military and civilian sectors, according to their respective advantages in resources, capital, equipment, and technology. This was the first time that all kinds of financial resources could be invested in joint ventures; plants, sites, and equipment (including deferred projects) were allowed to be converted into shares; and even technology could be appraised as capital stock and share profits. The *Measures*, however, stipulated "three unchanged" things, namely ownerships, relationships of administrative subordination, and financial relations. Although the *Measures* just put forward a joint venture rather than a joint-stock system, it was a necessary road towards the latter.

After the *Measures* was promulgated, local governments took the initiative to carry out many trial projects on a joint-stock system. For example, Shenzhen Baoan County Joint Investment Company implemented a joint-stock system in 1983 and changed its name to China Baoan Group Co., Ltd. in 1991; and Beijing Tiaoqiao Shopping Mall and Shanghai Feilo Acoustics Co., Ltd offered stocks to the public in July 1984 and November 1984, respectively. Following that, some small- and medium-sized state-owned enterprises in Guangdong, Liaoning, Shandong, Zhejiang, Tianjin, and other provinces and cities started to try the joint-stock system. Some companies engaged in employee stock ownership, and some used the system as a way of financing, while others regarded symbolic dividends as a kind of welfare to motivate employees.

Why did those companies introduce the pilots of a joint-stock system? The answer from local governments and enterprises was pretty forthright: They were forced to by circumstances. Since the enterprises had no money for development, they had no choice but to raise funds through stocks. Local governments and enterprises were pragmatic, and as long as they could get money, they would take risks to try new methods. As to the matters of how to regulate companies, disclose information, transfer stock rights, and get companies listed on stock exchanges, they did not give too much thought. The 120 "problematic stocks left over by history" in the Shanghai and Shenzhen stock exchanges were the side-effects of those pilot projects.

As for large- and medium-sized enterprises, they could receive money from the government and banks. At the beginning of reform and opening up, the central government decentralized power and transferred profits downwards, and at the same time carried out the management contract system with the surplus profits of contracted works left to enterprises, in order to allow more autonomy and more financial resources for self-transformation, self-accumulation, and self-development of the enterprises. If the state continued to implement the joint-stock system, there would be many tough problems to be solved as for how to coordinate between a joint-stock system and a contract system. As far as I can remember, it was in 1983 when the general manager of China Automobile Corporation, Rao Bin, sought financial help from CCB for the automobile industrial transformation during the Sixth Five-year Plan period. At first, the general manager intended to issue shares, but when my bank colleagues and I reminded him of many substantive issues such as financial disclosure, a board of shareholders, dividend sharing required by a joint-stock company, especially the issue of the relationship between higher authorities and the broad of directors, he felt frustrated and was at a loss what to do. At last, he gave up the joint-stock system and chose to float bonds instead.

China's reform and opening up policies cannot get away from ideological debates. With the implementation of joint-stock system pilot projects, debates arose around whether this system was socialist or capitalist in nature, whether it will lead to privatization, and whether this action will distract people from the socialist cause. Later, the report to the 13th CPC National Congress in November 1987 provided a conclusion: "various forms of a system of shares in enterprises have appeared during the reform. These include purchasing of shares by the state, collective purchase by departments, localities and other enterprises, and purchasing by individuals. This system is one means of raising money for socialist enterprises and can be further implemented on a trial basis." This document gave a pass for the reform towards the joint-stock system. In 1988, many local governments expanded their scope of pilots, but it did not last long. After the second half of 1988, China started to rectify its economy, and a political storm emerged one year later, which resulted in another debate on the nature of the system of shares. In May 1990, the State Council issued a document which demanded the continuous sound implementation of the joint-stock system, but encouraged people to neither scale up the pilots nor set up new pilot programs in general. In addition to equity participation and shareholding between enterprises, active pilots of which were still allowed, experiments on employee stock ownership would no longer be expanded. The State Council, however, promised to undertake supporting reforms for those which had issued stocks to the public in Shanghai and Shenzhen, which paved a way for building stock exchanges and opening securities markets in the two cities.

Liu Hongru (1992) made an incomplete set of statistics which indicated that at the end of 1991, the total number of pilot joint-stock enterprises of all kinds amounted to around 3,220 (excluding joint-equity cooperative enterprises in villages and towns and Sino-foreign joint ventures). Among these, pilot enterprises of institutional ownership added up to 380, accounting for 12%; pilot enterprises of employee stock ownership reached the number of 2,752, up to 86%; and pilot enterprises offered stocks to the public took up 2%. Among the total capital stock of the 89 enterprises which publicly issued stocks, state shares occupied 47%, institutional shares 29%, individual shares 14%, and foreign capital shares 9%.

At the beginning of 1992, Deng Xiaoping delivered a speech during his southern tour which laid a foundation for further reform and opening up in China. He urged Chinese people to further emancipate their minds, to be more daring in reform and opening up, to quicken the pace of economic development and not to lose any favorable opportunity. Deng mentioned in particular that "we allow people to reserve their judgment, but we must try these things out." His words were a great encouragement for the pilots of stock markets in Shanghai and Shenzhen. Later on, Liu Hongru (1992) cited Marx's words — share capital is "the most perfected form" which is "turning into communism" — which justified the joint-stock system by the classic argument of the founder of Marxism.

Now, some people criticize that China's practice contributed to deforming the stock market in regard to the stock ownership arrangement. During the pilot program of a stock system, China first set up state shares, institutional shares, and employee shares which turned to establish B shares afterwards.[32] This criticism reflected a lack of knowledge about China's stock market.

Individual shares aimed to let employees inside or outside an enterprise own shares. Because the stock system in China was initially established to satisfy the financial need for construction, and the money was primarily collected from employees of the joint-stock company as well as the general public. In a survey conducted in 1992, the investor structure of Shenzhen was as follows: Enterprise employees and functionaries accounted for 79%, workers 16%, and unemployed people 5%. In Shanghai, the structure of individual investors comprised 79.4% of enterprise employees and functionaries, 8% of investors from other industries, 6% of teachers, 4% of people without regular work, and 2.6% of self-employed people. At that time, rich private entrepreneurs seldom bought stocks, and most individual investors were workers who made a living on labor income. So people assumed then that shareholding by socialist workers was a characteristic of China's socialist stock market and was distinct from private ownership. Moreover, employee stock ownership was similar to a worker cooperative which was justified in the classic *Das Kapital*, and therefore it could evade the debates over whether the stock system was socialist or capitalist in nature.

State shares refer to the shares held by the government, which complies with the policy of "taking public ownership as the basis of the economy." Institutional shares are set up for the same reason as individual shares, with the only difference of shareholders being departments and enterprises. When the reformed stock system was piloted later, few individuals were rich enough to join, so the government had to ask several enterprises to be shareholders. Then, there was a Japanese book called *Corporate Capitalism* which specifically talked about cross-shareholdings between enterprises and affected the pilot programs in China. At that time, people believed that mutual shareholding between Japanese enterprises was of a capitalist nature, while in China since mutual shareholding happened between state-owned enterprises, there was no worry about changing the companies into capitalist ones. Besides, the central government granted power to enterprises and allowed them to keep a bigger share of profits. Consequently, the extra-budgetary funds of enterprises were increasing year by year. According to the statistics, the extra-budgetary funds in 1978 were RMB34.7 billion, equivalent to only 31% of the budget revenue; and in 1988, the extra-budgetary funds were RMB236 billion, accounting for 90% of the budget revenue. The cross-shareholdings and mutual investment between enterprises would produce similar effects and could also benefit the merger and reorganization of enterprises and enterprise groups.

B shares are foreign shares and to divide stocks into A and B categories was a practice directly learned from overseas stock markets.

The toughest issue was the circulation of stocks. At the moment, some people worried that the circulation of state shares would bring about the loss of state assets, and therefore the government had to prohibit the circulation of capital deposit and only allowed the issuance and circulation of shares by incremental capital at the initial stage of the pilot stock market. Consequently, state shares and institutional shares were temporarily not permitted to circulate. This "temporary prohibition," however, lasted for 15 years, resulting in the split share structure between tradable shares and non-tradable shares and a forbidden area for the successive China Securities Regulatory Commission.

At the initial stage, China's stock market encountered a contradiction particular to China, namely, to apply the management methods of a planned economy to solve the questions and conflicts appeared in the market economy. For example, when choosing companies to be listed, the Chinese government ought to give the chances to the most capable large- and medium-size enterprises in the market, but it set a quota for listed companies and allocated the quota, as a way of showing care, to the 120 small companies which were the earliest participants in the joint-stock reform and had problematic stocks left over from history. Take another example, the operation of a stock market has to comply with the law of supply and demand, and the initial boom prices in the stock market should be stabilized by listed companies issuing more shares; however, Chinese decision-makers reversed the order, and demanded to first restrain the share price before increasing issues in stocks. Besides, in a mature market, convertible bonds are usually issued by listed companies, but Chinese authorities asked non-listed companies to take a chance and then made those companies go public. There are still many other examples of the contradiction.

In conclusion, China's share-holding system started among a great number of ideological obstacles and under a great variety of political pressure. The joint-stock reform and the opening of the stock market in China were venturous and arduous works. The government must not only have the courage to overcome all difficulties in the way of socialist economy and remove all ideological barriers, but also bear the realities that debates over the nature of the stock market will never end and to apply the thinking of a planned economy to a market economy will create prejudices and misunderstandings.

Later, the CPC central committee repeatedly made it clear that the joint-stock system is an organizational form of property in a socialist society. Furthermore, the Third Plenary Session of the Sixteenth Central Committee of the CPC in 2003 stated that the country should "vigorously develop the mixed ownership economy participated in by state-owned capital, collective capital, and nonpublic capital, etc., realize the diversity of investors and make the joint-stock system the principal form of the realization of public ownership." Over 100 years ago, Marx regarded share capital as "capital of directly associated individuals," and praised it as "the most perfected form" which is "turning into communism." The idea of making "the joint-stock system the principal form of realization of public ownership" proposed for the first time by the CPC central committee was a significant theoretical breakthrough, representing an evolution of Marxism during China's practice of the stockholding system. Until 2005, when equity division reform and full circulation of stocks were carried out, China's shareholding reform and stock market walked out of initial confusion to make an epoch-making leap.

Finally, I would like to emphasize before ending this chapter that there are three important outcomes I would like to see happen as a result of this discussion of the joint-stock system. First, for China to become good at gathering and utilizing social funds to expand capital; second, for China to make good use of employee stock ownership which will benefit both fundraising and management; and third, for China to reorganize companies according to the joint-stock system and get them listed in order to secure property income for the citizens and enlarge the middle-income group.

4

Chapter

State Investment, State Intervention, Nationalization, and Privatization: Innovation of the Capital Formation Mechanism by China's State-Owned Economy

Prologue: The Earliest State Intervention in China and the Counter-Regulatory Effect of Economic Leverage

What impressed me most about state intervention was the three-year Great Leap Forward between 1958 and 1960 when Mao Zedong advocated "two targets" (the one obligatory to attain and the other aspired for) with quotas being increased at each lower level, which resulted in a seriously runaway capital construction. In 1962, Chen Yun and Deng Xiaoping presided over the meeting in the West Building at Zhongnanhai and discussed the measures for regulating the economy. The most immediate means of invention included: To close down, suspend, merge, or shift lines of production of problematic enterprises; to cancel unreasonable projects or reduce the staff; and sometimes even to directly increase or reduce investment according to the status of production. Deng Xiaoping named these measures as "special means for special times."

Another impressive incident was the three-year over-investment crowding out consumption. In 1962, there was a severe shortage of home-use hardware and consumer goods: Citizens could not find a place to buy an iron pan and an iron scoop, workers were unable to find a lunch box, and women had no hairpins to use. This situation created a great public outcry, and thus Premier Zhou Enlai had to spare some time from his tight schedule to host the State Council meeting and find ways to secure several tons of steel and aluminum from capital construction for the purposes of increasing the production of household hardware and other metal goods used in daily life. It sounds like a joke nowadays but the state intervention during the planned economy was exactly like this, so awkward and specific.

After the reform and opening up, the Chinese government learned to use economic levers. Initially, people still held the view that capital construction should be conducted only in a planned and proportionate way but not by a market principle. The market, however, was so strange that if you cannot make use of market levers, the market will mercilessly crush down your planned and proportionate development by its counter-regulatory effect. There was a true story which happened in Zhangjiakou City, Hebei Province. The city boasted itself as "a city of leather," and was the collecting and distributing center of leather from pastoral areas far and wide. The State Planning Commission established three large leather factories and introduced advanced leather splitting machines which could separate one piece of leather into three. The factories planned to purchase leather from supply and marketing cooperatives and turn it into leatherware. However, at that time, the government encouraged rural communes and production teams to run small factories by giving a favorable policy of "three-year tax exemption" to arouse their interests. Many rural communes and production teams took the chance to open small leather factories which purchased leather at a higher price but sold their products at a lower price than the three larger factories. Being poorly equipped, those small factories were unable to split leather for multiple uses, but due to the tax exemption, they could still make money. Their huge demand led to a shortage of leather in the supply and marketing cooperatives, and consequently the three large factories had to close down due to insufficient raw materials.

Now the Chinese government clearly knows that under a market economy, they have to not only rely on price mechanisms to balance supply and demand in the commodity market, but also regulate asset prices in the capital market to attract money capital and optimize the allocation of resources, in order to redistribute industrial production capability and promote the adjustment and optimization of production structure. Despite the fact that these market means have been criticized for their tortuousness, blindness, and anarchy for decades, they are irreplaceable in the real economy.

Now, let us get to the point and talk about the innovation of the capital formation mechanism in state investment, state intervention, nationalization, and privatization by the Soviet Union, China, and Western countries. The focus will be the tortuous course of China's state-owned economy in innovating the capital formation mechanism.

The Priority Development of Heavy Industry Creates a New Formation Mechanism for Government Capital in the Soviet Union

The economic systems in Western countries are mainly capitalist economies based on private ownership. After the October Revolution in 1917, Soviet Russia did the exact opposite by striving to build a socialist economy based on state-owned industry and collective agriculture, namely public ownership.

Soviet Russia launched a "Red Guard" attack on capital[1] for a short period after the October Revolution. The Soviet regime eliminated capitalism in cities and was able to distribute industrial products without compensation under military communism. The government, however, met frustrations when trying to practice the same in rural areas, so it had to resort to grain tax and exchange industrial goods for grains with farmers. Lenin drew lessons from this failure and promoted collective farms (i.e. public economy of collective ownership), trading industrial products of the state-owned economy for the agricultural products of collective farms.

It ought to be noted here that the socialist revolution conceived by Marx is like the one which happened in the developed capitalist countries such as the U.K. dating back to the 19th century. The Soviet Union, however, lagged behind in industrial development and its capitalism did not get fully established at that time. It will not benefit the socialist construction in the Soviet Union, if the country implements solely state ownership and discourages the development of capitalism. Lenin realized this fact and attempted to make a concession to the unpaid exploitation of capitalism by advocating capitalist redemption and state capitalism which could make use of foreign funds.

Lenin expressed his vision in his book — *State and Revolution* — that "as soon as the proletariat has won political power," "the whole of society will have become a single office and a single factory, with equality of labor and pay."[2] The Soviet government realized Lenin's dream in the state-owned economy. The state financed a great variety of state-owned enterprises in every sector of the society and implemented a highly concentrated planned economy which was called by Stalin as a "planned economy." Hence, a single government capital formation mechanism was created, which ushered in a new era of state-owned economy.

The economic construction of the Soviet Union experienced a phase of "priority development of heavy industry." Naturally, the law of economic development is to develop light and consumer goods industries first and then with the funds accumulated during the process to promote heavy industry. Stalin, nonetheless, did the opposite and came up with a slogan of "priority development of heavy industry." He said that "the reconstruction of industry involves the transfer of funds from the sphere of producing the means of consumption to the sphere of producing the means of production. Without this there can be no serious reconstruction of industry, especially in our Soviet conditions."[3] So starting from the Soviet Union, many countries including eastern European countries and China pursued a priority development of heavy industry by depressing domestic consumption and "tightening the belts for construction." Of course, for the Soviet Union, which suffered the hostility from and suppression by the imperialist powers, the merits for giving priority to developing heavy industry were to establish a complete range of economic system, enhance national strength, and gain victory in World War II so as to counter the fascist aggression of Germany, Italy, and Japan, although the citizenry's consumption was reduced. The Soviet Union was a backward agricultural country before the revolution, but Tsarist

Russia, after all, was greatly influenced by industrial civilizations. Therefore, it was reasonable that Lenin appreciated Fordism and Taylorism, and Stalin stressed the "Charter of the Magnitogorsk Iron and steel Combine" (i.e., an industrial system represented by the management mode of Magnitogorsk iron and steel enterprise), economic accounting, the system of one-man leadership, and the reliance on specialists in running factories. The state-funded industrialization of the Soviet Union offered an inspiration for practicing state intervention during the Great Depression by Western countries in the 1930s. Later, in the Brezhnev era, mathematical economics, which emphasized the optimized allocation of production factors, became popular, and a system of scientific and reasonable planned economy was gradually formulated, which enabled scientific planning to reach its full potential.

According to the statistics, Russia was a backward capitalist country before World War I. In 1913, the gross national product (GNP) of Russia was equivalent to only 6.8% of that of the U.S. Its national income per capital was one-sixth of that of the U.K. and less than one-fourth of that of France, and meanwhile its per capital output of major industrial products was only on a par with the least developed country (Spain) in Europe. Between 1928 and 1937, the priority development of heavy industry by Stalin enabled the Soviet Union to complete the industrialization within a decade, which took the capitalist countries in Western Europe a century, and turned the state into the No.1 industrial country in Europe. After suffering through World War II, the Soviet Union continued to develop and finally rose to be a superpower. In 1985, when Gorbachev came to power, Russia's GNP equaled 80% of that of the U.S., which was unprecedented in history (Fang Ning, 2007).

A planned economy, however, can hardly satisfy the changing demands of society. The problem was that the subjective judgment of planners was unable to reflect the objective reality of economic operation, and however clever a director of the Economic Commission may be, he cannot predict the supply and demand of thousands of products. The direct results of investment were more often than not that long-term investments could not receive immediate returns, short-term ones were unlikely to make substantial profits, and the high cost of regulation led to little success. The country came to realize the infeasibility of this practice in the 1960s. The Russian economist, Victor Glushkov, once said in 1964 that if all the Russians devoted to the plan-making work, it would not be until 1980 that they could complete the compiling of the plan for 1964.

Stalin not only prematurely proclaimed the realization of socialism in the Soviet Union, but also conceived a complete mode of product economy by regarding the abolition of the commodity economy as a token of achieving socialism in the book *Economic Problems of Socialism in the USSR* published in 1952. He said that "when instead of the two basic production sectors, the state sector and the collective-farm sector, there will be only one all-embracing production sector, with the right to dispose of all the consumer goods produced in the country, commodity circulation, with its 'money economy,' will disappear, as being an unnecessary element in the national economy."[4] Stalin also held the view that this kind of product economy had been established in the state sector, and the products manufactured within the sector only needed to be allocated by the state instead of being exchanged for money.

During the first half of the 1950s, the poisonous theory of getting rid of the commodity economy by Stalin spread widely. The Soviet Union, Eastern Europe, and China were all looking forward to the setting up of a single national economic body (comprised of representatives from state industry and the collective farms) as "a single and united sector, with the right at first to keep account of all consumer product in the country, and eventually also to distribute it, by way, say, of products-exchange."[5] It could be said to be a misunderstanding in the development of the government capital formation mechanism. The theory, nonetheless, attracted a generation of people with leftist thinking to change the ownership structure at an earlier date and realize a product economy by abolishing commodity economy.

In China, Mao Zedong first doubted about the notion of the means of production being not products. He wrote in the *Critique of Stalin's Economic Problems of Socialism in the USSR* in 1958 that "Stalin has not comprehensively set forth the conditions for the existence of commodities. The existence of two kinds of ownership is the main premise for commodity production. But ultimately commodity production is also related to the productive forces. For this reason, even under completely socialized public ownership, commodity exchange will still have to be operative in some areas." He especially mentioned that "to say the means of production are not commodities deserves study."[6]

Although Stalin admitted retaining commodity production, he called it "a special kind of commodity production" on various occasions. Stalin said that "our commodity production is not of the ordinary type, but is a special kind of commodity production, commodity production without capitalists, which is concerned mainly with the goods of associated socialist producers (the state, the collective farms, the cooperatives), the sphere of action of which is confined to items of personal consumption, which obviously cannot possibly develop into capitalist production, and which, together with its 'money economy,' is designed to serve the development and consolidation of socialist production."[7] When reading this passage, Mao Zedong commented that "the 'sphere of action' is not limited to items of individual consumption. Some means of production have to be classed as commodities. If agricultural output consists of commodities but industrial output does not, then how is exchange going to be carried out?" He specially pointed out that "in China not only consumer goods but agricultural means of production have to be supplied. Stalin never sold means of production to the peasants. Khrushchev changed that."[8]

In China, if this "special kind of commodity production" arranged by the planning agency was a beautiful vision in 1958, the three-year Great Leap Forward between 1958 and 1960 put all the means of production and consumption in short supply. As a result, the scarcest commodity would be supplied in a planned way (via purchase certificate). By the 1970s, the consumer goods purchased with certificates included: coarse food grain, flour, rice, cooking oil, sesame oil, cloth, wool, cotton, meat, eggs, sugar, soybeans, as well as the peanuts and melon seeds during the Chinese lunar New Year. Many industrial products were also supplied in this way, such as cigarettes, matches, watches, bicycles, sewing machines, and, later, TVs and refrigerators. Some items had to be obtained via a marriage certificate, such as beds, tables, chairs, wardrobes, hot water bottles and 555-brand alarm clocks. Purchase certificates became an expedient under the domestic tight supply. In those days, there was a popular joke: In 1962, Chen Yun proposed in the Meeting in the West Building at Zhongnanhai to increase the supply of nourishment to parts of middle- and high-ranking cadres, and later the meeting decided to provide an additional 1 kilogram of sugar and soybeans to cadres above level 17, and 1 kilogram of pork and eggs to cadres above level 13. The masses satirized those cadres as "sugar-soybean cadres" and "pork-egg cadres." Of course, this talk is beyond the scope of the capital formation mechanism, but it illustrates how the "priority development of heavy industry" and "belt-tightening on construction" have crowded out the production of consumer goods, and caused a man-made overall shortage of consumer goods and a period of low consumption level of the citizens. It was also the case in the Soviet Union, China, and Eastern European countries. The followers of Stalin, however, did not notice the causal relationship between priority development of heavy industry and the shortage of consumption goods. On the contrary, they drew a wrong conclusion and believed that the growth of production lagging behind the growth of consumption reflected a kind of superiority of socialism.

After all, the planned economy in the Soviet Union was different from that in China. During the Stalin era, namely, the socialist primitive accumulation period, the Soviet Union completed the industrialization and urbanization at the expense of farmers by "exploiting" them in a way more severe than capitalism. When Brezhnev came into power, the proportion of state-owned farms surpassed that of collective farms, agricultural population became a minority, and industrial accumulation no longer depended on the "exploitation" of farmers. Moreover, the industry of Russia was advanced enough to repay agriculture. In 1966, the government put into practice a guaranteed wage system towards all collective farms in the country, thereafter the welfare of the members of the collective farms was roughly the same as that of city workers in the state-owned enterprises.

A few years ago, Qin Hun touched upon the systematic defects in the Soviet Union's planned economy when talking about China's reform. He thought that although the "rational" planned economy of the Soviet Union could find an optimal solution to input-output function under operational research and linear programming, it was unable to adapt to the ever-changing consumer preference of each person; although the planned system could reach a static planned balance and eliminate the inevitable surplus and deficits which alternately occurred during the trial-and-error process of the market under an extreme condition, it would not create innovation incentives as the dynamically balanced market competition would; although the planned economy could make a large amount of products in an efficient way according to index in kind, it was far less good than the market economy when judged by utility gain efficiency. The fundamental problem was, just as Bukharin wrote in *The Economics of the Transitional Period*, that the planned economy must eliminate the so-called "freedom of labor" because the freedom of labor was incompatible with the properly organized planned economy and the planned allocation of the labor force. It was far more than the freedom of labor, and consumer sovereignty was also no longer in existence without considering personal preference. Individuals became "screws" on an integral machine, and labor, consumption, life, and even thought, displayed logically a tendency of being planned, which was a more serious consequence than the "soft budget constraints" described by Kornai. Because of this, the rational planned economy with the so-called "plan optimization" showed an apparently diminishing marginal benefit after the 1980s, and the Soviet-style planned economy came to an end and desperately needed a thorough reform and a new route (Qin Hui, 2008).

It is obvious that a planned economy is not as good as a market economy, not to mention the facts that the boom in technology, production, and consumption in Western market economy countries formed a contrast to the situations in the Soviet Union. Owing to the above-mentioned factors together with the internal political struggles within the Russian government, unsurprisingly, the Communist Bloc including the Soviet Union and the countries of the Warsaw Pact was doomed to failure.

State Intervention, Nationalization, and Privatization in Western Countries

In this part, we will talk about state intervention, nationalization, and privatization in the Western World where capital culture was created as capitalism was experiencing the Great Depression and deflation. We should start from the Great Depression in the U.S. in the 1930s and President Roosevelt's New Deal in 1933.

In 1929, the U.S. laissez-faire style of capitalism reached the height of its development. In that year, the U.S. GNP for the first time exceeded the target of USD100 billion with the per capita GNP of USD746.7, and its Engel coefficient reached 45%, so a lot of people bragged that capitalism had entered a phase of "permanent prosperity." Two U.S. presidents — Coolidge and Hoover — boasted that the United States had conquered poverty and "reached a higher degree of comfort and security than ever existed before in the history of the world."[9] However, the stock market crash of October 29, 1929 (also known as Black Tuesday) exposed at once the capitalist viruses, such as overproduction of capital, deteriorating enterprises, a rising unemployment rate, a fall in import and export trade, financial decline, and shrinking investment. Meanwhile, the Hoover administration believed that the market economy could ease the problems, so the government took a laissez-faire policy which only exacerbated the crisis. During the four years of Hoover's presidency, American GNP fell from USD104.4 billion in 1929 to USD55.6 billion in 1933, and national income fell from USD87.8 billion in 1929 to USD 40.2 billion in 1933. On the eve of Roosevelt's inauguration in March 1933, there was a wave of bank runs, and banks in 21 states of the U.S. announced closure or were going to close down, which made the Coolidge-Hoover prosperity a dead end. Samuelson satirized this economic bust in his book *Economics* as revenge by God on those excessively conceited people.

During the U.S. Great Depression in the 1930s, over-investment and under-consumption led to excess production capacity and, in turn, over-production brought about declining investment and eventually a financial crisis. How terrible is it if investors stop investing, banks no longer make loans, factories go bankrupt, and workers become jobless in a highly developed capitalist society! At that time, the Keynesian theory of government intervention was raised, and President

Roosevelt realized the idea with his policies.

In March 1933 when Roosevelt came into power, he asked banks to suspend business for a week, followed by the purchase of about 6,000 banks by the federal government to turn them into government-controlled banks. Therefore, to nationalize through government injecting money into enterprises is not a recent invention for the U.S. and the American government is not suddenly taking a "socialist road" today. Between 1933 and 1937, President Roosevelt ordered the government to invest USD12 billion in large-scale irrigation works, afforestation, road construction, and other public works at the expense of the financial deficit and national debt, as work-relief programs. The Tennessee Valley Authority (TVA) project was among these programs. It should be said that the Soviet Union's ten-year practice of state-funded industrialization which improved economic life, offered inspiration to the United States. Besides, with the fact of shrinking private investment, to replace private investment with government investment filled in the missing link of capital formation, which stimulated the investment demand of the government. On the other side, government relief and work relief created job opportunities and boosted purchasing power, which directly aroused consumption demand.

Of course, the effects of the state-centralized investment and work relief in Roosevelt's New Deal were less significant than expected. Someone reviewed afterwards and concluded that these programs had really driven demand and that what revitalized the U.S. economy was the Second World War. More importantly, the Roosevelt administration implemented a series of policies aimed at promoting equality. On the one side, the president introduced many policies to improve people's livelihoods and guarantee the basic lives of ordinary people, such as to build government-subsidized housing, to protect the right of freedom of association, to implement price controls over key commodities during inflation, to place the wages of workers from key industries under the control of the government by taking advantage of the wartime system, and to provide medical insurance, unemployment insurance, and social security. On the other side, the government raised taxes on the wealthy. The first step was to increase the federal tax levied on company profits (according to later statistics, the average tax rate rose from less than 14% in 1929 to over 45% in 1955). The second was to raise the income tax. The maximum rate of income tax was only 24% in the 1920s, but the rate rose to 63% during Roosevelt's first term and 79% during his second term. The third was to improve the estate duty. The highest estate tax rate, which started from 20% in 1929 and continuously grew to 45%, 60%, and 70%, ultimately achieved 77%. These measures reduced the concentration of wealth. The richest 0.1% of the U.S. population owned more than 20% of the national wealth in 1929, but this number was only 10% in the 1950s. Another result of these measures was that the median household income roughly doubled after 1929. For example, only one third of American families installed a home phone in 1936, while in 1955, 70% of families had a home phone and most families owned a car. In one word, Roosevelt's New Deal had turned the country with an extreme disparity between the rich and the poor in the 1920s to a middle-class society after the Second World War (Krugman, 2008).

After the Second World War, Western countries moved one step forward in state intervention to carry out nationalization. Under the influences of the Soviet Union and the victory of the anti-fascist war, people in the West were longing for socialism and there was a tendency to regard nationalization as a symbol of socialism. The governments of Western countries, in order to cater to their people, carried out large-scale nationalization by making national budgets fund huge investments, replacing private monopoly with state monopoly, and substituting private investment for the highly centralized state investment to create more space for the development of productive forces. The nationalized industries included the infrastructure sector (such as air transport, road transport, rail transport, gas, and electricity), raw materials sector (mining and metallurgy), financial sector (banks), key manufacturing sector (automobile industry), and emerging sector (atomic energy and aerospace). In 1965, the capitalist countries convened a World Capitalism Conference in Philadelphia and published *The Capitalist Manifesto*. It proposed to "learn from the experience of socialism where people are the masters, to realize a joint-stock people's capitalism; learn from the socialist welfare system, to implement a cradle-to-grave welfare capitalism; learn from the socialist planned economy, to carry out a planned capitalism with state intervention (Bian Hongdeng, 1997)." In many Western countries which were ruled by the Social Democratic Party, such as Sweden, the governments practiced cradle-to-grave socialism welfarism through the income redistribution function of taxes, which greatly eased the class contradictions and reformed capitalism. It is ironic that capitalist countries dared to learn from socialism without fear of being communized, while some leftist Chinese frequently stir up the dispute of whether the country should be part of the capitalist or socialist camp, lest it be contaminated by capitalist bacteria.

Things always reverse themselves after reaching an extreme, and the 20-year development of state intervention and nationalization brought about stagflation. Monetarists and supply-side economists criticized state intervention as a road to

Serfdom. In the 1970s and 1980s, neoliberalism became popular and privatization appeared successively in Western countries. In the 1980s, the "Reagan-Thatcher prosperity" emerged, as the information technology revolution and industrial structure upgrading developed in the Western advanced market economy countries. The United Kingdom during the administration of Margaret Thatcher privatized two-thirds of the state-owned enterprises. In 1986, when French President Jacques Chirac held the reins of government, he was determined to put into practice the privatization of the enterprises which had been nationalized in 1982 within two years. Compared to the previous nationalization, this privatization was another return from government capital to private capital in the capital formation mechanism. From then on, state intervention and privatization were used alternately by Western countries, which allowed the governments room to maneuver. By 2007 when the U.S. subprime mortgage crisis gave rise to the collapse of Wall Street, the Bush administration had to intervene heavily to rescue Fannie Mae, Freddie Mac, AIG, and Citigroup, and parts of these companies were again nationalized. The U.S. government's practice of using state intervention to save the economy made many fear that the U.S. was supporting socialist practices. The *New York Times* reporter, Thomas Friedman, author of the bestseller *The World is Flat*, said in a scoffing manner that "the U.S. and China are becoming two countries, one system."

Initial Government Capital Formation Mechanism: Allocation of Investment by Sector and by Region

After New China was established in 1949, the government proposed the "coexistence of multiple economic sectors." Since 1953, however, China implemented the first five-year plan by promoting a large-scale industrial construction centered on 156 major construction projects, and comprehensively learned from the Soviet Union to pursue a planned economy and expand the economy under public ownership, namely the state-owned economy. Old China was economically poor and culturally blank with a semi-colonial and semi-feudal economy, and had not established its own independent industrial system and national economic system. In 1954, Mao Zedong said: "What can we make at present? We can make tables and chairs, teacups and teapots, we can grow grain and grind it into flour, and we can make paper. But we can't make a single car, plane, tank or tractor."[10] In fact, according to the statistics, the industrial sector accounted for less than 10% of China's national economy in 1949, and the industrial products were not very large in number, including only 158,000 tons of steel, 1.89 billion meters of cloth, 2,000 sets of sewing machines, 4,000 sets of radio receivers, and 14,000 sets of bicycles.

The most significant feature of a planned economy is the centralization of national wealth to develop the economy. After the founding of New China, it took the country three years to restore its national economy and in 1953 the government started to launch large-scale economic construction. From 1953 to 1978, despite the mistakes of the three-year Great Leap Forward between 1958 and 1961 and the decade-long calamity of the Cultural Revolution, the government's investment in fixed assets of state-owned enterprises amounted to RMB760 billion, which increased national income from RMB70.9 billion in 1953 to RMB301 billion in 1978 and fiscal revenue from RMB22.29 billion in 1953 to RMB112.1 billion in 1978. By 1978, the proportion of industry reached 72.2%. According to the statistics released by the Leading Group for Financial and Economic Affairs of China, between 1949 and 1978, China's GDP increased from RMB46.6 billion to RMB362.41 billion, a growth of 7.78 times; industrial output value grew from RMB14 billion to RMB423 billion, a growth of 30.21 times; agricultural output value grew from RMB32.6 billion to RMB139.7 billion, a growth of 4.29 times; grain output grew from 113 million tons to 305 billion tons, a growth of 2.69 times; cotton output grew from 444,000 tons to 2.17 million tons, a growth of 4.88 times; steel output grew from 160,000 tons to 31.78 million tons, a growth of 198.63 times; coal output grew from 32 million tons to 618 million tons, a growth of 19.31 times; and generating capacity grew from 4.3 billion kilowatt-hour to 256.6 billion kilowatt-hour, a growth of 59.67 times. Within 29 years, China's GDP had grown by 8.43% annually on average, and the annual growth rate would be 7.78% if the data during the three-year (1949–1952) recovery of the national economy were deducted. In the first 30 years of reform and opening up, despite making some mistakes, China was able to produce automobiles in 1956, develop Daqing Oil Field and manufacture supersonic jets in the 1960s, and detonate the first atomic bomb in 1964. During the period from the founding of New China in 1949 to the beginning of reform and opening up at the end of 1978, there were still industrial structure problems, such as serious imbalances between light and heavy industries and a general short supply of consumer goods, but China took less time to make these achievements than Western countries, and it had established an independent and comparatively complete industrial system and national economic system, which paved the way for the further development of China.

In the first 30 years of New China, the country chose a planned economic system. The state was the main body of national investment and production, and enterprises were not independent producers. The investment and production of enterprises proceeded by following the government plan, and actually everything was determined by the government from human resources and property to production and supply. Plants and equipment were invested in by the state, raw materials and spare parts were allocated by the state, and products were also transferred by the state to the materials sector and the business sector for centralized procurement and marketing. Income and expenses were managed separately: All income of enterprises, including profits and depreciation, was turned over to the public finance; and all expenses, including capital construction and renovation costs, should be reported to the department of finance for financial allocation. The adjustment of manning quota of an enterprise should be approved by the competent national authorities and labor force was deployed by the state labor and personnel department. The government would guarantee job assignments of university graduates and their wages were issued based on national standard. The assigned job was euphemistically called an "iron rice bowl," but if you were not subject to the government's arrangement, you would lose everything to become a true "proletarian."

The State Planning Commission was in charge of national investment allocation then. But, how to constitute the capital formation mechanism of a state-owned economy considering the vast territory of the country, a great many ministries and local governments, and the requirement of "proportional development in a planned way" by the planned economy? After several years of trial and error, the government implemented a policy of "allocation of investment by sector and by region." In preparation of next year's investment plan of each sector, the investment of the previous year would be regarded as a base and an equal proportion of growth would be added annually, which was called a "base-plus-growth" method. The purpose of such an investment allocation was to balance the investment and production capability of each sector in different regions. Therefore, this investment system was an effective capital formation mechanism in developing the state-owned economy and was part of capital culture in the age of the planned economy, despite having been denounced for many years after the reform and opening up.

There was an argument at that time that the proportional and planned development of socialist national economy replaced the anarchy of production and competition of capitalism. People believed that the base-plus-growth method naturally complied with the planning method of a proportional development. In fact, this was a misunderstanding. Because the planned and proportional development calculated via the base-plus-growth method was against the objective economic law. Moreover, reproduction of an industry in fact will never develop in a proportional manner with that of another industry. It should be regarded as a law of investment activities. For example, there is no possibility that the investment in the production plant of power plant equipment grows proportionately with the money devoted to its user (the power station). Supposing the production capacity of a power equipment company is four installed generating sets with an installed capacity of 100,000 kilowatts per year and the first-year production has already satisfied the electricity demand of the whole society, if the service life (replacement period) of power plant equipment is 10 years, the simple reproduction of this power equipment company will annually create a social investment demand for accommodating 400,000-kilowatt equipment. That is to say, within the 10 years when the first 400,000-kilowatt power station is still in service, the entire society has to make additional investments to expand the power station into one with an installed capacity of 4 million kilowatts, otherwise the simple reproduction of the power equipment company will be impossible, let alone the proportionate expanded reproduction. The large-scale construction of the engineering industry during the Great Leap Forward in 1958 and the 10-year Cultural Revolution had resulted in a great deal of idle machinery. The problem was that the excess production capacity caused by widespread reckless investment during the Great Leap Forward and Cultural Revolution had covered up the overcapacity in the engineering industry, and as a result, the planning department and the industry did not spot the problem to reflect on the inherent defects of the "allocation of investment by sector and by region."

The objective of New China was to build a socialist country. Although the government advocated the redemption of capitalism and allowed a small space for capitalist development in the initial new democratic stage, China had entered a period of centralized planned economy in the pursuit of socialism with public ownership, after the country switched to the large-scale economic construction in 1953, especially after Stalin put forward the theory of product economy, "three-anti and five-anti" campaign was carried out to oppose the capitalist class, and Mao Zedong suggested the "General Line" for the transitional period of "one industrialization, three transformations."

The planned economy in China, the same as that in the Soviet Union and Eastern European countries, originated from the rigid socialist theory of opposing capital and business credit, and concentrating all the credit in banks. It talked about product economy and denied either commodity or commodity economy. China's planned economy was more centralized in that it included depreciation funds of fixed assets in income to be turned over to the Ministry of Finance and treated the renewal cost of fixed assets as capital construction funds which should be reported to the state for fiscal appropriation. Besides, Mao Zedong was constantly against revisionism during the first two decades of reform. It was reflected in the economic policies of opposing "passive equilibrium of national economy," "direct and exclusive control of enterprises by the ministry concerned," "trustization," "system of one-man leadership" and "inflexible administrative approach of controlling, blocking, and suppressing" in order to get rid of the unreasonable rules and regulations. It stressed that the government should take class struggle as a guideline to promote a large-scale mass movement, regard grain and the mass production of steel and iron as the focus of agricultural and industrial sectors, and replace the rational optimized allocation of resources with the development of five kinds of small industrial enterprises (iron and steel, coal, chemical fertilizers, cement, and machinery). Meanwhile, the rigidness in theories was also manifested in the following ideas: The emphases on public ownership and people's communes, and the priority development in heavy industry; the opposition against and the avoidance of capital by regarding all capital as "financial resources," state appropriated capital to enterprises as "investment" or "funds" (such as statutory funding), and fixed capital of enterprises as "fixed funds"; and the replacement of assets and liabilities in a balance sheet with debits and credits.

It was special that China set up a Construction Bank under the administration of the Ministry of Finance. The bank was responsible for state appropriation for and monitoring of the investment in national capital construction and wherever there was a construction project, there would be a Construction Bank to be built. Its financial supervision ranged from financial plan to fund appropriation, from budget management to final accounts, from prospective design and construction to the completion of a project, and from development units to construction units. In this way, the Contraction Bank was built into a department taking charge of all the investment (i.e. all the capital), to ensure the efficiency of investment under the circumstance of the national avoidance of capital. Since the bank developed its own system by distributing its branches around the country and implemented vertical management, it could monitor construction projects regardless of administrative divisions. For instance, the Anhui Bengbu bank branch which was responsible for financing the water control projects of the Huai River was able to appropriate money for the projects not only in Anhui, but also Jiangsu and Henan provinces. The Construction Bank served and was close to the grassroots, and accumulated a series of experiences in the effective use of capital, thus it had a great influence in investment. This advantage was a notable difference between the China Construction Bank and the capital construction banks and long-term investment banks in other socialist countries. That was why when the planning department intended to continue the absolute control over investment after the reform and opening up, the Construction Bank offered practical advice on managing investment by economic leverage from the market angle, and later on proposed the development of the capital market, and pioneered participating in the capital market and undertaking capital operation. We will elaborate the above issues in the following chapters.

The economic construction of New China experienced three large-scale excessive leaps in the growth of investment (a synonym for capital expansion). The first time was during the Great Leap Forward between 1958 and 1960; the second was around the later years of the Cultural Revolution from 1970 to 1975; and the third was in 1978 when the slogan of "going all out to make quick advances" was put forward and the 22 projects of importing excessive foreign technical equipment created a large amount of foreign debt. These three times of capital expansion all happened during the period of the highly centralized pursuit of a product economy with the primary cause being the top leadership. Senior leaders were anxious and eager to find a shortcut to the rapid development of socialism. Consequently, they felt a strong impulse to enlarge investment (capital) and pursued "high speed and high target" goals which often resulted in "production putting pressure on capital construction, capital construction diverting the pressure to financial department, and the financial department pushing the central bank to issue money when investment was growing larger and larger in a uncontrollable way." It should be noted that in the first two cases, some local governments, state-owned enterprises, and construction units did not want to rely on the assigned investment from higher authorities to form their construction capital, due to their enthusiasm to quickly and efficiently build socialism (in fact, the blindness in capital expansion). The local governments resorted to either the transfer of money from state-owned enterprises or surplus revenue (in practice, deficit spending), since they could count on no other financial resources. The local finance had to pay the bill if construction projects were unable to pay back the transferred money or there was no surplus in revenue, but the ultimate result must be that the Central finance urged banks to issue money to save the local finance. For those state-owned enterprises and construction units who had accepted fiscal appropriation, their additional demand of money would come from dishonest acquisition and the misuse of funds or misappropriation of bank loans. Their extra financial demand may also be satisfied by diverting the fund for heavy maintenance to capital construction, which would in turn increase costs. At last, those enterprises either were pressed to repay bank debts or paid less taxes and profits, which would still incur losses to the financial departments and banks.

There were diverse opinions towards the relationship between construction scale and national strength. Prior to the above three periods, the capital construction in 1956 exceeded RMB2.8 billion of the budget and additional financial credit of RMB3 billion incurred a deficit which was solved by banks issuing more money. Zhou Enlai concluded that "investment was too aggressive, management was too loose, capital was too dispersed, and the market was too tight," and he advocated "opposing a rush advance" in 1957. At the same time, when Chen Yun summed up the lessons learned in the economic construction of 1956, he pointed out that "the investment scale should adapt to the financial and material resources of a country, and the adaption determines economic stability." This is the origin of the famous principle of "construction scale should be compatible with national strength," which is also known as the "Theory on National Strength." Mao Zedong, nevertheless, regarded the 1956 economic construction as a justifiable advance instead of a "rush advance." During the meetings in Hangzhou and Nanning, Mao criticized Zhou Enlai and Chen Yun for opposing advances and blocking quick and efficient development. There were still many complaints about the adjustments to the three-year Great Leap Forward made by Zhou Enlai, Chen Yun, and Deng Xiaoping in 1962. Therefore, the mistake of excessive growth of investment was repeated during the 10-year Cultural Revolution.

Li Rui (1992) roughly calculated the losses incurred during the Great Leap Forward and Cultural Revolution in his book *Preliminary Study on Mao Zedong's Leftist Thinking in His Later Years*: In 1955, China's GNP accounted for 4.7% of the world total while the figure dropped to 2.5% in 1980; in 1960 China's GNP equaled that of Japan but only accounted for one fourth in 1980 and even one fifth in 1985 of Japan's GNP; in 1960 U.S. GNP was USD460 billion more than China's while USD3,680 billion more in 1985. Apart from the economic power, China lagged far behind Japan and Western countries in science and technology, and the gap was growing larger and larger. It was a serious and regretful result from the past 20-year leftist thinking and practice. According to statistics, the losses created during the Great Leap Forward were about RMB120 billion and around RMB500 billion during the Cultural Revolution. During the 30 years from the founding of New China to the Third Plenary Session of the 11th Central Committee of the CPC, China's total investment in capital construction amounted to RMB650 billion and fixed-asset investment was around RMB400-500 billion. Hence it can be seen that the loss of RMB620 billion during the two significant events was almost equivalent to all the capital construction investment in the first 30 years of New China. This did not include the intangible and incalculable losses, such as the losses caused by inappropriate talent training and the population explosion.

The over-expansion of investment in 1978 mainly resulted from the arrangement of foreign-funded construction by Hua Guofeng. He allowed government departments and local governments to borrow and repay convertible foreign exchange by independently signing contracts with foreign partners, which was not included in the plan of capital construction and was beyond the state budget. This decision made investment out of control, and at last, the debts were paid back by the state by taking money from the Department of Finance.

The above-mentioned three excessive expansions of investment, originating from either central authorities or local governments and grassroots enterprises, all forced financial departments and the central bank to issue money to solve the leftover problems. Despite different manifestations, these over-expansions were resolved by inflation filling the vacancy in the government capital formation mechanism. Therefore, after the reform and opening up, senior Chinese government leaders paid attention to the size of investment to prevent over-investment. This indicated that under a highly centralized planned economy, the plan was the law and the capital formation mechanism of local governments and enterprises had to conform to the plan of the central government, allowing no creativity.

It was impractical to include every investment into the plan of capital construction by way of "allocating investment by sector and by region," under the fiscal system of unified state control over income and expenditure. Although in the 1950s, the Ministry of Finance excluded four-kind expenditures (tech-organizational measures costs, expenses for the trial manufacturing of new products, labor protection costs, and expenses for miscellaneous construction) from the capital construction plan and the competent departments should submit an additional budget for the four items, there remained countless trivial investments in the economic life of China. By the 1960s, the government had to create three new channels to supplement the capital formation mechanism.

The first channel was to enable enterprises to draw and utilize by themselves parts of renewal funds, such as depreciation funds earmarked for industrial enterprises and the compensating funds for maintaining simple reproduction of the excavating and logging industry. The second one was the subsidies and grants for diverse small-scale innovation and renovation projects, such as grants to five-type small industrial enterprises and mobilization subsidies for producing deficient products, to support the existing enterprises to undertake transformation. The two capital channels will be detailed in Chapter 5.

The third financing channel was to allow the Construction Bank to provide loans for implementing small projects. For example, the Construction Bank started the business of small-project loans, including small technical loans, loans for regional building materials production, special loans for industrial exports production, domestic coordinate loans for introducing foreign equipment by short-term loans in foreign currency, special technical loans for textile products, etc. However, due to the principle of separate control over fiscal funds and bank credit, the Construction Bank cannot lend savings out and had to ask the Ministry of Finance and local governments to appropriate loan funds.

In conclusion, the investment system of "allocating investment by sector and by region" constituted the initial formation mechanism of state-owned capital, and renewal funds, renovation subsidies and loan funds were its supplements.

Loans for Small Projects: A Special Tool for Revenue Growth and Capital Innovation

Why in the first place did the government start loans for small projects? It was because in the 1960s when equipment replacement created serious debts in the accounts of enterprises, Sun Yefang appealed to leave depreciation funds to enterprises, but the Ministry of Finance did not amend the policy until much later. In 1964, the Shanghai Branch of China Construction Bank proposed to offer loans to the enterprises which were desperately in need of renewing their equipment. The loans were funded by the Municipal Finance Bureau and would be paid back through depreciation funds of enterprises in the future. This measure solved the urgent needs of local governments and enterprises, and was later promoted to the whole country. In 1972, the visit of the U.S. President Richard Nixon to China pushed the expansion of international economic exchange. In 1973, the Vice Premier, Li Xiannian approved the suggestion of the Ministry of Foreign Trade to run specialized factories and workshops of industrial exports and production bases of agricultural and sideline products as an experiment in certain selected enterprises, counties, and rural cooperatives. In some provinces and cities which had supplied the Hong Kong and Macau markets, production bases of fresh aquatic products and farm and sideline products were built. Production bases were also established in some pivotal production areas in the provinces and cities which had exported bulk agricultural products and produced valuable traditional local specialties. The construction costs of these pilot factories, workshops and production bases came from the loan funds for foreign trade appropriated by the Ministry of Finance and the special loans for industrial exports were lent out by the Construction Bank and would be repaid by the future profits. It was actually a subcategory of the small-project loan which was an invention of the Construction Bank to break through the planned economic system. Loans for small projects opened a new way for capital expansion and realized the growth in production and revenue through a different channel.

It should be noted that loans for small projects played a unique role in the state-owned capital formation mechanism of local enterprises. In addition to the positive functions of capital expansion, production growth and revenue increase for enterprises, the loans for small projects also expanded capital formation and enlarged fiscal revenue of local governments in the mid-1970s in Shanghai, Changzhou, Xiangfan, and Shashi, thanks to their flexible and vigorous financial works. Thus, there was a boom of learning from Shanghai, Changzhou, Xiangfan, and Shashi between 1975 and 1976. The flexibility in finance of these local governments was reflected in the fact that when their revenue exceeded the targeted figure, they would demand the central finance or provincial finance to set aside a portion of money. The money was not kept in reserve for future urgent use but as a fund to support small-project loans which would be offered to some inexpensive and efficient light textile projects with only one-year loan terms. For example, the Shanghai bicycle factory, Changzhou corduroy factory, Shashi thermos factory and bed sheet factory, Xiangfan cigarette factory, textile printing plant, and hosiery factory were able to expand the scale of production and substantially increase financial revenues through loans for small projects. Another smart practice of the local finance was to ask the corporate borrowers or their affluent partners in the same industry to repay the loan ahead of time and use this loan fund to solve the financial problems of other enterprises, when the local governments anticipated a huge fiscal surplus. Some cities turned the small loans over two or even three times a year. In this way, if the fund for small-project loans was RMB10 million, then the fund would triple or quadruple within just one year and add tens of millions of fixed capital to the municipal government, laying a foundation for long-term revenue growth. In those places, thus, loans for small projects became a special innovated form of government capital formation mechanism. It also should be mentioned that the reason why the small loans could turn into a supplementary measure for promoting production and fiscal revenue in those areas was also owing to the fact that state investment gave priority to heavy industry at that time and the textile and light industry could hardly get any loans. The serious shortage of textile products and general consumer goods in the lives of citizens created a vacancy for small-project loans to fill. The bicycle factory, corduroy factory, thermos factory, etc. funded by the small loans were everyday necessities of the people, and thus they were able to repay the loans and increase revenue within a short period by expanding production and satisfying consumption needs. Conversely, some cities in Northeast China did not grasp the essence and lent the loans to the heavy industry projects listed in the government's plan, which turned out to be bad debts and burdens on local finance.

There was a much-told story at that time that shortly after Xiangfan Municipal Party Committee Secretary Cao Ye took office, he asked Zhang Tixue of the Provincial Party Committee for some financial support. Zhang Tixue replied, "There is a cigarette factory in Xiangfan, and it is a treasure bowl. You should make good use of it!" As soon as Cao Ye went back to Xiangfan, he did research on the cigarette factory. Cao Ye applied for the loans for small projects to expand the factory and turned the small cigarette plant with an annual output of tens of thousands of boxes into a major tax-paying company producing 150,000–200,000 boxes of cigarette per year. The factory was so lucrative that it became an important pillar for production and revenue increase of Xiangfan City, and in turn substantially expanded the city's loan funds. It was a typical example of innovating the state-owned capital formation mechanism by taking advantage of loans for small projects.

Under the highly centralized planned economy, China implemented a policy of "large-scale fiscal allocation with small-scale bank loans," which suppressed the financial innovation activities of the banking sector. On the contrary, the financial sector, as a major investor and a representative of public ownership, was deeply concerned about capital returns (taxes and profits handed over to the state by enterprises). Consequently, the financial sector came up with many brilliant ideas about financial innovation, and the "loans for small projects" and the later "loans circumventing credit ceiling" were the best examples. It indicated that all financial innovation was closely related to the innovation of the capital formation mechanism. During that time, the China Construction Bank was under the administration of the financial sector and had the chance to participate in the operation of loans for small projects. So it was reasonable that the bank was very skilled at maneuvering financial tools and undertaking financial innovation, after the reform and opening up. It should be said that the bank's accomplishments during this period were largely attributed to its participation in financing activities.

Innovation in Capital Formation Mechanism: A Contract System

The Third Plenary Session of the 11th Central Committee of the CPC in 1978 signified a new era of reform and opening up. The committee believed that a serious defect in the economic management system since the founding of New China was the over-centralization of power and the central government should give more decision-making power in operation and management to local governments and enterprises in a bold manner and a managed way. "To decentralize power and transfer profits downwards" was determined as the keynote of the economic system reform. This proposal was reflected in the relationship between central finance and local finance as the policies of "a division of revenue and expenditure between the two levels and each level was responsible for balancing its own budget" implemented in 1980 and "separate categories of taxes, designated scope of revenues and expenditures, and responsibility contracts at different levels" implemented in 1985. The central government also expanded the autonomy of enterprises by retaining a portion of profits to be placed at the disposal of enterprises, and carried out the two fiscal policies of "transforming fiscal grants in capital construction into repayable loans" and "replacing profit delivery of enterprises with taxes." The measures of "reducing taxes to give more profits to enterprises" and "repaying loans before paying taxes" adopted during the policy of tax for profits added more financial autonomy to enterprises. Although these measures enhanced the enthusiasm of enterprises to complete the state plan, they brought about many problems, such as unfair work allocation, uneven burdens on different taxpayers and wages eroding profits, therefore the state-owned enterprises reform in 1985 concentrated on the separation of government functions from those of enterprises, and ownership from management. After 1987, the central government started to promote a contracted managerial responsibility system (or contract system), when the new tax system and the policy of replacing tax delivery with taxes increased the burdens of enterprises, and the incentive function of taxation and enterprise vitality were weakened. The key of the contract system was to contract out works in accordance with the state plan: To try out an input-output contract system in sectors like the petroleum sector, a contracted management system in large- and medium-sized enterprises, and a leasing contract system in small enterprises. In 1988, the central committee expanded the system of dividing revenue and expenditure between the central and local governments to an all-round fiscal contract system (including progressive incremental revenues, sharing in total revenue, sharing in total revenue and increased revenue, progressive quota of turned-in revenue, fixed quota of subsidy, etc.), which further motivated the local governments. The most notable feature of the contract system was to encourage local governments, government departments, and enterprises to exceed the production target, and apart from the prescribed portion which would be turned over to the central government, surplus profits were left over to contractors, namely, local governments, government departments and enterprises, to make investments. The reform of this period was later known as the "planned commodity economy" and the core of this economy was to admit enterprises as comparatively independent producers. The contract system greatly stimulated the enthusiasm of local governments, government departments, and enterprises. Local governments possessed more stand-by financial resources, government departments gained the money and energy to practice input-output contracts, and enterprises also acquired the financial resources and vitality for self-renovation, self-accumulation, and self-development. They accumulated more and more reserve funds for arranging extra-budgetary investments. During this period, the proportion of the central financial income to the total fiscal income dropped substantially, and the investments for capital construction by the state finance decreased. Against such a backdrop, various forms of the surplus from contracted works became an important part of the state capital formation mechanism.

After the reform and opening up, profit retention and surplus profits were the largest investment resources within and out of the government plan at first. In 1979, urban and rural residents had weak spending power (their total deposit amount was only RMB21 billion), and there were neither consumer goods nor a consumption service industry. Against such a background, if the central government intended to change the 30-year priority development of heavy industry and unbalanced structure between heavy and light industries and accumulation and expenditure, it had to count on the affluent enterprises which increased their financial capabilities by winning more autonomy. Much needed public baths, shops, kindergartens, continuation schools, schools for children of employees, nursing homes, as well as affiliated companies for absorbing children of employees were built up by making use of the retained profits and surplus profits of those enterprises, and thus a whole system of "enterprises burdened with social responsibilities" was established in some large- and medium-sized enterprises. Although this system was repeatedly criticized later on, it contributed the initial capital to the construction of consumption service facilities outside the government structure and constituted the capital formation mechanism for consumption service facilities at that time.

The policy of the "decentralization of power and the transfer of profits to enterprises" and the contract system of this period greatly motivated government departments, local governments, enterprises, and public institutions to pursue income growth and increase their reserve funds. The contract system, nevertheless, had some flaws: First, enterprises focused on short-term interest and would conduct the behaviors of overusing equipment, overissuing wages and bonuses, and predatorily using corporate resources; second, contracting enterprises were only responsible for surpluses instead of deficits, and the separation between ownership and management on the base of state ownership denied the property rights of enterprises as legal persons and only acknowledged the managerial authority of the state-owned enterprises. These enterprises were not independent producers of commodities with completely autonomous management rights in a market economy and thus they were not enterprises in a real sense. For local governments, since the contract system fixed the revenue to be handed over to the central, a fragmented economy with regional closure and segmentation was intensified.

Another significant result of "the decentralization of power and the transfer of profits to enterprises" and the contract system was an increasingly reduced central fiscal income. The financial deficits in 1979 and 1980 were RMB13.54 billion and RMB6.89 billion, respectively, and although this number declined in the following years, the ratio of fiscal revenue to GDP and ratio of the central fiscal income to national income manifested a straight downturn. In 1978, the proportion of the state revenue in GDP was 31.1% but it went down to 12.3% in 1993. The share of central fiscal revenue in total fiscal revenue declined from 40.5% in 1984 to 22% in 1993.[11] The financial constraints of the central government forced itself to seek financial support from local governments. The fragile central finance was unfavorable to the stability of the whole country, and to reform the tax-contracting system became an objective requirement for the development of a socialist market economy, which paved the way for the financial restructuring towards a tax-sharing system in 1994.

To Transform Fiscal Grants into Repayable Loans and Credit-Based Investment: A Return of Bank Functions

The capital formation mechanism of the 1980s in China featured the intervention of credit in investment. Bank credit was common in Western market economies but experienced a bitter and tortuous course in China.

We know that traditional socialist economic theories discriminate against business credit and the participation of credit funds in investment. For a long time, the Chinese people have clung to the doctrine that said that only the incremental national income, namely, fiscal revenue, could serve for long-term social investment, while credit funds from banks were limited to short-term purposes. This was the famous "golden rule" held by the Chinese people for over 30 years after the founding of New China — a "clear division between short-term and long-term funds, and separate management of public finance and banking system." Meanwhile, people accepted Marx's view that "business credit is what capitalists grant each other" and now that there were no capitalists in a socialist system, and so there was certainly no business credit either. As early as the 1950s, all kinds of horizontal funds transfers between enterprises were prohibited, and sales on account and payment in advance were completely banned. On the contrary, the Chinese government advocated collection with acceptance and cash on delivery. The decision-makers of China thought that by centralizing all the credit to banks and replacing business credit with bank credit, China would save all the tortuous calculation and enter into what Stalin called a "socialist product economy." However, the hasty rejection of credit denied not only reasonable sales on account and payment in advance, which were necessary for commodity economy, but also bills and clearance. It is just because of this denial that in the first 40 years of New China, people avoided talking about capital, and thus the country lacked a culture of capital and credit.

After the reform and opening up, the Chinese people rethought their traditional understanding of credit. When the government gave more rights to state-owned enterprises, it advocated horizontal economic links, allowed business credit, and worked to get banks involved in investment by substituting bank loans for fiscal appropriation in capital construction. Why did the government propose replacing fiscal appropriation with bank loans? This happened due to pressure from the theoretical circle. At the same time, a Hungarian economist criticized socialist state-owned enterprises for being "thirsty for investment," and the causes were the soft budget constraint and the meticulous care of socialist governments for their enterprises. Theorists put forward the idea of strengthening the budget constraint towards enterprises and expanding the autonomy of enterprises to turn them into independent business accounting units, responsible for their own profit and loss. The corresponding reform was the "replacement of profit delivery by tax payment," namely, to require state-owned enterprises to pay taxes instead of submitting their profits to the administration. Another policy was to repay capital with interest after the capital construction projects, funded by bank loans instead of fiscal appropriations, were put into operation. People believed that if one could not return the loans, one did not dare to borrow money, which would help to scale down the capital construction. The representative of this theory in the academic circle was Ma Hong whose theory was very aggressive.

The second cause for promoting the replacement of appropriation by loans in capital construction investment was that the National Construction Committee (NCC) had the enthusiasm to implement such a policy. The economic plan was formulated by the State Development Planning Commission (SDPC) while the NCC was responsible for managing construction sequence and concentrating all the resources to complete projects. Under the system of projects invested in by state appropriation, the construction projects asked for more money as soon as they wanted some, and regarded state investment as an endless source of money. The NCC thought that to change state allocation into bank loans might restrain the projects' endless demand for money since the repayment responsibility was increased. At that time, Gu Mu served as the Director of the NCC and appreciated the intensive knowledge of the Construction Bank on capital construction projects by frequently stating that the "China Construction Bank is a good friend of our NCC." Gu thought of making the Construction Bank fall under the collective administration of the Ministry of Finance and the NCC when the state appropriation was replaced by bank loans. The NCC believed that to have another subordinate body familiar with capital construction was an advantage to its construction management. Logically, the NCC was very active in promoting this policy.

The reform of loans for fiscal allocations was discussed several times among the SDPC, the NCC, and the Ministry of Finance. Later on, senior government officials approved this reform, and Hu Guofeng, the then Premier, made it clear that "fiscal appropriation for capital construction investment would be gradually substituted by bank loans and the change would start from this year (1979)." During March and April 1979, The Shanghai Xinguang Dyeing, Weaving, and Shirt Manufacturing Mill volunteered to join the pilot program when it heard that profits resulting from starting production ahead of schedule belonged to the enterprises in the experiment of loans for fiscal allocations. One copper band factory discontinued its request for state appropriation for fear of being unable to repay the money when it knew that fiscal allocations would be replaced by bank loans. This verified the initial wish of reducing endless state investment by implementing a reform of substituting state allocation for loans.

The reform of loans for fiscal allocations was a breakthrough in the original planned economy. In April 1979, Deng Xiaoping proposed replacing fiscal appropriations with bank loans and he regarded banks as a lever for economic development and technological innovation in a meeting of the provincial and municipal first party secretaries during the period for the Central Working Conference. He pointed out: "Banks should also get involved in promoting national economy, but they now just work as accountants without fully playing their due roles. For small investment with immediate returns, bank loans are more proper than state allocation. If the investments required by factories are less than several hundreds of thousands, a bank can lend money to them and the loans can be repaid within several years. If this scheme is proved to be workable, bank outlets should be increased to a wider area." Deng specially talked about the Construction Bank and its leverage effect. He said that the so-call "Construction Bank" should not only work out accounts, but also have to seek new business opportunities and deal with economic works.

For the planned fiscal system, to change state allocation for capital construction investment into loans from the Construction Bank would not impose a heavy burden on financial departments. The Ministry of Finance said that this reform was just a change of fund supply. It did not alter the planned system of "allocation of investment by sector and by region" of the SDPC and the Construction Bank indeed possessed abundant experience from participating in supervising investment in capital construction and undertaking equipment loans for many years. As a result, in August 1979, the SDPC, the NCC, the Ministry of Finance and China Construction Bank collectively asked for the approval from the State Council to carry out pilot programs in the textile industry, tourism industry, and other industries, in Beijing, Shanghai, and Guangdong Province. This pilot project of loans for fiscal allocations was expanded to the whole nation since 1985.

It also needs to be mentioned that before this reform, the deposits in the Construction Bank could only be used for short-term construction loans, i.e., working capital loans, and no fixed-asset loan (investment loan) can be made there. Since the policy of "decentralization of power and transfer of profits to enterprises" was promulgated, China experienced a tight fiscal balance. Therefore, President Li Xiannian presented on several occasions that the Construction Bank should be more flexible in its business and would lend to one person the idle deposits of the other person. It was the policy of loans for fiscal allocations that restored the banks' credit function by allowing bank credit to get involved in investment.

There was an interlude during this reform. In 1979, when Li Xiannian hosted a meeting discussing expanding consumption by suppressing accumulation, the textile industry demanded more investment. At that time, central finance bore a deficit of RMB18 billion, so the Minister of Finance, Wu Bo, told the head of the Central Bank, Li Baohua, that "the textile industry need money but the financial department really does not have any. Can you lend us RMB2 billion to fund the Construction Bank to make loans to the textile industry?" Li Baohua replied: "We are also banks and we should also support the textile industry. How about letting our People's Bank of China directly set aside RMB2 billion for providing loans?" In this way, Li Xiannian decided to make the central bank grant RMB2 billion in loans to the textile industry every year and the loans were called "middle- and short-term equipment loans" (later, the loans were issued by the Industrial and Commercial Bank of China [ICBC] on the central bank's behalf when ICBC was first set up in 1983). Following that, based on the instruction from Li Xiannian, the Construction Bank also offered small construction loans about RMB2–3 billion per year and the Bank of China annually provided USD300 million of short-run foreign exchange loans to export enterprises. As a result, the deformed structure of "large public finance and small banking system" was changed fundamentally and China entered into a new era of "relying on banks to support construction."

The biggest merits of the reform of loans for fiscal allocations and the engagement of credit in investment were to restore the role of enterprises as independent commodity producers in a market economy and urge most enterprises to accelerate capital turnover and enhance economic performance by teaching them that the capital could not be used without compensation and interest was the opportunity costs of the capital. Another important contribution of the reform was to activate all the functions of banks by breaking the 30-year prohibition of using fixed assets only for state appropriations rather than bank loans.

To be more specific, the economic reform centering on decentralizing power and transferring profits to enterprises at the beginning of the 1980s incurred an increasingly declining proportion of fiscal income in GDP and that of the central fiscal income in total fiscal revenue. The financial embarrassment made the traditional system of a unified state control over income and expenditure based on fiscal allocation, unable to sustain itself. The most practical contribution of the reform of loans for fiscal allocations and the engagement of credit in investment was to give priority to indirect finance in the investment and financing policies during the 10 years of the seventh and eighth five-year plans. By mobilizing citizens to make savings in banks, China successfully completed the social fixed-asset investment of RMB8.1 trillion (quite a large portion was accomplished by bank loans) and thus realized the growth miracle of the nation's economy during this period.

Of course, the reform of loans for fiscal allocations has its absurdities and distortions. First, a newly built enterprise with no capital base would ask for bank loans and the bank actually approved its borrowing request. The loan was in fact repaid by tax since the enterprise could use pretax profit to pay back the money. In this way, debt was considered as equity and the relationship between debt and equity was reversed, which caused the excessive debts of enterprises in the 1990s. Although absurd, it constituted the most important capital formation mechanism of this period. Second, bank loans were issued on the basis of deposits, but the investment loan quota was determined by the NCC. "Allocation of investment by sector and by region" was changed into "allocation of investment and loans by sector and by region" and banks made loans to the projects according to the instructions from the NCC. This was a distortion. Overall, in spite of the weakness in the reform of loans for fiscal allocations, its merits overweighed its demerits considering the return of bank function. From then on, credit-based bank loans became a major component of the capital formation mechanism.

It is worth noting that the changes in the national income distribution after the reform and opening up played a vital role in the participation of bank loans in investment. In the first 30 years of New China, the rural areas implemented a collective ownership and the income of farmers was really low. The income distribution in the urban areas was a performance-linked pay system in name but a low-income system in reality. In the enterprises and public institutions of cities, college graduates could only earn RMB50–60 per month, similar to the wages of employees with a lower educational background, showing a strong egalitarian characteristic. The low wages remained the same for a long period after 1962, which caused the low savings rates of Chinese citizens. The rural and urban residents' deposit balance was only RMB21 billion at the end of 1978, only equal to 5.79% of that year's GDP. In the distribution pattern of national income, residents were not the principal contributors in national saving and thus by no means the main providers for investment, neither were enterprises, during the early period of New China. Only the government could play both roles at the same time: Savers and investors. This was a unique feature of China's national income distribution.

After the reform and opening up in 1978, the income distribution pattern underwent changes. Deng Xiaoping proposed allowing a part of the people to become wealthy first, excluded the transportation for sale over a long distance from speculation and profiteering, and allowed farmers to find jobs or do business in cities. At the same time, enterprises broke the "big rice bowl" system of equalitarian treatment by paying higher wages together with bonuses to their competent employees. The growth of employment rates and the decline of dependency ratios together with the above factors collectively boosted the rapid increase of the savings of urban and rural residents. In 1987, the balance of savings deposits of urban and rural residents reached RMB433.4 billion, taking up 36.23% of that year's GDP (RMB 1. 2 trillion), increased by 20 times compared to the number of 1978 of RMB21billion. Savings became an important source for banks to support economic development through loans. Meanwhile, many theorists regarded household saving deposits as a potential trouble and worried that the residents would snap up consumer goods in the market. According to the statistics of 1995, the newly increased household saving deposits amounted to RMB810 billion and the year-end balance reached RMB2.966 trillion, equivalent to 50.7% of that year's GDP (RMB5. 848 trillion).

The continuous increase of household savings reflected a substantial improvement in people's wealth since the reform and opening up. A series of reforms relating to the decentralization of power and the transfer of profits to enterprises reworked the distribution pattern of national income and fundamentally changed the transfer mechanism from savings to investment. This indicated that after the reform and opening up, the Chinese government was no longer the main body of savings and investment, and residents and enterprises took the government's places as savings contributors and investment contributors, respectively. The separation between the two kinds of contributors provided a broader room for financial reform and demanded an effective social financing system to simultaneously give full play to the roles of banks and the capital market and lead the transition of savings towards investment.

The Investment Boom between 1982 and 1992: The First Contest between Market and Planned Commodity Economies

Decision on Economic System Reform made during the Third Plenary Session of the Twelfth Central Committee of the CPC clearly put forward in October 1984 that socialism practiced a planned commodity economy on the basis of public ownership and demanded the development of a socialist commodity economy beyond mandatory planning. But this document restricted commodity economy only to the product field and especially emphasized that "under socialism, labor force, banks, land, and mines are not commodities." This was a result of historical limitation.

But the expansion of capital had no end. Although the government called China's economy a "planned commodity economy," the economy was by no means a market one. Since the market was full of vitality and energy, it wanted to break through the restriction of being planned. The most notable events were the four investment booms between 1982 and 1992.

1. The first investment boom occurred when enterprises and local government used their stand-by financial resources to make investments after the policy of decentralizing power to lower-level governments and granting more profits to enterprises in 1982.
2. The second one was the credit boom caused by four banks competing to offer loans on the basis of deposits when the state appropriations were replaced by bank loans in 1984.
3. The rise of financing through securities, investing through trust companies, and establishing financial institutions by local governments between 1987 and 1988.
4. The fourth boom was created by various investments from outside the government structure and the government's' enthusiasm in building development zones after the southern tour talks of Deng Xiaoping between 1992 and 1993. The real investment accounted for 147.8% of the budget, and 8,700 new development zones were built in reality despite only 119 having been approved by the state beforehand.

The four investment booms all happened during the transitional period from a centralized economy to a market economy. Different from the previous three investment expansions which were fueled by the investment impulses of higher authorities, these four expansions were carried out under reasonable instructions from the central government, but the problems of these four investment expansions laid in local governments, government departments, and enterprises. So the investment boom took place in spite of the fact that the higher authorities clearly demanded control over investment scale. Another difference was that the sources of the four investment booms were mainly extra-budgetary funds and bank loans.

The excessive growth of investment during the reform and opening up was a result of the ameliorating of production relations and the arousing of greater enthusiasm of local governments, government departments, and enterprises to build a socialist society during the process of decentralizing power and transferring profits downwards. Meanwhile, many policies of this time were transitional in nature or incomplete, and thus many systematic defects which were conducive to the excessive growth of investment were exposed during the implementation. As the central government motivated enterprises and local governments to devote themselves to socialist construction, the blindness accompanied with this motivation encouraged the excessive growth of investment in various aspects, which became the impetus to make use of the limited financing sources scattered in government departments, local governments, enterprises and banks to expand investment. The problem was that government departments, local governments, and enterprises possessed just a little money and intended to only invest in local areas or their own business instead of other provinces or by means of a joint venture. They were short-sighted and did not consider their sustainable capability when making investments. Just imagine under the conditions that more than 2,000 counties demanded development and several hundreds of thousands of enterprises asked for reform, how could investment not over-expand?

The investment boom during 1982 to 1992 exposed two problems:

The first one was that the planning department did not admit the role of economic leverage in investment and it had no idea about how to adjust investment by using economic leverage. The mainstream thinking at that time was that investment in capital construction could only be arranged by the state and was free from the impacts of economic leverage. As a result, the planning department and competent authorities diverted all their attention to distributing the dozens of billions of budgetary investment and bank loans instead of guiding the social investment of hundreds of billions. The planning department neither led the extra-budgetary funds to the state-guided plan by using a series of encouraging and restrictive policies via the distribution system, nor encouraged local governments and enterprises to raise funds from multiple sources for the construction projects.

The planning department felt completely at a loss what to do with the suddenly emerged hundreds of billions of extra-budgetary investments. At first, the department set quotas to restrict the capital expansion for fear of the excessive growth of investment, and then collected energy and transportation funds and construction tax from the extra-budgetary funds in order to compensate for the shortage of funds in the budget. Later on, the government worried that the extra-budgetary funds would take up the existing investment scale, so it stipulated "10 leaving out"[12] and "5 exclusions"[13] with the hope of controlling the investment scale by ruling out several occasions in measuring the size of investment. In brief, the government neither encouraged nor led the extra-budgetary capital to support the key projects in the state's plan, but regarded the extra-budgetary funds as a threatening force to the government's plan to be restricted and prevented.

Consequently, the investment distribution system just led the government departments, local governments, and enterprises to ask for projects and compete for investment, and this stimulated the expansion of investment. This system was not beneficial to the control, leading, and managing of investment by the state.

The second problem was that government departments, local governments, and enterprises took advantage of the counter-regulatory effect of some improper fiscal and taxation policies to facilitate the repeated constructions, when they saw opportunities in market demand and gained the impetus to expand capital.

The fiscal contract was an example. Local governments were at the same time taxpayers and tax gatherers, which deformed some economic levers to become catalysts for investment expansion. The Chinese government set a high tax rate for some products (such as televisions and refrigerators) to suppress investment, however, to contract fiscal targets to local governments encouraged investment growth since high-tax products now were turned into an important source of fiscal revenue for local finance. During this period, local governments and enterprises introduced more than 100 color TV production lines, 56 refrigerator production lines, and 200 granite production lines, which were all high-tax products and attracted excessive investment, resulting in overcapacity, market saturation and sluggish sales.

Taking the input-output contract system as another example, this method motivated different sectors to increase production, and stimulated them to seek financial resources from or contend for investment with local governments and broaden social funds. On occasion an investment would be made to increase some unnecessary product processing capability, for the purpose of adapting to the existing interest pattern of certain areas or enterprises. For instance, to introduce 11,000 tons of ethylene went against the economies of scale, but the competent department in the central government gave in to the local governments and introduced 5 similar projects, which turned a microeconomic unreasonable expansion into a macroeconomic one.

The same thing happened in the reform of materials allocation structure. To grant the allocation power of products from small enterprises to local government was intended to arouse the enthusiasm of local governments, increase production, and invigorate the material market, and yet it encouraged excessive investment towards small enterprises from the local authorities.

Financial reform initiated from the replacement of state appropriation by bank loans in capital construction investment and the participation of credit in investment. This reform took the initiative in supporting economy and enlivening finance, and opened a door for investment expansion via credit. For one thing, the reformed financial system enabled local government to use bank loans as a means of investment expansion, while the slogan "more savings, more loans" put forward by the central government deteriorated the inborn defect of credit-based loans. For another, the vision of the central bank to build four major national banks (the Bank of China, the China Construction Bank, the Industrial and Commercial Bank of China, and the Agricultural Bank of China) into universal banks, endowed the four specialized banks with broader financial strength to collect social funds to support production construction by way of bank loans through their diverse operations.

The four banks all wanted to win a favor from local Party and government departments by credit loans, so they competed to issue loans, which caused a credit boom. Moreover, the two-way countermeasures which boasted of both controlling the balance of new loans and limiting the fixed-asset loan disbursement, were less effective than expected. In fact, neither the planning department nor the central bank devoted to monitoring the real data of the annual fixed-asset loan disbursement in the four banks, and even bank statistics, showed no information on loan disbursement size. A more serious problem was that the Chinese central government once agreed to leave the financial funds of certain provinces and cities to local projects as a favorable policy to the local governments, which in fact was equal to increasing a credit quota for the local area, but gradually evolved into an unwritten principle of "local funds to be used for local projects." In reality, this action encouraged the financial separation between different provincial governments and, to a larger extent, indulged the excessive growth and the blindness of investment.

Any economic reform would inevitably bring about the dispersion of capital and thus urge government departments, local governments, and enterprises to raise funds for long-term investment, since the reform was aimed at arousing the enthusiasm of the above-mentioned parties and increasing their financial capability and vitality. The financing boom induced by the financial reform between 1987 and 1988, the investment fever of trust companies, financial craze caused by local governments striving to run financial institutions and the emergence of more than 700 financial companies, all contributed to the high growth of investment. Between 1992 and 1993, when Deng Xiaoping visited southern China, he said "development is the absolute principle," which motivated all positive factors in construction and development and attracted the growth of various investments from outside the government structure. In the aforementioned two times of investment booms, the primary investors were state-owned enterprises, and government departments and local government played leading functions. This reflected the impact on the rigid planned economic system and the inability of the old system to adapt to market disciplines during the economic transition when government departments, local governments, enterprises, and banks, made use of the financial products and instruments borrowed from the mature market economy, in the pursuit of motivations for construction and development.

Those investment booms were almost all accompanied by rises in inflation which were finally solved by implementing tight financial policies to control the investment scale and take the economy back on a healthy track. The investment craze between 1992 and 1993 exposed many defects in the transitional reform policies of department responsibility contracts, local fiscal responsibility contracts, and state appropriation for bank loans. After the adjustment by financial macro-control in 1993, a series of reforms were carried out, which gave birth to the tax-sharing system, modern enterprise system, foreign exchange settlement system, the separation between commercial banks and policy banks, as well as securities and insurance markets, and it thus further promoted the innovation of the capital formation mechanism.

The economic reforms of a socialist society also have their merits, that is, the market-oriented reforms can motivate all the positive factors. These reforms, however, demanded that the planning department, the financial department, the central bank, and other comprehensive departments accommodate the changes, harness the reform by using the economic levers, and lead all kinds of financial resources mobilized by various reform measures in the right investment direction. On the contrary, if the comprehensive departments cannot adapt to the reform policies, foresee the potential power of all positive factors, make the best of the favorable environment to practice the powerful macro-control system and measures, skillfully utilize various economic levers to promote the beneficial and abolish the harmful, and lead the enthusiasm towards investment in the right direction, it would lead to the deviation from the reforms and create the blindness of arbitrary capital expansion.

Prelude to a Market Economy: Financial Macro-Control and Tax Reform

At the beginning of 1992, Deng Xiaoping put forward a series of visions to speed up the reform and opening up and develop a socialist market economy, which was a major breakthrough compared with the planned commodity economy

12 years earlier. In October of the same year, the 14th National Congress of the CPC proposed the establishment of a socialist market economic system, which completely solved the long-term ideological misunderstanding towards a market economy since the reform and opening up. *Decision of the Central Committee of the Chinese Communist Party on Setting Up the Socialist Market Economic System* made during the Third Plenary Session of the 14th Central Committee of the CPC in November 1993, pointed out that to build a socialist market economic system was to make the market play a basic role in resource allocation under the state macro-regulation. Since then, the relationship between government and the market came into public notice, which provided a theoretic foundation for the reform towards a market economy in 1993 and 1994. China's reform towards a socialist market economy started under very tough conditions. It first met with the overheated economy and inflation in 1993 and dispersed capital resulting from the previous policies of decentralizing power and transferring profits downwards and various contract systems. At that time, Zhu Rongji was the executive vice-premier of the State Council. He had to deal with the inflation and dispersed capital first, which was a necessary preparation for the economic transition. And then in 1994, Zhu Rongji carried out a series of radical policies, including the tax-sharing system, modern corporate system reform of state-owned enterprises, foreign exchange settlement and sale system reform, and the separation between policy banks and commercial banks, on the basis of the strengthening of financial macro-control in 1993, which started the transition towards a socialist market economic system in the financial area.

The first task of the preparation for an economic transition was to control inflation, or to be more precise, to reinforce financial macro-control, bring down inflation and eliminate economic overheating. It dated back to 1992 when the southern tour speech by Deng Xiaoping aroused people's enthusiasm to pursue economic construction and development which also was accompanied by the blind growth of various extra-budgetary funds. The stock craze, real estate craze, and development zone craze emerged in the second half of 1992. In 1993, the total fixed assets investment rose by 61.8% and the investment rate was as high as 43.3%. The rapid growth of total social demand created a tension in the infrastructure and basic industry, the gap between demand and the supply of electricity, petroleum products, and building materials was growing larger and larger, and the railway carrying capacity of important trunks could only satisfy 40% demand. The overheated economy caused serious inflation. In 1993 and 1994, retail price increased by 13.2% and 21.7%, respectively, the fastest and highest rising rates since the reform and opening up. Meanwhile, there were also problems of excessive input of currency and financial disorder. In the first half of 1993, M1 and M2 rose by 36.5% and 54.1%, respectively, displacing an unusual growth rate of money supply. The currency issuance was RMB55billion more than the number of the same period of the previous year, and RMB44 billion more than that of the inflated 1988. The phenomena of indiscriminate collection of funds, unselective inter-banking lending, and arbitrary increase of interest rates became increasingly severe. The bank deposits growth showed a declining trend, and the four major banks illegally issued short-term loans, most of which flew to the real estate industry and stock markets.

In view of the overheated economy and increasingly high inflation rate, the central government sent 13 ministers to conduct investigations in 26 provinces and cities, which resulted in 13 articles that were to be discussed in the State Council. Zhu Rongji was the executive vice-premier responsible for national economic works and he said in a joking way: "13 is not a lucky number, we should add a few more articles." This was the No. 6 document (also known as "16 articles document") released by the CCP Central Committee and the State Council in June 1993 about improving the economic situation, with the primary tasks being to intensify the financial macro-control, combat inflation, and eliminate economic overheating.

The implementation was not successful at the very beginning. In order to put the "16 articles document" into practice, Zhu Rongji assumed the position of Governor of the People's Bank of China in June 1993, to enhance economic macro-control via financial means with the rectifying of financial order as a breakthrough. He announced the following measures: 1. To resolutely investigate and punish the illegal activities, such as the indiscriminate collection of funds, unselective inter-banking lending, and arbitrary increase of interest rates in order to block the illegal channel for capital loss; 2. Under the principle of a tight loan supply, to secure the necessary funds for state-owned enterprises, key construction projects, and agricultural development; 3. To raise the lending and deposit rates successively in May and July 1993, reopen the business of inflation proof savings deposits in order to speed up capital withdrawal and stabilize citizens' expectation. In July 1993, the central bank took back the loan size adjustment right up to 7% from provincial branches and centralized the allocation and relending rights of credit loans, the formulating and adjusting rights of the benchmark interest rate, as well as the issuing power of money and gave these rights to the head office of the People's Bank of China. These measures effectively controlled the economic and financial disorder. In 1994, the central bank suddenly stopped making an overdraft for the government and offering special-purpose loans. It should be said that the reinforcement of economic micro-control and the rectification of financial order in 1993 laid a good foundation for the comprehensive economic reform in 1994.

The second task of the preparation of an overall economic reform was to deal with the dispersed capital, namely, under the circumstances of the sharp decline in central fiscal revenue and extremely dispersed capital, the central government reformed the tax system by implementing a tax-sharing system, regulated the allocation relationship between the central government and local government, created a fair competitive environment for enterprises, centralized more financial resources for the central financial department, and strengthened the capability and function of the central government in regulating the economy.

It was said in the above, under a planned economic system of state-monopolized revenue and expenditure, all income of an enterprise would be turned over to the state in the forms of tax and profits, and the national financial resources were highly centralized in the hands of the central government. The reform and opening up set the keynote of decentralizing power and transferring profits to enterprises, expanded the autonomy of enterprises with a gradual implementation of various management contract responsibility system and tax farming system, and transferred the financial system from "a separated revenue and expenditure between the central and the local governments" to "an all-round fiscal contract system," which played a huge role in promoting the enthusiasm of local government and accelerating the economic development. However, since the contract system fixed the revenue to be handed over to the central authority, the proportion of the central fiscal revenue to the total fiscal revenue decreased constantly, from the 40.5% of 1984 to the 22% of 1993. The increasingly small amount of central fiscal revenue forced the central government to borrow money from local government or overdraw from banks. The contract system also reinforced a fragmented economy with regional closure and segmentation. Meanwhile, uneven burdens on different enterprises also impeded the further development of independent management of and fair competition between enterprises. Therefore, to completely change the contract system, reform tax and fiscal systems, and straighten out the relationships among the state, enterprises, the central financial department and local financial departments, became objective requirements for developing a socialist market economic system.

In 1994, on the basis of strengthening the financial macro-control, the state carried out a large-scale tax reform. This reform clarified the confused relationship between tax and interest in the previous policy of tax for interest, and distinguished between the responsibility of government as a social administrator and that as state-asset owner by separating profits from tax. The new tax reform formed a modern turnover tax with added-value tax as the main part and consumption tax and business tax as the supplement. State-owned enterprises took 35% of total profits to pay income tax, and the contract responsibility system and tax-contracting system were abolished. Meanwhile, in consideration of the tax reform, state-owned enterprises introduced new enterprise financial rules and accounting standards, established the state assets investment income distribution measures of sharing profits according to contributions and leaving the profit after tax to enterprises, and adopted an international financial statement system. This reform played a positive role in regulating the profit distribution method, rationalizing the income distribution relationship between the government and enterprises, guaranteeing a stable growth of national revenue, and creating the level playing field required by the development of a socialist market economy for enterprises.

In 1994, the fiscal management system of a tax-sharing system between the central and local governments was implemented. The main point of this system was "three divisions and one return," namely, to divide central tax from the local tax (divided into Central Tax, Local Tax, and Shared Tax between central and local governments in terms of tax categories), divide the scopes of administrative power and expenditure between the central and the local parts, divide the central administrative organs from the local ones, and establish the tax return system from the central to the local governments. The tax-sharing system was the largest tax reform since the founding of New China, and a breakthrough of the traditional thinking of "decentralizing power and transferring of profits." It regulated the financial relationship among different governments, promoted the annual growth of the two proportions (the proportion of fiscal revenue in GDP and that of the central fiscal revenue in the national fiscal revenue), and effectively facilitated the establishment of a socialist market economy by motivating governments of various levels to participate in financial affairs and boost the growth rate of the central financial income. In the first year of the new tax system, the direct income of the central government accounted for 55.7% of total government revenue, 27.6 percentage points higher than the number in 1992.

According to Xiang Huaicheng, the Executive Vice-Premier Zhu Rongji personally led a team of government officials from relevant departments to work out accounts face-to-face with 13 provincial governments for more than two months during the tax-sharing reform, and Xiang Huaicheng followed the team to visit most of the provinces, excluding Guangdong and Hainan provinces. The two-month visits were by no means easy trips, and working overtime or even overnight frequently happened. Zhu Rongji said jokingly afterwards that "during that period, we travelled all around, and tried our best to convince the local governments and enterprises. Sometimes, we have to eat humble pie, and at other times, we may employ both hard and soft tactics. The task was finally done, but I lost almost 5 pounds of weight."

The tax-sharing system focused on the establishment of a decentralized tax-sharing system to solve the problems of weak financial strength, the disordered fiscal system, and the seriously inadequate financial regulation ability of the central government, which were formed in the 15 years before the reform and opening up under a fragmented administrative relationship. The system also correctly handled the two basic relationships between governments and enterprises, and between the central government and the local government, and laid a foundation for both the transition of financial functions in order to adapt to a market economy and the deepened overall reform with a proper relationship between the government and market. The most obvious merits of this reform were that under the financial constraints of the central government, a vast majority of capital could be centralized in the hands of the central government who was no longer at the mercy of local governments by gaining the right to allocate funds. When talking about the tax-sharing reform of 1994, many people considered this tax reform as a great leap in the financial system.

When dealing with inflation and dispersed capital, the central government also carried out a reform in financial system by separating policy banks from commercial banks, and using credit policies to adjust the economic structure. In 1994, the state built three policy banks in succession — China Development Bank, Agricultural Development Bank of China, and the Export and Import Bank of China — and thus changed the money supply mechanism of commercial banks forcing the central bank to issue money. In the following year, the central bank insisted on an appropriately tight monetary policy and practiced a series of financial macro-control measures conforming to the market rules to fundamentally resolve the financial problems. Besides, in view of the situations of a sharp decline of foreign capital, a decreasing trend of foreign trade, and a severe shortage of foreign exchange reserve in 1994 (the trade deficit in 1994 was USD12.2 billion, while the foreign exchange reserve in 1993 was just USD21 billion, unable to sustain the two-year trade deficit), the central government implemented a system of selling and purchasing of foreign exchange through banks in the foreign exchange receipts and payments of domestic institutions. Under the collective action of this practice and other policies, like export rebates, China's trade surplus and foreign exchange reserve increased year by year.

The Transformation of Operation Mechanism in State-Owned Enterprises: To Build a Modern Corporate System

To build a modern corporate system was the direction for reforming state-owned enterprises indicated by the CPC during the Third Plenary Session of the 14th Central committee of the Party, but since the state-owned enterprises had developed under a planned economic system, this reform was a complete change.

The theoretical basis for the state enterprises management under a planned economy was *The State and Revolution* written by Lenin — Once the proletariat seized power, the state should manage the whole society by deeming it as a plant and a management office. The management method by each government department towards the state-owned enterprises under a planned economy was basically as follows: The State Development Planning Commission (SDPC) approves projects, the financial department appropriates funds, the banks act as cashiers, the industrial sector takes charge of production, the material and commercial sectors control the supply of raw materials and the products sale, and the personnel department manages personnel changes. Moreover, the state-owned enterprises under a planned economy, especially the large state-owned enterprises (such as, large steel mills, automobile plants, logging plants, and mining and oil fields), assumed almost every social function by acting as public security organs and funding schools and hospitals, in addition to production works. The state's governance towards enterprises was a kind of decentralized management of each department responsible for a certain part. This was a typical bureaucratic style of work. It resulted in not only a separation of power and the checking of interests among different departments, but also weak communication and buckpassing between them. Since property rights cannot be transferred, the suspension of operation or the merger and acquisition of enterprises had to get the state's approval, which involved the interests of managers and operators and thus could not be easily given.

After the reform and opening up, the Chinese government implemented a planned commodity economy and successively carried out a series of reform policies: In 1979, pilot projects of expanding enterprise autonomy were conducted in Shougang Corporation and another seven state-owned enterprises, which denoted the beginning of the state-owned enterprises reform; in 1979, reforms of "loans for fiscal allocations" and "replacement of profit delivery by tax payment" were put into practice; in 1981, the government smashed the "two iron rice bowls" (i.e., industrial enterprises eating from the rice bowl of the state and the workers from the rice bowl of enterprises) by practicing an economic responsibility system; in 1984 the central government narrowed the scope of mandatory planning while it gave more space for instructive planning and market forces; and after 1987, contracted managerial responsibility system was promoted nationwide. Between 1981 and 1984, the Chinese government allowed some overproduced products and a certain proportion of other products prescribed by the state to be sold through the enterprises' own channels at market prices instead of state-set prices, which was called a "double-track pricing system." In 1992 some pilot enterprises of sharing-holding reform were successively listed on the stock market at home and abroad. The reform of decentralizing power and transferring profits to enterprises enlarged the autonomy of enterprises, but the enterprises were still acknowledged as relatively independent commodity producers. The rights of enterprises, however, had not been expanded much during the reform. Although enterprises could directly arrange production, supply and marketing, and dispose of the overproduced products and budget surplus, they had to repay capital with interests after the reform replaced fiscal allocations with loans, and pay taxes as a substitute for profits delivered to the state. There was no exception for joint-stock enterprises and listed companies. It seemed that the listed companies were subject to market competition, but in fact not only the competitive enterprises but also the uncompetitive ones could not be weeded out through competition. The management mechanism was still based on a bureaucratic administration, incompatible with the market rules. After all, although the Chinese government all the time talked about public ownership, the government did not truly understand the concept or know how to be a shareholder.

In 1994, when Zhu Rongji announced the reform of state-owned enterprises, he faced two major challenges: Excessive debts of enterprises, and heavy social responsibilities of enterprises resulting from "enterprises performing social functions." Therefore, the central government had to take several years to first lighten the heavy social burdens and reduce excessive debts. There were mainly four tasks for the state-owned enterprises.

To help out with the excessive debts of the state-owned enterprises

In 1994, the Company Law of China officially came into effect and it required the building of a modern corporate system featuring "clearly established ownership, well defined power and responsibility, separation of enterprise from administration, and scientific management." The first problem concerning the property rights was how to get the state-owned enterprises out of over-indebtedness. Actually, this problem was a result of the confusion between debt and equity during the reform of replacing fiscal appropriation with bank loans. The own capital (equity capital) which should be appropriated by the state was obtained through loans. Consequently, a large number of state-owned enterprises were running under heavy debts in the absence of equity capital. In 1995, many articles pointed out that the problem in the state-owned enterprise reform was the ambiguous property right. I said at that time that "to talk about ownership and property rights, we have to first make clear the capital relationship. Who offers the funds? How much would the contributor offer? Without capital, what is the point of talking about property rights? If the capital is not replenished, how to clarify property rights?" In fact, higher authorities understood the situation. When Zhu Rongji initiated the reform of state-owned enterprise in 1994, he decided to pilot the "optimization of the capital structure" in 18 industrial cities (later expanded to 100 cities), and the main target was to ease the heavy debts by transferring debts into investment capital. It was the premise for building a modern corporate system by clarifying equity ownership. According to the accounts of 1995, to reduce the debt ratio by 20 percentage points required an injection of RMB850 billion government capital, but the financial embarrassment made it difficult to replenish the state-owned capital. From 1994 to 1998, despite the fact that the central government took several years to encourage enterprise mergers, regulate bankruptcy procedures, suspend repayment of bank loans and interests, write off bad debts and give subsidized loans for technological transformation projects, these measures could not fundamentally get the enterprises out of trouble. On the contrary, the over-indebted enterprises increasingly lacked capital funds. Their deficits expanded year by year and finally a comprehensive loss occurred in 1996. Until the end of 1997, the central government confirmed the three-year reform and trouble-shooting targets of state-owned enterprises. In August of 1999, the government determined to implement the "debt-to-equity swap." After five years of practice, the reversed relationship between debt and equity was eventually set right.

To separate between major and auxiliary businesses, downsize staffs to improve efficiency, and reduce the social responsibility of enterprises

The state-owned enterprises undertook complicated and extensive major and auxiliary businesses, and were burdened with heavy social responsibilities. The irrational corporate structure of "being all-inclusive whether being large or small," has always been an obstacle for the state-owned enterprises to participate in market competition. The enterprises launched the nationwide movement of "breaking the three-irons" (the iron rice bowl, the iron wages, and the iron chair of the cadre),[14] and ushered in the three reforms of the employment system, the income distribution system, and the cadre and personnel system in order to facilitate the employment and dismissal of staff members, the increase and deduction of pay, and the promotion and demotion of higher management officers, whereas the central authorities gradually discovered that the complicated and extensive major and auxiliary businesses were the root causes for the redundant personnel and low efficiency of state-owned enterprises. Therefore, a major step for the reform of the state-owned enterprises was to separate major and auxiliary businesses, and detach the auxiliary social responsibilities from the major production business in order to lessen the burdens of the state-owned enterprises. After this reform, catering, entertainment, trade and commercial institutions, as well as other service organizations, which had been originally attached to the state-owned enterprises, were separated out, and hospitals, vocational schools, property management offices, and other social service units became independent. According to later incomplete statistics, more than 4,000 enterprise-backed primary and secondary schools, over 400 public security organs, and more than 2,000 hospitals were detached from enterprises. In this way, both enterprises and government were back to their prescribed roles and the property right of auxiliary institutions became clear after this reform. Some sources said that more than 90% of sideline institutions were turned into non-state-owned holding companies, in which staff shares accounted for 57% of total equity. Clear property rights pushed the operational mechanism of enterprises through profound changes, and the employees' consciousness of market competition and surviving the crisis were greatly enhanced. Some enterprises took advantage of the property rights exchange market during the separation of subsidiary business for major business to bring in competent investors, which added fuel to the further development of the enterprises. After the reform, the structure of state-owned enterprises was adjusted and optimized, so the enterprises could divert more material and financial resources and energy to main businesses in order to achieve high efficiency. Later, in order to highlight core business, the reform of "downsizing for efficiency" was put into practice. During this period, the staff of the state-owned enterprises decreased from as much as 70 million to 40 million, a drop of 40%. This downsizing significantly improved the labor productivity, promoted the transformation of employment and income distribution mechanisms, and created conditions for enterprises to grow larger and stronger and increase their market competitiveness. The largest problem brought along with the reform of downsizing for efficiency, however, was that when the state-owned enterprises buy off the employee service years and get their employees laid off, these jobless employees could not receive sufficient compensation and social security. Although later on the central government carried out the re-employment project as a remedy, a large number of employees were left at the bottom of society due to the lack of property placement and necessary social security. Zhu Rongji revealed in a speech in 2002 that the number of laid-off workers between 1998 and 2000 was 25.5 million.

To reorganize and upgrade small- and medium-sized state-owned enterprises

In the reform of state-owned enterprises, how to pull tens of thousands of enterprises out of the over-indebtedness was a big problem. It has to be mentioned, the *Decision on Some Issues concerning the Improvement of the Socialist Market Economy* announced in the Third Plenary Session of the Fourteenth Central Committee of the CPC in 1993 pointed out that for the general small state-owned enterprises, some could implement contract operation or leasing management, while others could be transformed into joint-stock companies or even sold to other organizations or individuals. How could these enterprises dig themselves out of excessive debts and losses under the circumstance that state-owned enterprises operated on borrowings due to a lack of capital and were constantly burdened with high interest rates? Quanzhou City was overwhelmed by the heavy burdens and became the first to sell dozens of local enterprises to the China Strategic Holdings, a Hong Kong company headed by Oei Hong Leong. In fact, it was debt restructuring and there was no such a problem of the loss of state assets. But to sell state-owned enterprises and state assets was a sensitive topic for the Chinese people. Under the influence of a public ownership for over 40 years, some people criticized this sale by Quanzhou as a squandering action. Later, the overseas listing of the China Strategic Holdings aroused a "China Strategic Crisis" (which will be detailed in Chapter 16). It was also in the year of 1993, when Chen Guang, the Municipal Party Secretary of Zhucheng, Shandong Province, reformed 288 local enterprises above the county level by selling out the net assets to employees and up until July 1994, 272 enterprises had completed the reform. Some people satirized Chen Guang by calling him "Chen Sold-Out." In July 1995, when the Shandong provincial government held a provincial meeting on the reform of the county-level enterprises in Zhucheng City, the Zhucheng reform model was justified. But the criticism towards Chen Guang from certain Beijing leftist magazines made the relevant departments soon change their mind by saying that "to sell out is not a panacea for all." Of course, you could choose not to sell, but you have to be always burdened with a deficit. Here, I have to explain the "ice cream principle." It is said that the property of state-owned enterprises is just like ice cream, you have to sell it as quickly as possible lest it will melt. But now another "ice cream principle" comes out: One would rather hold an ice cream and see it melt before one's eyes than sell it to others. The reality is that if you sell five Yuan worth of ice cream at a price of three Yuan, some people will criticize you for creating the erosion of state assets; if you keep the ice cream until it melts and the nation's asset is indeed lost, no one will criticize you for anything. It indicates that some people do not actually care about the loss of state assets and are willing to be misers holding the melting ice cream instead of selling it. These people cannot get rid of the ideological constraints. In 1996, Hong Hu, the Deputy-Director of the State Commission for Restructuring the Economic System, conducted an investigation in Zhucheng City and made the conclusion that the reform orientation was correct, the reform measures were powerful, the effects were remarkable and the public was satisfied. In March of the same year, Zhu Rongji, Vice Premier of the State Council and member of the CPC Central Committee Political Bureau Standing Committee, led officials from the nine ministries to Zhucheng City for another investigation. Zhu Rongji appraised the corporate reform of Zhucheng in a meeting in Qingdao and asserted that there was no loss of state assets in Zhucheng.

In September 1995, the Fifth Plenary Session of the 14th CPC Central Committee passed the *Suggestions on the Formulation of the Ninth Five-Year Plan for the National Socio-Economy Development and the Long-Term Objectives by 2010* (hereinafter referred to as the *Suggestions*). The *Suggestions* put forward a new idea of "invigorating large enterprises while relaxing control over small ones," and pointed out that the government should "focus on building the entire state economy, and implement a strategic reorganization of state-owned enterprises through the flowing and restructuring of stock assets." The reorganization should orientate towards market and industrial policies, invigorate major enterprises while allowing more flexibility for minor ones, integrate the optimization of state-owned assets distribution structure and corporate organizational structure with that of the investment structure, and form mechanisms of mergers, bankruptcies, and the downsizing of staff for efficiency in order to prevent the loss of state assets. The government should discriminate between different occasions, and accelerate the reform and restructuring of small state-owned enterprises, through reorganization, combination, merger, stock cooperative system, lease, contract management, sale, and many other forms.

In the reform of state-owned enterprises, although small- and middle-sized enterprises were in the majority, their small total assets facilitated the reorganization. After the *Suggestions* of the CPC Central Committee were announced, there were constant ideological struggles, and the local government also faced the severe reality of having no money to either replenish capital or cover the deficit and repay bank loans, thus the practices of "selling the whole enterprise," "operators and workers holding shares," and even "transferring enterprises with no asset" were promoted throughout the country. In 2003, Li Rongrong wrote in an article that "a great variety of means were used to loosen control over and enliven small state-owned enterprises, and 86.1% of the small enterprises had completed the reform. Through the policy of bankruptcy and closedown, a large number of loss-making and insolvent enterprises and exhausted mines withdrew from the market, which directly promoted the strategic reorganization of the state-owned economy and the establishment of the mechanism for survival of the fittest." There was a report in 2008 which said that the property rights reform of small- and medium-sized enterprises around the country was basically put into place, and the majority of enterprises in Sichuan, Chongqing, and Shaanxi had completed the reorganization. Taking Sichuan Province as an example, the number of small- and medium-sized state-owned enterprises dropped from 14,000 to 820, a decrease of 94%, between 1998 and 2005.

To pilot the modern corporate system in large state-owned enterprises

In November 1994, the State Council approved the pilot projects of the modern corporate system in more than a hundred enterprises. It signified that the state-owned enterprise reform transferred from the temporary solution of decentralizing power and transferring profits to system innovation in order to shape a basis for the development of the socialist market economy. The *Suggestions* of 1995 came up with the idea of "focusing on a batch of enterprises and business groups, and by taking capital as a link, uniting and leading a number of the enterprises to transformation and development, in order to form economies of scale and give full play to the leading role of the enterprises in the national economy." However, since the relationship between a modern corporate system or a joint-stock system and diversified investment subjects was unclear during that period of time, the pilot enterprises failed to attract or organize more private capital through the shareholding system and other organizational forms. As a result, the investment subject was single and 80% of the enterprises were transformed into solely state-owned corporations. The pilot projects "were not very successful" and "government functions were mixed up with enterprise management" (Zhang Zhuoyuan, 1999). Until 1996, the central government proposed the "three reforms and one strengthening" in order to reform, reorganize, restructure and strengthen the management of the state-owned enterprises. In 1997, the report of the 15th Party Congress stated that "We shall cultivate and develop a diversity of investors in order to push the separation of administrative functions from enterprise management and change the way enterprises operate," "readjust and improve the ownership structure" and explore multiple forms of public ownership in its realization.[15] Later the reform of enterprise through stock system was gradually promoted. More than 2,000 state-owned large- and medium-size enterprises successively undertook the pilot projects of the modern corporate system, and a substantial part of enterprises formed business conglomerates with international competitiveness. In 1999, the state decided to put into practice a strategic adjustment of state-owned economy. After 2000, when enterprise management was detached from government functions and the reforms were accelerated, China made larger steps in the reform towards the modern corporate system. It was not until several rounds of integrations and reorganizations of large state-owned enterprises that 123 large central enterprises were finally formed under the State-owned Assets Supervision and Administration Commission.

If we analyze deeper, we could find that the solution to the difficulties in the reform of state-owned enterprises towards the modern corporate system was to shift the operation mechanism. First, to accommodate business operation to the market. An inherent weakness of Chinese enterprises was being small and scattered, and the enterprises were inexperienced in operating in the capital market since they had been brought to life under the planned economy free from market competition. Once the planned economy was transformed into a market economy, every enterprise would regard itself as an independent cell of the market economy. At first, the state-owned enterprises were short-sighted, and only paid attention to the small market. Their "market infantilism" would inevitably make the enterprises treat their partners from upstream and downstream businesses as competitors, which would hinder industrial consolidation and the centralized management of business groups. Every enterprise wants to be the leader and thus both upstream and downstream enterprises focus on their own development, which will definitely result in scattered forces and a loss of advantages. This situation was common at that time and the most typical one was the "four petrochemical enterprises of Nanjing" widely reported in 1997. The four enterprises were Yangzi Petrochemical Company, Yizheng Chemical Fibre Company, Jinling Petrochemical Corporation, and Nanjing Chemical Corporation, which were respectively affiliated to China Petro-Chemical Corporation, Ministry of Chemical Industry, Ministry of Textile Industry, and Nanjing Municipal Government. Since the four petrochemical enterprises operated under separate authorities in the old administrative system, they could hardly overcome their narrow vision of the small market and only focused on self-development by finding overseas partners to expand their business. Just as the media described, these enterprises were about to "fight an international war in the domestic market." On the eve of the 15th National Congress of the CPC, after the intervention by the central government, the State Council decided to reform these four petrochemical enterprises into large ones with the economies of scale, and consolidate them into leading conglomerates with international competitiveness in major industries to serve as a sample of win-win partnerships and being industry pacesetters. Although this forming of large enterprise groups was not a result of market forces, a major breakthrough was to remove the institutional and managerial barriers in enterprise organization. Under such a fragmented and segmentary system, the mergers and acquisitions of large enterprises could not be realized without the intervention by the central government.

Second, to establish an effective incentive mechanism for enterprise managers and to be able to efficiently select and secure capable managers. The competition in the modern market economy comes down to talent competition. This competition does not exist among general staff but high-level management professionals and "a good general is usually harder to find than an army of one thousand." The keys are two words: Appointment and reward. The later reflects the value of the former. China's enterprises follow the thinking of official rank standard, and when a company selects its top managers, seniority must be given top priority. Thus, the young talents cannot be promoted and the outstanding senior managers, especially entrepreneurs, cannot be remunerated generously. For a long time, the Chinese people did not consider the opportunity cost in talent deployment and were not good at placing the capable person at a suitable post. The opportunity cost resulting from the poor personnel arrangement is far larger than the loss of state assets. Of course, there is a problem of "talents being difficult to be controlled." Some leaders are accustomed to the submissive and flattery subordinates and therefore cannot tolerate the obstinate and unruly talents.

The key to the talent deployment is to discard the prejudice of equalitarianism, and establish an incentive mechanism. When Longping High-tech Agriculture Corporation was listed, some people talked about the tens of millions of shares held by the founder, Yuan Longping in a jealous way; when Stone Group Corporation carried out management buy-outs, people again guessed the market value of the stocks in the hands of its Chairman, Duan Yongji; when Sina, Sohu, Netease were listed in the U.S. stock market, someone discussed about the wealth of the respective leaders of Wang Zhidong, Zhang Zhaoyang, and Ding Lei. It was obvious that others were envious of the above talents. Although management buy-outs and a share option plan have certain risks, there will always be one who is brave enough to take the risk if the reward offered is attractive enough. However, only the bravest one can get the huge reward, and without either great efforts or outstanding achievements, one will be unable to receive the generous reward. People who get used to the traditional system of state-owned enterprises, tend to consider share option as a kind of costless welfare and right, and believe that as long as one is assigned by higher authorities, even if the person is good for nothing, he can enjoy the fruits of others' work. Consequently, quite a number of state-owned or state-controlled enterprises under the old system, as well as a group of inappropriately reformed listed state-controlled companies which still followed the old system, displayed a situation of "rich leader but poor group." These enterprises can hardly build "generally wealthy teams" as leading private firms can.

Speaking of "rich leader but poor group," we have to mention the famous case of the "Tobacco King" of Yunnan, Chu Shijian, who embezzled public funds after invigorating Yuxi Hongta Tobacco Group. Yuxi Hongta Tobacco Group was a local state-owned enterprise in Yunnan Province and known as Yuxi Cigarette Factory before being reformed. When Chu Shijian served as the Factory Director in 1979, the factory was just a semi-mechanized workshop only with a fixed asset of RMB10.65 million and an annual output of 275,000 boxes of cigarettes. Chu Shijian had worked as Factory Director for three years and carried out three major reform policies. The first one was to renovate the income distribution system. In 1982, Yuxi Cigarette Factory promoted a system of "contracted performance-linked salary and bonus" by relating the workers' salary and bonus to the production volume in order to completely abolish equalitarianism in distribution. Second, to change the system of tobacco planting being administered by the agricultural sector, tobacco purchasing price being set by the Price Bureau, and cigarette sale being monopolized by the Tobacco Bureau.

In 1985, Chu concurrently held the posts of Factory Director of the Yuxi Cigarette Factory, Manager of the Yuxi Tobacco Branch Company, and General Director of Yuxi Area Tobacco Monopoly Bureau. He established the famous mode of "three-in-one" by consolidating the above-mentioned three organizations into one and opened a "high-quality tobacco production base" to directly guide the tobacco cultivation. This action connected every link in the tobacco industry from tobacco cultivation, tobacco production to sales, and utilized the profits from the cigarette factory to support tobacco planting, so that farmers could benefit directly. In 1988, a major earthquake struck Yunnan. To immediately improve the economic situation of Yunnan, the central government gave special approval to the city for the development of the tobacco industry and clearly stated that others could also try the "three-in-one" mode invented by Chu Shijian. As a result, Chu undertook a large scale of mergers and acquisitions of tobacco factories in Yunnan to expand the production capacity, and opened exclusive stores to sell the products, which turned Chu Shijian from an entrepreneur into an industrial magnate. Third, to introduce advanced equipment. The cigarette factory purchased cigarette units from Molins Tobacco Machinery Group of the U.K. in 1981, and later continuously introduced 89 sets of the world's leading equipment from the U.K., Germany, Italy, Japan, and the Netherlands.

Within just 17 years when Chu Shijian was acting as the Factory Director, he turned a small local tobacco factory into the first in Asia and third in the world cigarette group. The factory was also a nationally well-known enterprise and financial pillar for the local government. By 1994, one of its famous brands, Hongtashan, had opened 12,000 exclusive shops, and could annually produce 2.18 million boxes of cigarettes and generate profits and tax revenue of as much as RMB20 billion. Yuxi Cigarette Factory was rated as a first-class national enterprise, and Chu Shijian won the title of "National Outstanding Entrepreneur" and "Top Ten Man of National Reforms," and the lifelong honor of "Golden Ball," among many others.

Surprisingly, in February 1995, the Central Commission for Discipline Inspection of the CPC received an anonymous report about one of Chu Shijian's relatives getting involved in a bribery case. In July 1995, Yunnan provincial government appointed a new Chairman of the Yuxi Hongta Tobacco Group and

Chu Shijian was arrested for a trial in 1997. In January 1998, the Xinhua News Agency carried a report about the serious economic crimes committed by the former Chairman of the Yuxi Hongta Tobacco group, and Chu Shijian was accused of embezzling public funds of about USD3.55 million with other leaders of the group (Chu received USD1.74 billion). It was reported that Chu Shijian confessed to the procuratorial personnel: "The new chairman will take over the group in July 1995, and I thought I have to transfer the signing authority to the new chairman then. I have devoted my whole life to the group and have to think about the rest of my life. I cannot have suffered for nothing, so I decided to embezzle over USD3 million and told other group leaders that it was enough for our latter lives." Many people in the Yuxi Hongta Tobacco Group thought that Chu had taken the money he deserved at the time when he should not have.

Chu's candid confession to the procuratorate aroused a wide discussion around the country. Chu Shijian made a huge contribution to the Yuxi Cigarette Factory when he was in power for the last 10 years. The factory created RMB99.1 billion in profits and tax revenue for the state, achieved a brand value of RMB39.8 billion, and solved the employment of half the population of Yunnan Province. Finally, the central leadership decided that his merit cannot offset his faults, while his defects cannot obscure his virtues. In 1999, Chu Shijian was sentenced to life in prison. Two years later, Chu's sentence was commuted to 17 years' imprisonment. In 2002, he was approved for medical parole due to severe diabetes.

In 1997 when Chu Shijian was arrested, the State Tobacco Monopoly Bureau issued a "double control" policy which withdrew the "three-in-one" mode and closed Hongta exclusive shops. According to statistics, since 1999, the output of flue-cured tobacco in Yunan Province was reduced from 2.3 million to 1.1 million within three consecutive years, and the annual sales volume of Hongtashan dropped sharply from its peak of 900,000 boxes to 300,000 boxes.

Ma Jun, the defense lawyer for Chu Shijian, did the math for Chu Shijian: During the 17 years when Chu acted as the Factory Director, he created a total of RMB80 billion profits and tax revenue for the state, but his total personal income was only RMB800, 000. Ma Jun believed that the objective reality which aroused the feeling of unfairness in Chu, apart from subjective factors, led to Chu's crime. Ma Jun had a famous saying that "the annual income of such a contributive leader of a state-owned enterprise can hardly compete with the pay for a single performance of a singer!"

Ma Jun said: "In China's fights against corruption, the government focused more on the entrepreneurs who made a fortune by trashing their enterprises, namely the so-called 'rich leader but poor group.' The state-owned enterprises reform and economic development aimed to eliminate the situation of 'rich leader but poor group' and create more and more 'rich leaders and rich groups.' Chu Shijian has committed a crime and should face legal consequences, but his crime was after all different from that of a rich leader of a poor group. Chu turned not only his little group but also the large group (the province or even the state) into rich ones. When he intended to also enrich his own family by moving some wealth from his little group, he was caught by others."

Ma Jun further expanded his idea by borrowing the "cat theory" from Deng Xiaoping: "The defendant Chu Shijian resembles the cat which is good at catching mice but steals fish on special occasions. Compared with the cat which also catches mice but frequently steals fish or which does not catch a mouse but usually steals fish, Chu shijian was totally different. Why cannot we give the capable cat some fish before the cat steals fish?"

Of course, the embezzlement of more than USD30 billion by Chu Shijian was indeed a case of corruption and negligence and Chu's merit could not offset his faults. However, from his case we can see that the establishment of an effective incentive mechanism was very important.

Counterfeit Short-Term Lending and Loans Beyond the Credit Ceiling: The Last Contest between Market Economy and Planned Economy in Currency Field

After the reform and opening up, along with the financial reform and the involvement of credit in investment, the central bank imposed a credit ceiling with a view to leading and regulating the support of bank credit to economic development, controlling money flow, and establishing a normal financial order. Meanwhile, in some coastal cities and areas where the market economy and non-state economy developed rapidly and vigorously, capital was increasingly in great demand and normal credit funds could not satisfy the financial needs. Consequently, counterfeit short-term lending (namely, to use short-term loans for long-term investment) and loans above the credit ceiling emerged to meet the financial demand for operation, which created for a time investment expansion.

In 1993, when the Vice Premier Zhu Rongji rectified the financial order, he focused on cleaning up illegal lending, fake trust, and loans above the credit ceiling in order to get tens of millions of capital back into normal production and circulation channels in the speculation market. The illegal activities of counterfeit short-term lending and loans bypassing the credit ceiling continued despite repeated prohibitions. In 1995, Zhu Rongji decided to impose severe punishment on several typical violations as a warning to others. I was working for the China Construction Bank at that time, and after making investigations on the loans above the credit ceiling in Zhejiang Province, I found that the problems of counterfeit short-term lending and loans bypassing the credit ceiling were very complex there and closely related to the policy of local government to enliven its economy, the defects in credit control system and the non-market interest rates, not just a matter of operational violation.

According to my findings, the once popular illegal activities of counterfeit short-term lending, fake trust, and loans above the credit ceiling in coastal cities appeared as early as the mid-1980s. They were financial pillars for the impressive growth of the non-state economy in these areas and in reality breakthroughs in the initial credit control system. At that time, since there was no real estate market and securities market, the loans beyond the credit ceiling did not get involved in speculation, so I called it a "special case" in the capital formation mechanism and believed this "special case" was a real reflection of the last contest between a market economy and a planned economy in the currency field.

The problem originated from the credit control system. The system was initially an instructive plan for the financial field and a guidepost for controlling the year-end bank loan balance. Back in 1983–1984, the financial revenue and expenditure were tight, and the investment in capital construction was cut down. The central bank complained about the deformed pattern of "large public finance but small banking system," and there was a proposal of "linking deposits with loans, and more deposits, more loans" in financial reform. As a result, banks in different areas started to provide a large number of fixed-asset loans to support capital construction and technical innovation. As a result, the credit loans ran out of control at the end of 1984. From 1985 on, the state demanded the carrying out of dual-track control over the scale of fixed-asset investment and credit loans, but the implementation was difficult. The reasons were that the credit ceiling only limited the year-end loan balance but could not control the "excessive loans in the middle of the year," and technical renovation loans could be reloaned after being withdrawn. In fact, these loans were not subject to the fixed-asset loan ceiling. According to the survey of the Bureau of Statistics, many banks possessed a considerable amount of "other investment loans" which were not calculated in the fixed-asset loan size. Therefore, although the government called for the control over the investment scale of fixed assets between 1985 and 1988, the investment quota was exceeded every year.

Despite a less stringent credit control system in the initial implementation, the system greatly limited the bank loans in the coastal provinces and cities where the market economy enjoyed a rapid development. At that time, in the Guangdong and Fujian provinces, and later in Shanghai, due to a lack of construction funds, the local governments asked for approval from the central government for a policy of "local funds for local use," which was a breakthrough in the credit control system and in reality created a favorable regional policy of "more deposits and more loans." This practice aroused attention from cities with prosperous market economies (especially Jiangsu and Zhejiang Provinces), but those cities without the favorable policy could not follow suit. These local governments thus made every endeavor to search for funds in order to develop the economy. "Financing fever," and then "bonds fever," and "financial fever" occurred successively. The local governments first issued municipal bonds to raise funds and then turned to run trust companies and various financial companies for collecting a portion of funds to support local construction after the central authorities banned the issuing of local bonds. During the rectification in 1989, more than 300 trust and investment companies utilized short-term lending capital to support long-term investment, which was a prototype of loans beyond the credit ceiling.

In Jiangsu, Zhejiang, and other places where a market economy and a non-state economy grew prosperously and financial awareness was awakened comparatively early, the credit control system in fact played a role of restricting the development of the market economy and production. In those cities, the economic development was based on the non-state economy (the proportion of the non-state economy accounted for two-thirds of the economy in Zhejiang and Jiangsu provinces) and markets (Zhejiang owned over 4,000 large markets out of 8,000 around the country), and so was the growth of bank deposits. However, the credit quota was decided on the basis of the "base-plus-growth" method, and the credit control system complied with the patterns of a planned economy and a state-owned economy rather than those of a non-state-economy and a market economy. As long as there were no large projects and large enterprises, there would be no sufficient loans. Even though the size of loans increased a little bit, it was far from enough to satisfy just state-owned enterprises, let alone non-state and market economies. Those cities held little hope for the increase of loan quota. The deposits grew quickly in those cities while the loan quota lagged behind, so the banks in those cities usually transferred their deposit surplus to the bank branches in other cities to support loan projects. Thus, the local Party and government officials in the former cities were not pleased.

Due to the rapid development of the market economy in coastal areas, local governments, enterprises, and banks found opportunities in market supply and demand, and proposed some projects which suited the practical requirements of the market. At this point, owing to the insufficiency of loan quota, the urgent need of local governments and banks to use deposits to support local economic development gave rise to the emergence of counterfeit short-term lending, fake trust, and other kinds of loans to bypass the credit ceiling.

What is the definition of a loan beyond the credit ceiling? It is a loan which is issued through bypassing the credit limit. It should be said that the credit control system imposed on the state-owned commercial banks, as a major monetary means, played a certain role in macro-financial control. The system could control the total amount of credit and suppress the overheated economy for one thing, and ensure the concentration of funds on important projects and promote the healthy development of the economy for another, at the earlier stage of economic reform when the state-owned economy was at the dominant place, and financial institutions were not in a great number and offered just simple financial products.

In the mid-1990s, the central government advocated "a socialist market economy," which incurred huge changes in the economic and financial areas. I concluded these changes as methods of "breaking the four kinds of dominance" in the financial field: 1. Breaking the dominant place of the non-state economy by encouraging the growth of the non-state economy which accounted for one-third of the total economy nationwide, and two-thirds in coastal areas; 2. Breaking the dominant place of state banks, as the medium- and small-sized commercial banks, urban credit cooperatives, and non-bank financial institutions sprang up and contributed 30% of the total new loans in 1994; 3. Breaking the dominance of indirect financing between banks by the development of the capital market, bonds, stocks, funds, and other kinds of direct finance; 4. Breaking the dominance of deposits and loans through the diversified development of financial products. In 1994, the financial assets except loans in China's four major specialized banks accounted for 46% of the total newly increased assets, owing to the diversified business development of banks. The "breaking of the four kinds of dominance" increasingly reduced the function of the credit control system as a monetary policy tool, and gradually turned the system into an obstacle to the market economy. A great variety of conflicts thus occurred, and the credit control system was increasingly unable to meet the needs of the market economy and financial reform.

To lend out loans beyond the credit ceiling mainly happened in the state-owned banks, where there was a huge gap between deposits and loans, through basically two ways. The first way is that banks will lend the funds to the subsidiary companies of county- or city-level financial departments who will then entrust banks to make loans to enterprises. The other way is that when enterprises demand a higher deposit rate (for example, a monthly interest of 12 ‰), which cannot be satisfied by banks due to the interest rate control, the banks will resort to fake trusts who will organize tripartite trust agreements to be signed among depositors, banks, and loan customers, and banks will ensure the depositors that all the risks incurred by the entrusted loans will be solely borne by the banks. But the practice of "lending out excessive loans in the middle of the year (quarter) but suppressing the loans back to the credit limit at the end of the year (quarter)" was regarded as a normal operation rather than an illegal activity. Sometimes, when enterprises could not repay their loans, the outstanding bank loans would surpass the credit quota, and banks would stagger the time for calculating the credit size and reduce the loan amount by dispatching loan balance.

To lend out loans by bypassing the credit ceiling reflected various conflicts inside and outside banks caused by the credit control system under the socialist market economy.

First, the pressure from local government. Many local governments demanded the launching of some new projects to meet the market demand based on the development of the local market economy, and emphasized the principle of "local funds for local use" to prohibit local banks from funding the projects of other provinces. Some other local governments publicly called for a narrowing of the huge gap between deposits and loans in banks, which would have meant to make full use of the deposit surplus to prevent banks at a higher level from transferring the money to other areas. At that time, the China Construction Bank had the largest deposit-loan gap among other state-owned banks and was most frequently asked to transfer money to the bank branches in other places. Several counties and cities even called on local enterprises to not save money at the China Construction Banks for fear that money from local enterprises would be transferred to other places. Many counties and cities supported the establishment of foundations and encouraged enterprises to independently raise funds. It was said that the capital raised by enterprises amounted to RMB4 billion in Zhejiang Province in the first quarter of 1993. Some counties and cities issued a document which said the raised funds with a monthly interest rate lower than 15‰ can be included in costs. Until 1995, certain counties and cities still urged local banks to ask for loans, including loans beyond the credit ceiling, from upper-level banks by means of a government bonus: According to the amount of newly increased loans, fixed-asset loans will be rewarded with a 5‰ bonus, and working capital loans will be rewarded with a 2‰ bonus; the bonus will be included in the costs of borrowing enterprises.

Second, various financial institutions sprang up and fiercely competed with each other. The support from local governments to run financial institutions was regarded as a way out for local construction companies by centralizing social funds. Urban credit cooperatives and trust companies were first set up, and then branch institutions of commercial banks other than specialized banks were established, owing to the efforts of various parties, in order to divert deposits from specialized banks, link loans to deposits, absorb social funds, and support production and construction. The increase of financial institutions was an achievement of financial reform, but unfair competition existed among financial institutions. The core issues for the competition were loan size and interest rate. Small- and medium-sized banks imposed no credit quota and were regulated through the asset-liability ratio, and for these banks, more deposits means more loans. The deposit and loan interest rates in credit cooperatives can fluctuate. In fact, it was not a secret that many financial institutions used abnormal means to win customers, stirred up a war of interest rates, and expanded their financial shares.

Third, financial consciousness of enterprises was awakened and enterprises started to pursue a market-oriented interest rate. They usually demanded from deposits a portion of additional income (called "handling charges"), larger than the general interest rate. This pushed the banks to undertake entrusted loans which bypassed the credit ceiling in order to adapt to the increasingly high interest rates.

Fourth, banks also have the demand to increase loans out of their own interests. There were three reasons: 1. To issue more working capital loans, especially to those clients who often possessed comparatively large deposits, which was an important requirement for stabilizing primary customers. Among the state-owned banks, the China Construction Banks had a small proposition of liquidity loans and thus were greatly in need of such a kind of loans; 2. To stabilize the banks' connection with their clients by means of higher interest rates of entrusted deposits; 3. To increase the earnings of banks and their employees, improve working conditions, and implement electronic management by making use of the handling charge (or interest margin) of entrusted loans.

After all, the rapid development of the market economy in coastal cities objectively required the increase of loan funds and these loan yields in reality had the possibility to outnumber the average rate of profit. This was the most important objective condition. Moreover, the pressure from government, the requirements[16] from upper level banks to basic level banks during the transition of specialized banks to commercial banks, and the practice of small- and medium-sized commercial banks implementing an asset-liability ratio management, all became a kind of catalyst for the emergence of loans beyond the credit ceiling.

In 1995, when I conducted an investigation of Zhejiang Province, some counties and cities there allowed a certain proportion of working capital loans over the credit limit, after the central bank abolished the monthly monitoring of the quarterly loan size, so the deposits grew substantially. One bank branch in a county-level city implemented an asset-liability ratio management method, after getting the approval from the provincial bank branch. The county-level bank branch was allowed to issue the working capital loans amounting to 40% of the newly increased deposits, and thus deposits soared and almost doubled. It was learned that the loans bypassing the credit ceiling in many cities mainly aimed to support the non-state economy and market economy, and the loan type was mainly working capital loans, usually accompanied by collateral or guarantee. Many bank branches believed that individuals would incur the least risks to banks, followed by collectives, while the state-owned enterprises were most likely to pose risks. At that time, the overdue rate of the whole Construction Bank system in Zhejiang Province was only 2.41%, and the quality of credit assets of Zhejiang Province ranked the first around the country.

Through my survey in Zhejiang, I also found that the problem of issuing loans over the credit limit was a historical holdover. The financial rectification in 1993 cleaned up the illegal short-term loans and called back the speculative funds in the real estate and stock markets, but a large number of loans over the credit limit issued to the enterprises with insufficient working capital became a part of operating funds which participated in the normal turnover of those enterprises. Although the central authorities said that banks would not be blamed for the excessive loans issued in the past, the authorities did not increase the loan quota by making allowances for this portion of loans. Therefore, the lower bank branches continued the practice of lending out loans beyond the credit ceiling and the indebted enterprises had to borrow new loans to repay their old debts which could not be gotten back at once. The fundamental solution to the problem of loans beyond the credit ceiling, a solution believed in by the banks around the country, was to reform the credit control system and implement an asset-liability management system.

When Zhu Rongji rectified the financial order in July 1993, he ordered the dismissal of the directors of banks which had lent out loans beyond the credit ceiling. But the actual situation of the excessive loans was very complicated, especially in Zhejiang and Jiangsu provinces and other economically developed areas, where the local governments, local financial institutions, and central bank branches had usually approved or given tacit permission to the lending activities. In some areas, the bank loans beyond the credit ceiling were made after the local Party and government organs coordinated with the financial sector, central bank, and audit offices. It was ironic that an illegal business won favor from almost all the departments and authorities, except the policy-makers. It also indicated that the credit control system was divorced from reality, the market, and the general people.

It is clear now that the problems of "loans bypassing the credit ceiling" and "counterfeit short-term lending" seemed to lie in the banks, but in fact they resulted from local governments deliberately breaking the investment and loans limits set by the Planning and Economic Committee through manipulating the financial sector and banks in order to develop market economy and expand capital. But, if we only consider the financial operation, to issue securities, raise funds, run financial institutions, lend out loans bypassing the credit ceiling, and undertake counterfeit short-term loans, all were innovations in the capital formation mechanism. It also indicates that there is but one step from innovation to violation and from truth to absurdity. The problem is that the financial administrative authority cannot see the root cause and may cut the wrong tree down by just punishing the cadres. At that time, Wang Qishan was the president of the China Construction Bank, and he repeatedly stressed: "We should be practical and realistic in investigating the illegal loans and find out the cause for loans beyond the credit ceiling and counterfeit short-term loans." Later, Zhu Rongji listened to Wang's report and finally agreed to legalize the loans over the credit ceiling issued in the past, and replace the credit control system with the asset-liability management, which solved the problem by a system reform and propelled the healthy development of economy and finance.

The Proactive Fiscal Policy between 1998 and 2004: State Intervention to Fight Deflation

In 1997, the inflation rate of China dropped to 0.8%, and China's economy achieved a soft landing in preparation for take-off. A financial crisis, however, suddenly occurred in Southeast Asia, and the deteriorating external environment brought about deflation in China in 1998. This was the first deflation to occur during China's transition into a socialist economy.

It should be said that when the Southeast Asian financial crisis affected China during the latter half of 1997, the crisis did not receive sufficient attention. In March 1998, the National People's Congress and the Chinese Political Consultative Conference were convened. At that time, the fiscal deficit occurred year after year, and various parties advocated for deficit reduction, so the two meetings decided a moderately tight fiscal policy. But shortly after the two meetings, the impacts of the Southeast Asian financial crisis spread wider and wider. China promised to not devaluate its currency in order to stabilize the global financial market and the international monetary system, which further weakened the commodity prices, increased the unemployment rate, frustrated the exporting of products, and brought about sluggish economic growth in China. Two month later, in May 1998, China's fiscal policy had to undertake an adjustment and reform. When the monetary policy could hardly play any role, the central government turned to implement a proactive fiscal policy in order to stimulate domestic demand and boost economic growth. In June 1998, the Standing Committee of the National People's Congress passed the budget adjustment proposal and officially declared the transition from a moderately tight fiscal policy to a proactive one. This decision actually restarted the state intervention by using fiscal policies as the means of regulation and it made the state investment restore the leading role in the formation mechanism of core social capital, after the central government advocated the policy of "construction relies on banks, and meals on finance" and the finance department retreated from economic construction in the mid-1980s. The state intervention of this time was different from the previous ones. The state was faced with a great variety of savings and investment subjects under a socialist market economy, and the financial regulation was intended to activate demand and consumption and promote exports and investment through various regulatory measures including more financial investment. One way was to increase the financial deficits by RMB100 billion. At that time, the central bank issued RMB100 billion more long-term treasury bonds for construction and the central government used the "national debt projects" invested in by the state to stimulate investment demand and promote the capital input from all parties of society. Proactive fiscal policy and prudent monetary policy, thus, came into being and lasted for as long as seven years.

Of course, the implementation of the proactive fiscal policy was not smooth all the way. The actual situation at that time was: An excess of industrial products, inadequate effective demand, a declining average profit rate of industrial enterprises, a lack of new investment opportunities, prudent investment and loans by enterprises and banks, and an obstacle in the transition of savings to investment. In the face of these unprecedented problems, the response measures of the government seemed relatively inadequate. Moreover, for a long period of time from the founding of New China until the reform and opening up, the macro-regulation towards investment by the government mainly focused on the control of investment scale and the prevention of investment overheating. And since the state leaders stressed "construction relies on banks" in the mid-1980s, the central government stuck into a predicament of "meals on finance," which further weakened the regulatory function of finance in the national economy. The 40 years of shortage economy taught the China's government how to deal with shortage and control demand inflation, but the government did not know how to handle surplus and initiate demand, especially how to make corresponding policy preparations. In 1998, China started to carry out a proactive fiscal policy, mainly to increase the issuance of treasury bonds and transfer savings into investment. Then, the government directly invested fiscal appropriations in non-profit, large-scale hydraulic projects, infrastructure projects, and public works, as a replacement for the shrinking enterprise and private investment, in order to strengthen the intervention in the economy. At that time, some scholars worried that the projects funded by the national debts would force out private investment, but this worry was unnecessary. The reality was that enterprises made no investment and banks lent out no money, and thereby the national debts projects emerged to fill the vacancy in the capital formation mechanism. While implementing a proactive fiscal policy, the government also adopted a series of supplementary measures, mainly including the following measures:

1. To let the China Development Bank issue financial bonds and increase policy loans.

2. To use financial discounts as a lever to start huge bank loans. The government gave discount government loans to some enterprises which needed support during their renovation and reformation projects, and intended to use a small portion of interest subsidies to stimulate a large amount of investment and loan demands. Among the newly issued treasury bonds, RMB9 billion were used for discount loans for technological upgrading. It was estimated that the RMB9 billion bonds could stimulate RMB180 billion investments for technical transformation.

3. To standardize government procurement. During the past shortage period, the government emphasized control over institutional purchasing power and government expenditure to ensure market supply. But now, the government had

to give full play to the positive role of government procurement in expanding domestic demand. This measure would not only cut down expenses, but also bring into play the size effect of the government market purchasing behavior.

4. To establish financial credit guarantee fund. Some local governments regarded fiscal revolving funds as financial credit guarantee funds, in order to promote enterprise investments and bank loans. This could further activate the economic leverage in establishing a financial guarantee system for small- and medium-sized enterprises and promoting the development of high-tech industry.

5. To refund export taxes and reduce or remit taxes in order to encourage investment.

6. To adjust the depreciation policy. To allow the accelerated depreciation of new equipment, and thus to stimulate investment by increasing the depreciation rates or shortening the depreciation life.

7. To make use of the government-invested companies and industrial state-holding corporations, and undertake capital operation during the joint-stock reform of state-owned enterprises, the listing of companies, the transfer and expansion of public shares by using capital as the linkage.

After 1998, the government enlarged the financial input by means of national debts, and fueled economic growth by using state investment to drive private investment. Examples are as follows:

1. To increase the investment in highway and railway construction and the development of small towns along the traffic routes in order to promote the economic development along the traffic lines. However, the total length of china's railways was just 62,000 kilometers in 1998, and the Ministry of Railways planned to invest RMB230 billion before 2000 to extend the railways to 68,000 kilometers. Statistics said that between 1998 and 2001, the Chinese government built or started building a large number of key infrastructure projects, including new railway lines of 4,000 kilometers and double-track railways of 1,988 kilometers. Meanwhile, during those four years, the government also increased 25,500 kilometers of highway mileage, strengthened more than 30,000 kilometers of embankments of large rivers and lakes, and relocated over 2 million populations living along the Yangtze River. Here I only want to explain that with the construction of highways and railways, to invest more money in the construction of small towns along the traffic routes will boost the agricultural industrialization in different regions and facilitate the transfer and employment

of a group of agricultural surplus laborers. This will provide a bridge to absorb the rural labor force and organize and lead the industrialization of agriculture, which will finally become a new economic growth point in China.

According to the 2004 statistical bulletin, under the support of the central government, 150,000 kilometers of inter-county and rural highways were reconstructed and the drinking water problem of 50.2 million people was solved. A report in 1998 about the construction of the Beijing-Kowloon railway said that this railway, which stretched over 2,381 kilometers, consumed an investment of around RMB40 billion. Since its construction was started in 1993, the urbanization in the areas along the railway had geared up. In 1996, the average GDP growth rate of major cities along the railway was 2.9 percentage points higher than that of the whole country and 6.4 percentage points higher than that of the provinces along the railway, and the revenue of these cities grew by 28.7%. The average per capita net income of the rural residents in the villages along the railway was RMB2,167, RMB267 more than that of the national average, and increased by 18% by vertical comparison (price factor has been removed). The per capital net income of urban residents living in the cities along the railway reached RMB4,872, RMB492 higher than that of the national average, and grew by 16.2% by vertical comparison. Compared to the average growth rate of the per capita net income of urban residents and that of rural residents in the areas along the railway, the national average growth rates were 9% and 3.4% lower, respectively. The statistics of the Beijing-Kowloon railway provided powerful evidence for the need to increase investment in highways and railways, as well as proof of the expansion of domestic needs.

2. To increase the investment in urban infrastructure construction. The urbanization in China lagged behind its industrialization, and the relationship between industrial construction and urban construction was not properly dealt with for a long period of time. After the reform and opening up, many new cities were built and deficiencies in urban roads, water supply, and drainage facilities and public transportation facilities existed in these cities. The expansion of investment in the public projects, including urban highways, water, power, gas, communications, and public transportations, would not only stimulate urban consumption, but also increase the employment and re-employment in urban areas. The best example was the power supply. At that time, many power distribution and substation facilities for urban residents were made in accordance with the comparatively low power load standard of public building design between the 1950s and 1980s, which impeded the

consumption of high-power household appliances. It was not uncommon that many urban residents bought air conditioners and microwave ovens, but could not use them. Later on, investment was made in the renovation of the power supply system and power distribution and substation facilities to transform low-voltage grid and substation facilities, and update old housing wires. This action not only employed a group of electrical workers, but also expanded the market for high-power household appliances. The sales of household appliances and the income from power supply were increased, which correspondingly enlarged the state's revenue from the two activities.

3. To enlarge the investment in water conservancy construction and afforestation, along with the post-flood reconstruction, in order to make great progress in returning the grain plots to forestry, afforesting the barren hills and wasteland suitable for afforestation suitable for afforestation, and constructing other ecological projects. The government combined investment growth, the welfare-to-work program, and the depletion of inventory together in order to expand domestic demand.

4. To increase educational investment represented the state's support for public works and was also an effective intervention measure. At that time, the high school graduates of China numbered 3 million per year, but only 1 million could be admitted to universities since there were not enough universities. After 1998, the investment in education was increased and the mode of privately-run universities with government subsidies was advocated, which not only attracted private investment in education but also increased employment. The newly built universities and colleges provided education for hundreds of thousands of students and postponed the employment start time of these students, which eased the employment pressure on hundreds of thousands of people and enhanced the quality of the reserve labor force.

From 1998 to 2004, China's central bank issued RMB910 billion in long-term treasury bonds for construction in seven consecutive years, which effectively boosted domestic needs and promoted the healthy and stable operation of the national economy. The price of commodities was relatively stable, employment rates grew substantially, the balance of payments recorded a "double surplus" within several consecutive years, and the economy continued to maintain near double-digit growth. Some people, therefore, said that the seven-year implementation of the proactive fiscal policy was a period of China's rapid economic and stable development. The achievements of the proactive fiscal policy were as follows:

1. Maintained sustained and rapid economic development. According to the data from the National Bureau of Statistics in 2005, the economic growth rates between 1998 and 2004 were 7.8%, 7.2%, 8.4%, 7.2%, 9.9%, 10.7%, and 9.9%, respectively (at constant prices). The most direct benefit was to drive GDP growth by 1–2 percentage points. Statistics indicated that the national bonds contributed 2% to the economic growth rate of 7.8% in 1998, 1.5% to the growth rate of 7.2% in 1999, and 1% to the growth rate of 8.4% in 2000. No matter how much the contribution of the treasury bonds was, to drive the GDP growth under inflation was an accomplishment of the proactive fiscal policy.
2. Increased the resident income and stimulated consumption. Since 1999, the Chinese government raised the salaries of employees in the government and public sectors and increased pensions to retirees, scaled up the fiscal transfer to the central and western regions, and established an allowance system for remote areas. The household consumption rate increased by 6.54%, 9.1%, and 10.1% between 1999 and 2001, and by 13.3% in 2004 (10.2% in real terms).
3. Maintained a steady growth in imports and exports. Ever since 1998, the Chinese government gradually increased the export rebate rates of certain commodities and made the average export rebate rate reach 15%. Meanwhile, the improvement in management of processing trade and the expanding of the import and export rights of manufacturing enterprises effectively stimulated exports.
4. Promoted the optimization of economic structure. First, to support the technological innovation and the development of high-tech industries which conformed with the orientation of industrial policies, through tax relief, discount government loans, and other preferential policies. Second, the central government invested more money in the infrastructure construction and ecological environment construction in central and western areas. For instance, in 2000, the investment in central and western China increased by 13.8% and 14.4%, 5.5 and 6.1 percentage points higher than the national average. In 2004, the growth rates of investment in the central and western areas were 30.2% and 26.6%, 4.4 and 0.8 percentage points higher than the national average.

Statistics said that from 1998 to 2001, through the efforts of the use of government bond funds to leverage the inflow of supporting funds, the volume of total investment in the 8,600 government bond-financed projects reached nearly RMB3 trillion, and thereby a group of important projects were finished, and the economic growth potential was enhanced with the economic growth rate maintained above 7% for several consecutive years. Now, the Qinghai-Tibet railway was opened to traffic and the west-east natural gas transmission project was officially put into operation. To consider the overall net effect of the proactive fiscal policy in fiscal expansion and tax reduction, the policy raised the economic growth by 2.0, 2.8, 3.2, 0.5, 0.6, and 0.9 percentage points between 1998 and 2003. This indicated that in the later years of the proactive fiscal policy, due to the significant increase in fiscal revenue, the net effect was comparatively weak. It also reflected that with the gradual recovery of social investment and the growing internal dynamism in economic development, the dependence on the proactive fiscal policy declined. Therefore, to alter the orientation and strength of the fiscal policy in 2004 and to move towards a prudent fiscal policy in 2005 were proved to be entirely correct methods.

When the government implemented a proactive fiscal policy, people worried most that the government bond-financed projects would exert a crowding-out effect on private investment, and thus there were always voices to advocate putting an end to the proactive fiscal policy. It now appears that the seven-year proactive fiscal policy had little impact on private investment. For me, I think the crowding-out effect mainly existed in the capital market. The proactive fiscal policy indeed eased the deflation to a large extent by taking advantage of the government bond-financed infrastructure constructions and the western development which were worth hundreds of billions to leverage several trillion in supporting loans, when banks faced limited credit quotas and dared not to easily lend out money in order to control risks. The biggest flaws of the proactive fiscal policy, however, were to make the financial authorities have a misunderstanding over the temporarily narrowed gap between loans and deposits, and cause the authorities to relax the construction of the bill market, bond market, investment funds market, futures market, and other financial markets. In general, the proactive fiscal policy made a great contribution in fighting deflation while the prudent monetary policy was inadequate in building a healthy economy. Thus, the latter policy left some regrets in both the development of the fictitious economy and the capital market and the perfection of the financial market structure.

In order to harness the deflation in 1998, the central government carried out a series of reforms in the institutional consumption system, including salary, housing, health care, education of employees. We knew that under the planned economy, employees received low salaries and maintained low consumption, and the housing, health care and education expenses of employees were all shouldered by the state based on a low standard. After the transition to a market economy, the control over the income distribution system of wages and bonuses was gradually relaxed and the income of workers increased significantly (of course, a large income gap existed among workers, due to the big difference in corporate profits). The lagged reform in the housing, health care, and education systems of employees was also an important factor in restricting consumption and fostering deflation. A significant measure in controlling deflation taken by Zhu Rongji in 1998 was to speed up the reform in housing, health care, and education systems and lead the transition of investment by enterprises and public institutions and institutional consumption to private investment and consumption. Since the reform and opening up, Chinese residents earned more and more and their demand to upgrade the consumption structure was great, especially in terms of housing consumption. In 1998, the State Council ordered Party and government organizations to put an end to the 40-year welfare housing distribution system and advocated the monetization of housing distribution, which brought about the real estate boom which continued for the next 10 years. This played a huge role in stimulating housing consumption. Due to the fact that there may be problems of overly depending on the market in the reform of housing, health care, and education systems, the central government stressed the establishment of people-orientated policies to improve people's livelihoods and the construction of housing and health care systems in order to ease over-marketization. But generally speaking, the reforms were more helpful than harmful. It should be said that these reforms were necessary. They played a huge role in adapting to marketization, increasing workers' income, leading the transition of the institutional investment and consumption to private investment and consumption, releasing various demands and motivations of the formerly restrained private investment and consumption, and getting the deflation under control.

There was one thing special in the deflation of 1998, that is, the excessive debts of state-owned enterprises discouraged banks from offering loans to distressed enterprises. Although advocating the encouragement of mergers and the standardization of bankruptcy procedures, the central government was reluctant to implement debt-to-equity swaps and thus the deflation was further intensified. Until the latter half of 1999, the central government decided to found four financial asset management companies and applied debt-to-equity swaps to the overdue loans (namely, the non-performing loans of banks) of a considerable part of overly indebted large- and medium-sized state-owned enterprises, which not only solved the excessive debts of the enterprises, but also optimized the enterprise capital structure. The debt-to-equity swap would in turn enhance the debt-paying ability of enterprises and became a major force in increasing bank loans and controlling deflation. The topic of debt-to-equity swaps will be discussed in Chapter 7.

Strategic Adjustment of the State-Owned Economy and State-Owned Enterprises Reform

After the reform and opening up, China started its reform in the state-owned economy. In general, the reform was a complex and arduous process and it went through four stages after 1979.

The first stage was the "decentralization of power and the transfer of profits" between 1979 and 1984. This reform, mainly through enlarging the autonomy of enterprises, put into practice the measures of profit retention and profit contracts to encourage enterprises to meet targets and realize production and revenue increases on the basis of the replacement of profit delivery by tax payment.

The second stage was the separation of ownership and control between 1985 and 1993. Through the implementation of a contracted managerial responsibility system, enterprise management was separated from government administration, and ownership was separated from management power and, therefore, state-run enterprises would become state-owned ones. Meanwhile, the policy of "loans for fiscal allocations" was fully implemented and a group of state-owned enterprises was transformed and listed through the pilot program of a joint-stock system. After the first two stages of reform, the state-owned enterprises obtained, to a certain extent, the financial resources and vitality in undertaking self-renovation, self-accumulation, and self-development, in comparison with their pervious situations under the highly centralized management.

Between 1994 and 1999, the state-owned enterprises reform entered into the third stage of a clearly defined ownership.

Since 1999, the reform moved into the fourth stage, namely, strategic adjustment of the state-owned economy. The central government put forward the need to implement strategic adjustment in the layout of the state-owned economy, and concentrated the state capital in the fields related to national security and the lifelines of the national economy in order to enhance the controlling power, influence, and leading role of the state sector. The adjustments were made according to the principle of "refraining from doing some things in order to accomplish other things." The reason why the central government proposed the strategic adjustment was because state capital was insufficient in major industries and key fields while it was widely spread in other sectors.

The unreasonable allocation of resources forced the government to redirect investments of state capital to ensure the rational flow. The fundamental targets were to concentrate the state-owned capital in the fields related to national security and lifelines of the national economy, by withdrawing government capital from certain industries and fields, and at the same time to make room for the injection of private capital. So the focus of the adjustments was to first reduce the investment of state capital in some sector before making full use of it in others.

The state-owned enterprises reform focused on the withdrawal of the state capital from certain sectors, but how to retreat? The inevitable question was that during the withdrawal of state capital and the introduction of private capital in some sectors, there would be a problem of transferring a group of state-owned enterprises and state capital to private enterprises. Although it was not explicitly stated, the reform was intended to privatize the state-owned enterprises, as had been done by Western countries, and replace state-owned capital with private capital.

In 2003, the State-owned Assets Supervision and Administration Commission of the State Council (SASAC) was established, and it was responsible for the strategic adjustment of the state economy and the unified management of state capital. The founding of the SASAC represented the separation of public management from ownership in the organization of government for the first time, identified the representatives of the state-owned assets contributors, and basically realized the integration between asset management and the governance of personnel and work. Since then, state-owned enterprise reform entered a new phase.

To privatize state-owned enterprises, however, was not as easy in China as in Western countries with a market economy, since China's reform was constrained by power, knowledge, and ideology, especially the ideological constraint which was ubiquitous. Although the higher authorities concluded that there was no loss of state assets in the sales of small state-owned enterprises in Zhucheng City, there were still some leftist articles on this issue by 2001. The mergers and acquisitions of state-owned enterprises by private enterprises, such as the acquisition of Xinjiang Tunhe by Xinjiang D'Long Group and the acquisition of Guangdong Kelong by Shunde Greencool, faced a similar situation. In 2004, Professor Larry Lang from the Chinese University of Hong Kong questioned the direction of state-owned enterprises reform concerning the drain of state assets. Many non-mainstream economists echoed his opinion and petitioned for an investigation on this problem disclosed by Professor Larry Lang. At that time, Zhang Wenkui from the Development Research Center of the State Council firmly responded that the direction of reform cannot be denied in spite of the problems in the state-owned enterprises reform. Therefore, this controversy triggered by the question from Professor Larry Lang developed into an important part of "The Third Grand Debate on Reform." Later on, Zhao Xiao from the SASAC criticized Larry Lang for being less informed about China's situation, and acting "as a bull in a China shop." Professor Zhang Weiying from Peking University responded to Professor Larry Lang by saying that "We should be kind to the people who contribute to the society."

It was inevitable that there would be some specific contradictions and questions in the strategic adjustment of the state economy and the privatization in certain sectors. For example, how should state investments withdraw while private investments could step in? There was no set pattern and the government had to learn by doing. The government should let small enterprises try independently during the strategic adjustment, and accepting both success and failure for that experience is what the government wanted. The second question was whether the state-owned enterprises should be sold and how much should they be sold for during the privatization? The decision-making power was in the hands of the government or the government officials. There could be a win-win situation if the officials acted properly, but rent-seeking behaviors may also exist among different levels of officers. Another question was how to place the senior managers in the reformed state-owned enterprises? In the acquisition of Western companies, employees would receive a Golden Parachute by employers buying off the service years of the employees. But Chinese enterprises practiced an official rank standard with business leaders being quasi-bureaucrats, and the process of the redemption of state-owned enterprises was more complex and costly than the seniority buy-outs in Western companies.

During the strategic adjustment of the state economy, there was also a task of regulating privatization and protecting the enthusiasm of private capital in participating in the national economy. In the past few years, many privately-controlled companies ran into equity disputes, which usually represented a contest between new and old systems. It was always the case that private capital was in an inferior position. The old system side, despite its disadvantages, tried to regain initiative through its extensive connections in the old system. So when the holders of state shares were in a tight corner in a joint-stock company, they had to turn to their private counterparts for help. Once state shareholders were out of trouble, however, those companies would force the private economy to step down on the excuse of prohibiting the loss of state assets. Therefore, the government ought to regulate privatization and protect the active participation of private capital in order to ensure that the state asset is willing to withdraw from ownership of business while the private capital can come in as a replacement and enjoy development free from the discrimination and disruption from the force of habit.

Another implication of privatizing state-owned enterprises was to expand equity transactions to the transactions of corporate right of control. In fact, the capital market of any country can never be called mature if no corporate right of control is traded and transferred. Only with the flow of corporate control, can resources be really optimized, and asset restructuring, adjustment of industrial structure, and synergy effects be truly realized. Being state-controlled is not always the story, and the government should push forward the corporate control transactions, along with the strategic adjustment of the state economy and the reduction of state-owned stocks, through the engagement of private enterprises, management buy-outs (MBO), and investment banks.

In November 2006, the *Guiding Opinions of the SASAC about Promoting the Adjustment of State-owned Capital and the Reorganization of State-owned Enterprises* clearly stated the objectives of state capital restructuring and reorganization of state-owned enterprises: To maintain the absolute controlling power of the state economy in major industries and key fields related to national security and national economic lifelines, including the military, electric fencing and electricity, petroleum and petrifaction, telecommunications, coal, civil aviation, and shipping; to enhance the leading role of the state-owned economy in basic and pillar industries, such as equipment manufacturing and non-ferrous metals industries; to maintain the necessary influence of the state-owned economy in commerce and trade circulation and other industries and hold dominant shares by the state in the industry pacesetter enterprises which have larger influence or special functions.

According to the article "To steadily promote the state-owned enterprises reform on a new start" written by the former SASAC Director Li Rongrong in *Seeking Truth* magazine in August 2007, the accumulative sales revenue of China's state-owned enterprises in 2006 reached RMB16.2 trillion (RMB18 trillion in 2007), 50.9% higher than that of 2003, with an average annual average growth rate of 14.7%; the profits amounted to RMB1.2 trillion (RMB1.62 trillion in 2007), 147.3% higher than that of 2003, with an average annual average growth rate of 35.2%; the taxes turned over to the state added up to RMB1.4 trillion (RMB1.57 trillion in 2007), 72% higher than that of 2003, with an average annual average growth rate of 19.8%. As of the end of 2006, the gross asset of state-owned enterprises in China totaled RMB29 trillion, 45.7% higher than that at the end of 2003, with an average annual growth rate of 13.4% (at the end of 2007, the total assets of China's state-owned enterprises increased by 23.1% compared to the number of the previous year, the debt-to-assets ratio was 57.3% and the return on equity was 8.5%).

On the whole, the primary achievement of the state-owned enterprises reform was to facilitate the concentration of state-owned capital on the major industries and key fields essential to the national economy and state safety. In 2003, there were 150,000 state-owned enterprises, but the number was reduced to 119,000 at the end of 2006, 31,000 less than the total number of 2003, with an average annual decrease of 8%; however, the average assets of the state-owned enterprises reached RMB240 million, an increase of 84.6% compared to that of 2003 with an average annual increase of 22.7%. Although the number of state-owned enterprises was decreased, the majority of them realized an invigorated development under loose government control. The overall quality and competitiveness of the state-owned economy continuously increased and its controlling power, influence, and leading role were also greatly strengthened.

There was a clear tendency of state-owned capital concentrating in the energy, raw materials, transportation, military, major equipment manufacturing, and metallurgical industries, among others. In 2006, over 80% of the national assets of central government-run enterprises were concentrated in the above-mentioned industries, and these enterprises were responsible for the country's production of almost all the crude oil, natural gas and ethylene, and provided all the basic telecommunications services and most value-added services. Those enterprises contributed approximately 55% of the state's total electricity production, 82% of the total air transportation turnover of China's aviation industry, 89% of the national waterway cargo turnover, 48% of the total auto production, 60% of the national production of high value-added steel, 70% of the country's hydroelectric equipment production, and 75% of the thermal power equipment manufacturing in China. In addition, as of the end of 2006, the country had implemented a system of policy-related bankruptcy to 4,251 long-term insolvent state-owned enterprises, solved the placement of 837 workers, and completed 80% of the workload of policy-guided closure. In 2008, the target of policy-mandated bankruptcy was basically finished.

Another major achievement was to accelerate the joint-stock system reform of state-owned enterprises to make the mixed ownership economy the principal form of the public ownership system. As for the corporate system reform in the central government-run enterprises and their subsidiaries, the proportion of reformed enterprises increased from 30.4% in 2002 to 64.2% in 2006. Since 2003, 33 central government-run enterprises have gotten listed through IPO in overseas markets.

Large enterprises related to petroleum and petrochemicals, telecommunications, transportation, and metallurgy were listed overseas. The joint-stock system reform in each province, region, and city was also further geared up. During the four years between 2003 and 2006, there were successively 78 times of open recruitment of 81 senior management positions in the enterprises directly controlled by the central government. In 2007, another 22 executive positions in the central government-owned enterprises were offered to both domestic and overseas talents, and a market-oriented employment mechanism complying with the modern corporate system was initially set up.

In the face of the widely distributed state-owned enterprises, China's government had long suggested fostering 30 to 50 large companies or groups with international competitiveness. Four years after the founding of SASAC, there were 77 central government-controlled enterprises participating in the 41 reorganization efforts, and the number of the central government-owned enterprises was reduced from 196 in 2003 to 157 in 2006. It was said that another 80 to 100 enterprises would be adjusted or restructured by 2010. In 2006, the number of central government-run enterprises with a sales revenue over RMB100 trillion was 21 and that of the ones with a profit above RMB10 billion was 13, which increased by 12 and 7, respectively, compared with the number in 2003. In 2006, 13 central government-controlled enterprises including Baosteel Group were listed in the *Fortune Global 500*, 7 more than in 2003. Among those enterprises, Sinopec Group, China National Petroleum Corporation (CNPC), and China Mobile Communications Corporation moved up to 23rd, 39th, and 202nd places in 2006 from 70th, 69th, and 230th in 2002, respectively.

In January 2007, Singapore's *Lianhe Zaobao* published a review article by Han Fangming and he thought that "under today's globalization, the competition of national strength among different countries is to a large extent the long-term business confrontation among enterprises. Large enterprises can save the market transaction costs by undertaking economy of scale or economy of scope, significantly reduce the cost of government regulation, and enhance the research and development capabilities. In this matter, the Chinese government has never followed the specious fallacy of 'market fundamentalists.' It is very wise; otherwise, if the government adopts the shock therapy to sell out overnight all the large enterprises essential to the economic lifeline, China's status and the future of China's citizens will become fragile owing to the loss of economic strength."

In September 2010, Li Rongrong stepped down as the director of SASAC. During his seven-year tenure at SASAC, he reduced the number of the central government-controlled enterprises to 123 from 196. By the end of 2009, the total assets of those enterprises jumped to RMB21 trillion from RMB7 trillion, the net assets increased to RMB8.4 trillion from RMB2.9 trillion; the operation revenue reached RMB3.36 trillion; the profits grew from RMB240.5 billion in 2002 to RMB815.1 billion in 2009; the annual tax contribution exceeded RMB1 trillion; and 30 central government-controlled enterprises entered the *Fortune Global 500*. He Liangliang from Phoenix Television commented on Li Rongrong by saying that "Li is a capable man." Many other commentators believed Li Rongrong deserved the praise.

The biggest controversy about Li Rongzi during his rule at SASAC was the seven-year policy of "the state advancing as the private sector receded" (or privatization). Some people argued that in the past seven years, the central government-owned enterprises occupied the majority of resources in national economic activities, controlled the absolute say in social economy, and gained the pricing power of the commodities pertinent to national interest and people's livelihoods. This caused the slow development of the non-state-owned enterprises whose contribution rate to GDP was 65% and tax contribution rate was 61% (according to the data of 2008), and created an even more difficult environment for the growth of medium- and small-sized privately-owned enterprises. It was an undeniable fact that the rising dominance of China's state-owned enterprises was at the expense of the once-vibrant private sector. This situation could harm the balance and stability of national economic ecology and seriously erode the cornerstones of the law of the market economy: Fairness and efficiency. Meanwhile, according to the report released by the China Europe International Business School, the salary at the A-share listed state-owned enterprises in China nearly doubled that at privately listed companies (including overseas-listed Chinese companies). In contrast, the listed state-owned enterprises were less efficient than the listed private enterprises, and the average return on net assets of the former accounted for only 37.7% of that of the latter.

On September 5, 2009, Li Rongrong revealed that the annual increase of the profits in the central government-controlled enterprises was RMB159 billion, and the annual growth of the total compensation for the senior executives above the level of vice president in these enterprises was around RMB46 million in the "Top 500 Enterprises of China Release Conference and Corporations Summit" in Hangzhou. He believed that these increases were reasonable, but the compensation for the senior managers in the central government-owned enterprises became a topic of public controversy.

5

Chapter

A Depreciation Fund as a Ready Accumulation Fund for Expanded Reproduction

Prologue: "Ghost Hunting"

This chapter will focus on depreciation and also simple and expanded reproductions as well as the crowding out of investment in the former by that of the latter. This activity recalls the "ghost hunting" activities organized by Xu Yi, Bank President of China Construction Bank (CCB), from my time when I was working with him there.

In 1958, nine years after the founding of New China, the CCB was incorporated in the Ministry of Finance to become an Account Division for Capital Construction, and thus my colleagues in CCB and I had the chance to get experience with the macro-economy. However, books were the only source for people to understand accumulation, social reproduction, and simple and expanded reproductions back then. It was not until the leftover problems from the three years of the Great Leap Forward (1958, 1959, and 1960) had been solved that people really gained access to those macro-economic issues.

The Great Leap Forward gave birth to the over expansion of investment in capital construction in 1958. Mao Zedong advocated setting "two targets," the one was a must to attain and the other was one to aspire towards. The investment quota was being increased at every lower level and, as a result, investment in capital construction had expanded massively. In addition, during the movement, the Ministry of Finance accepted Mao's criticism about performing purely fiscal functions, and put forward a slogan of "more revenue, more expenditure, more construction; much more revenue, much more expenditure, much more construction." By 1959, the investment quota and revenue had grown while the commodity supply was still in short supply and becoming more and more lacking. Li Xiannian was the then Vice-Premier, responsible for finance and trade affairs, and at the same time the minister of the finance department. Li Xiannian asked the officers in the Ministry of Finance: "Currency is said to be the symbol of material goods, isn't it? How come money is spent, but there are no goods? There is something fishy!" He called on the department to hunt the "ghost." The Ministry of Finance instructed Xu Yi who was Financial Secretary of the Account Division for Capital Construction and President of the CCB to form a "ghost hunting group" responsible for researching the relationship between capital construction investment and economic growth as well as financial revenue and expenditure. The group members included Tian Yinong, Wang Zhuo, Chen Baosen, liu Biao, Hu Jing and I, among others.

Under the leadership of Xu Yi, we carefully read Karl Marx's *Das Kapital* many times. We found the following passage in Volume 2 of *Das Kapital*:

> *On the basis of socialised production the scale must be ascertained on which those operations — which withdraw labour-power and means of production for a long time without supplying any product as a useful effect in the interim — can be carried on without injuring branches of production which not only withdraw labour-power and means of production continually, or several times a year, but also supply means of subsistence and of production.*[1]

In another place, Marx further elaborated the scale of production when assuming a communist society:

> *The question then comes down to the need of society to calculate beforehand how much labour, means of production, and means of subsistence it can invest, without detriment, in such lines of business as for instance the building of railways, which do not furnish any means of production or subsistence, nor produce any useful effect for a long time, a year or more, while they extract labour, means of production, and means of subsistence from the total annual production. In capitalist society however where social reason always asserts itself only post festum great disturbances may and must constantly occur.*[2]

In *Das Kapital*, Marx made a thorough analysis on the great disorder caused by excessive investment in capitalist society. Similarly, in our not well-planned socialist society, over expansion of investment and long-term input without any output also brought about a great disturbance. It was the "ghost hunting" activities that made us realize the huge power of Marx's theory about the feature of capital construction of "no output, only input" described in *Das Kapital*, and deeply understand that excessive monetary input in capital construction but without corresponding output would lead to economic and financial disorder.

In the "ghost hunting" activities, Xu Yi led us to re-examine the relationship among industrial and agricultural output value, investment in capital construction, financial credit receipts and payments, and materials supply and demand, and came to the conclusion that the size of capital construction investment was too large, the ratio of light to heavy industry was imbalanced, a budget deficit existed instead of a budget surplus, credit expansion was supported by the issuance of money, and the national economy was seriously disproportionate. In a report to Li Xiannian, Xu Yi pointed out that the great disturbances which were caused by excessive input in capital construction without corresponding output, occurred in many aspects of the economy at that time. At last, Xu summarized: "Passion for investment is commendable while rules cannot be violated." However, this report of "ghost hunting" was not revealed due to the struggle against rightist deviations in the Lushan Conference.

The aggressive investment during the three-year Great Leap Forward brought about the five-year adjustment of the national economy. An important lesson learned from this investment expansion was that capital construction investment during the Great Leap Forward pursued only expanded reproduction rather than simple reproduction, resulting in massive debts in the updating of urban industrial equipment and the expansion of excavating and logging industries, and thus the government had to take out more money to compensate for simple reproduction during the adjustments after 1961. The Ministry of Finance offered RMB37 billion in total to commission CCB to solve the problems of incremental investment at every lower level and excessive investment growth left over during the Great Leap Forward.

In 1962, the Party Central Committee and the State Council drew a lesson from this experience: Any works of socialist economic construction, whether to draw up plans, implement economic administration, or undertake material supply, must first focus on simple reproduction and then expanded reproduction.

I tell this story because Chapter 1 said Marx discovered that the depreciation fund or sinking fund is both a compensation fund and an accumulation fund, but the expansion nature of capital made Chinese enterprises, competent departments, and officers from the State Planning Commission responsible for "conscious social regulation," naturally apply compensation funds to accumulation, namely expanded reproduction, which frequently resulted in runaway increase in investment and great disturbances in social economy. The runaway increase in investment during the Great Leap Forward was the result of expanded reproduction crowding out simple reproduction. In the late 1979s, the double expansion of investment in both capital construction and innovation was another kind of runaway investment.

The "ghost hunting" activities led by Xu Yi enlightened me in my lifelong research in investment and capital. It is also because of this "ghost hunting" that CCB started to focus on investment scale and the cadre from the Ministry of Finance and CCB learned a profound lesson on excessive investment. The troubles made by government departments, local governments and enterprises on a micro-economic level will be solved by the Ministry of Finance and the CCB on a macro-economic level. This "ghost hunting" and the discussion on the concept of investment with the State Planning Commission made us deeply understand Marx's words: On the basis of public ownership, society has to calculate beforehand how much it can invest in capital construction without detriment to existing production. It becomes the theoretical basis for my study on investment throughout my life.

Marx: The Depreciation Fund Is Also the Accumulation Fund for Expanded Reproduction

Some people may question: How can we regard the depreciation fund as a new form of the accumulation fund, since the depreciation fund is just a kind of compensation fund and the stock of existing capital in the capital formation mechanism? It is right that the depreciation fund is used to replace the portion of value gradually transferred to products through the wear and tear of fixed capital. The reason why the depreciation fund is considered as a compensation fund is because fixed assets repetitively perform the same functions in social reproduction whose value is transferred to products through wear and tear and compensated through the selling of the products, and the depreciation fund will be used for the renewal of fixed capital and transformed into new fixed capital which will be renewed in kind (this renewal will bring about massive moral depreciation) at the end of the useful life of old fixed assets. But this is just one side of the story.

The other side of the story is that the compensation of fixed assets in value and those in kind are different in time. During the depreciation of capital, the depreciated capital "dies" in name only, and the use value of the remainder can continue to function in production as long as the capital does not wear out and must be replaced; while the nominally "died" capital, i.e. depreciation allowance, can still be used for accumulation and expanded reproduction as long as it serves for no immediate compensation.

A depreciation fund is both a compensation fund and an accumulation fund. The one who discovered this law was none other than Marx. In this way, depreciation has been incorporated into the capital culture.

How did Marx find that depreciation funds are at the same time funds for compensation and accumulation?

When Marx wrote *Das Kapital*, he had already discovered that the compensation of fixed assets in value is inconsistent with that in kind in terms of time. In his letter to Engels on August 20, 1862, he wrote:

One point about which you, as a practical man, must have the answer, is this. Let us assume that a firm's machinery at the outset = £12,000. It wears out on an average in 12 years. If then £1,000 is added to the value of the goods every year, the cost of the machinery will have been paid off in 12 years. Thus far, A. Smith and all his successors. But, in fact, this is only an average calculation. Much the same applies to machinery having a life of 12 years as, say, to a horse with a life — or useful life — of 10 years. Although it would have to be replaced with a new horse after 10 years, it would in practice be wrong to say that 1/10 of it died every year. Rather, in a letter to Factory Inspectors, Mr Nasmyth observes that machinery (at least some types of machinery) runs better in the second year than in the first, at all events, in the course of those 12 years does not 1/12 of the machinery have to be replaced in natura each year? Now, what becomes of this fund, which yearly replaces 1/12 of the machinery? Is it not, in fact, an accumulation fund to extend reproduction aside from any conversion of revenue into capital? Does not the existence of this fund partly account for the very different rate at which capital accumulates in nations with advanced capitalist production and hence a great deal of capital fixe, and those where this is not the case?[3]

More than 10 days later, Engels replied to Marx on September 9, 1862: "Likewise the question of wear and tear is where, however, I rather suspect you have gone off the rails. Depreciation time is not, of course, the same for all machines. But more about this when I get back."[4] Unfortunately, this topic was not touched upon afterwards.

Five years later, on August 24, 1867, Marx reminded Engels about this issue again:

"I am again obliged to seek your advice on one point, as I did many years ago.

Fixed capital only has to be replaced in natura after, say, 10 years. In the meantime, its value returns partially and gradatim, as the goods that it has produced are sold. This progressive return of the fixed capital is only required for its replacement (aside from repairs and the like) when it becomes defunct in its material form, e.g., as a machine. Prior to that, however, these successive returns are in the capitalist's possession.

Many years ago I wrote to you that it seemed to me that in this manner an accumulation fund was being built up, since in the intervening period the capitalist was of course using the returned money, before replacing the capital fixe with it. You disagreed with this somewhat superficially in a letter. I later found that MacCulloch describes this sinking fund as an accumulation fund. Being convinced that no idea of MacCulloch's could ever be right, I let the matter drop.

His apologetic purpose here has already been refuted by the Malthusians, but they, too, admit the fact.

Now, as a manufacturer, you must know what you do with the returns on capital fixe before the time it has to be replaced in natura. And you must answer this point for me (without theorising, in purely practical terms).[5]

Two days later, Engels wrote back to Marx and explained: "There is no doubt that the manufacturer is using the replacement-fund on average for 4½ years before the machinery is worn out, or at least has it at his disposal." He continued: "Regarding the economic significance of the matter, I am none too clear about it, I do not see how the manufacturer is supposed to be able to cheat the other partners in the surplus-value, that is, the ultimate consumers, by thus falsely representing the position — in the long run."[6] Engels sent two schedules for machinery to Marx the next day and told Marx that if the depreciation rate is 10%, a capitalist could "increase his machinery by 60% and without putting a farthing of his actual profit into the new investment."[7]

Marx, thereby, concluded in *Theories of Surplus Value*: "The sinking fund, i.e., the fund for wear and tear of the fixed capital, is, in my opinion, at the same time a fund for accumulation."[8]

Later, when commenting on Malthus, Marx cited the words of Malthus on McCulloch: "Mr. McCulloch…conceives that the introduction of machines into any employment necessarily occasions on equal or greater demand for the disengaged labourers in some other employment, …In order to prove this, he supposes that the annuity necessary to replace the value of the machine by the time it is worn out, will every year occasion an increasing demand for labour."[9] Marx then commented: "The sinking fund itself can, indeed, be used for accumulation in the interval when the wear and tear of the machine is shown in the books, but does not actually affect its work. But in any case, the demand for labour created in this way is much smaller than if the whole capital invested in machinery were laid out in wages, instead of merely the annual wear and tear. MacPeter is an ass—as always. This passage is only noteworthy, because it contains the idea that the sinking fund is itself a fund for accumulation."[10]

Marx asserted: "Hence where much constant capital, and therefore also much fixed capital, is employed, that part of the value of the product which replaces the wear and tear of the fixed capital, provides an accumulation fund, which can be invested by the person controlling it, as new fixed capital (or also circulating capital), without any deduction whatsoever having to be made from the surplus-value for this part of the accumulation (see McCulloch). This accumulation fund does not exist at levels of production and in nations where there is not much fixed capital. This is an important point, It is a fund for the continuous introduction of improvements, expansions, etc."[11]

In another place, Marx added: "We have seen that where capitalist production is developed, that is, where the productivity of labour, the constant capital and particularly that part of constant capital which consists of fixed capital are developed, the mere reproduction of fixed capital in all spheres and the parallel reproduction of the existing capital which produces fixed capital, forms an accumulation fund, that is to say, provides machinery, i.e., constant capital, for production on an extended scale."[12]

In conclusion, the sinking fund or depreciation fund is not only a compensation fund but also an accumulation fund for expanded reproduction.

Accelerated Depreciation: Speed Up Compensation for Advanced Capital

Accelerated depreciation is an advancement of the capital formation mechanism. It fully takes into account the rapid development of new technology and the possible moral wear and tear, features accelerated replacement, and aims to ensure for enterprises the renewal of fixed assets in the form of technical improvements.

At first, capitalist society will set aside depreciation funds in accordance with the average use life of fixed assets. This method can help enterprises to stabilize costs and make excess profits by expanding the life expectancy of machines if technological changes are minor. On the contrary, if there is a dramatic technological change, this depreciation method can no longer compensate the moral depreciation resulting from early obsolescence of technology and equipment, and thereby expose the problems of this method of long depreciation life, low depreciation rate, and high risk.

The first industry which revealed those problems was the military industry. During World War Two, Western countries took the initiative in speeding up depreciation and shortening the service life of equipment in military industry enterprises, in order to encourage capitalists to make investments and production in the military industry. The Bulletin "F" in 1942 promulgated by the U.S. government reduced the depreciation life of fixed assets in military industry enterprises to 5 years (from 20 to 30 years). Then, during the Korean War, accelerated depreciation was again applied to the military industry enterprises by the U.S. government. The merit of this method is that the compensation of original capital is secured before tax payments and profit distribution. The downside, however, is the massive loss of taxes owed to the government. Consequently, after the wars, Western governments postponed the accelerated depreciation.

After the Second World War, capitalist enterprises encountered some outstanding problems when recovering from the effects of the war: Heavy tax burden, excessive dividends, low depreciation rate, extended service years of equipment, huge debts from equipment replacement, and inadequate compensation for fixed assets. In the meantime, the rapid development of science and technology in the postwar years called for a new form of compensation investment since the low depreciation rate could hardly make up for the moral wear and tear caused by the early obsolescence of technology and equipment. It revealed that the old depreciation system could no longer satisfy the need of the compensation fund. Since enterprises required accelerated depreciation, the government had to choose between a low depreciation rate which would continue the heavy tax burden and bring about a persistently depressed economy or even paralyzed economy, and a high depreciation rate which would increase the compensation fund.

In 1985 when I joined the Investment Policy Seminar of the Economic Research Center of the State Council, I studied accelerated depreciation. I found that after the Second World War, governments in Western countries generally sped up depreciation, and intended to use less total tax to encourage capitalists to give up a portion of dividends for the purpose of equipment renewal or replacement. The government made use of the increase in industrial orders in engineering, steel, and other industries to show a multiplier effect in order to beat economic recession and achieve economic recovery. Western countries, such as the Federal Republic of Germany, Japan, France, and the United States, chose the accelerated depreciation.

At that time, Zhang Yuping from the investigation department of the CCB compiled a book called *Selected Investment Statistics of Fixed Assets of Foreign Countries (1954–1980)*. The book showed the proportion of the depreciation funds of fixed assets to Gross National Product (GNP) in Western countries (see Table 5.1).

Table 5.1 Proportion of depreciation funds for fixed assets to GNP in Western countries (%)

	U.S.	U.K.	France	Germany	Japan
1954	8.82	7.83	9.37	8.07	7.28
1960	9.06	7.61	8.79	8.83	10.66
1977	12.12	11.26	11.23	11.18	13.03

Source: Investigation Department of CCB, *Selected Investment Statistics of Fixed Assets of Foreign Countries (1954–1980).*

From the above table, we can see an upward trend of the proportion of depreciation funds in Western countries. Of course, this growth may also result from the increase in the total fixed assets, but the change from low depreciation rate to accelerated depreciation must be an important reason.

The Ministry of Finance in Japan believes that accelerated depreciation is a good way to develop financial resources. In 1986, I made an investigation into the automobile industry in Japan. Japanese people thought that the accelerated depreciation practiced in the Japanese automobile industry substantially increased the proportion of depreciation funds in the own capital of enterprises. The proportion was 50% in 1960, 66% in 1961, 71% in 1962 (calculated based on the statistics of 12 factories), and 74% in 1964 (calculated based on the statistics of 15 factories), which accumulated a large number of funds for the great development of the automobile industry in 1968. Among the investments in the Japanese automobile industry, the proportion of own capital investment was 50% in 1960s, increased to 70%–90% in the 1970s, and further raised up to 95% in the mid-1980s. This indicates that accelerated depreciation played an indispensable role in strengthening enterprises' financial capability in self-transformation and self-development.

The statistics of the U.S. reveal another aspect of the function of accelerated depreciation. In 1962, the American government revised the depreciation policy by establishing a guideline life of equipment which brought about an annual decrease of USD1.5 billion in tax payments, but the profits obtained through stimulating investment were three times as large as the tax decrease. In 1971, the Nixon administration relaxed the depreciation policy, which would lead to a tax reduction of USD3.9 billion per year. In 1981, the Reagan administration further shortened the depreciation period of automobiles from 3.5 to 3 years, industrial equipment from 8.6 to 5 years, and factory building from 23.8 to 15 years. The benefit gained by enterprises from tax cuts was USD9.7 billion in 1982, USD18.8 billion in 1983, and over USD30 billion in 1984, but the government believed that accelerated replacements would bring greater economic and financial benefits to the United States.

The move from a low depreciation rate to an accelerated depreciation rate was a breakthrough of the capital formation mechanism in speeding up the compensation for advanced capital. It replaced the high-risk equal-annual payment depreciation with accelerated depreciation and enabled enterprises to first compensate for initial capital before making accumulation, paying taxes, and allocating profits. It increases the compensation fund and promotes the positive cycle of reproduction by speeding up depreciation. Of course, this compensation fund, as Marx has said, is not only the fund for the wear and tear of the fixed capital, but also a fund for accumulation.

Technology Transfer Fee: Mechanism for Intangible Assets Compensation and Accumulation

Science and technology developed quickly after the Second World War, and Western developed countries produced a great number of scientific and technological innovations, including new equipment, new technology, new processes, new material, and new products. The trade in technology rose along with this trend, and there were demands for the transfer of technical achievements, production technology, know-how, software, etc. In the meanwhile, some enterprises in Western developed countries spontaneously transferred technological achievements through technology trade and adopted technology transfer fees to compensate for the investment in the trial production of technology. The charge for technology transfer was generally composed of two parts: One was the one-time transfer fee of technical patent, widely known as "initial down payment," which will be charged once the transfer agreement becomes effective; the other is the recurring technology transfer fee collected according to a certain proportion of annual output, also known as "royalty." This charging method was soon accepted by the society and protected by the law in the economic life of society. It becomes an important part of intellectual property protection.

This transfer of technology facilitates the technological progress. In one aspect, the popularization of science and technology turns science and technology into productive forces of society and brings about huge economic benefits to both society and enterprises. In the words of Alan Greenspan, the technological promotion turns what is "scarce and expensive" into something "cheap and common." In the other aspect, the rapid advances in the high tech field and the substantial increases in technical experiment investment (in which intangible assets occupy a considerable proportion) require new forms of technology transfer and intangible assets compensation and accumulation mechanisms.

A technology transfer fee has, therefore, come into being. It is a compensation system of technological investment and a supplement to the capital formation mechanism of intangible assets, and for the society a system for the establishment and the stable operation of science and technology development funds in the national economy. It constitutes the investment and costs of intangible assets for the enterprises which introduce new technology while an effective form for the compensation and accumulation of intangible assets for the enterprises which disseminate the technology.

The Detour on the Way to the Development of Depreciation Fund and Fund for Simple Reproduction

Since the first five-year plan of large-scale economic construction in 1953, New China implemented highly centralized planned economic and fiscal systems. All income of state-owned enterprises, including profits and depreciation, should be turned over to the financial department. Spending on each item by these enterprises, whether the investment by newly-built enterprises in capital construction or the renovation and reformation investment by long-established enterprises (including the renewal of factory buildings and equipment) had to be reported to the state finance ministry for approval and budgetary provisions in the form of capital construction plan.

Such a highly centralized kind of management was difficult to be implemented. Economic activities change day after day, and it is impossible to include every investment of all enterprises in a national capital construction plan without any errors or omissions. This rigorous policy frequently met with opposition from the industrial sector since the promulgation in 1952. During the three-year Great Leap Forward between 1958 and 1960, this system was abolished with the practice of decentralization. In this period, Mao Zedong advocated setting "two targets," the one obligatory to attain and the other aspired for, with the investment quota was increased at every lower level, and thus the investment in capital construction expanded massively. Moreover, in practice, people regarded capital construction investment as investment in expanded reproduction, and therefore many economic sectors used the planned provisions for capital construction to invest in expanded reproduction, especially in new projects. As a result, investment in simple reproduction was crowded out and could not be guaranteed and there was a huge debt from equipment replacement.

The adverse impact from the incremental investment at every lower level in capital construction during the Great Leap Forward was revealed in the economic adjustments in the early 1960s and mainly reflected in the inadequate investment for maintaining current production level.

First, the debt caused by equipment update in long-established enterprises was exposed. The earliest cases were the debts from the maintenance of automobiles, industrial boilers, and diesel engines in the four major cities of Tianjin, Beijing,

Shanghai, and Shenyang, and the outstanding renovation costs for rolling stock in the Ministry of Railways. So the state finance ministry appropriated RMB1.3 billion for three consecutive years for repaying the debts incurred by equipment update.

In the meanwhile, many other long-established enterprises also suffered from equipment replacement debts. At that time, Sun Yefang suggested that the central government leave depreciation funds to enterprises to ensure the simple reproduction of fixed assets. His advice aroused a discussion on depreciation funds and simple reproduction in the economic circle, especially in the biweekly economic symposium hosted by *Red Flag* magazine. I was working for the CCB then and joined the discussion with Xu Yi, President of the bank. I organized a team to investigate the simple reproduction in dozens of sectors and provided over 10 investigation reports to the biweekly meeting.

The shortage of investment in sustaining simple reproduction also disclosed the outstanding expenses for the expansion in excavating and logging industries. According to the regulation of that time, building new mines and forests was a function of capital construction and the expansion of existing mines and forests was to be conducted according to the national capital construction plan. However, the capital plans usually focused on developing new mines and forests without making proper arrangements for the expansion of old ones. So the old mines and forests lived off their past gains and created huge debts in the expansion works.

Dong Biwu then wrote a poem to describe the situation and the closing line said "To act rashly is of no use." In order to solve the investment for the expansion of old mines and forests, the financial department stipulated in 1962 that the expansion expenses of coal mining and forest harvesting could be drawn from the costs of coal and wood according to a certain percentage of output as a fund for maintaining simple reproduction, and this fund would be independently used by competent departments instead of being approved by the state according to the national capital construction plan. It was very beneficial for regulating the production of mines and forests. The nature of this fund was said to be the capital construction fund and it was not included in the state budget. Similarly, oilfield maintenance costs, namely the costs for drilling injection wells around oilfields to increase pressure and thus maintain original oil extraction capacity when the oil resources and oil productivity decreased, were also drawn from the costs of crude oil according to a certain proportion to the crude output. These measures guaranteed the funds for simple reproduction and were necessary supplements to the capital formation mechanism during the planned economy period.

The Party Central Committee and the State Council summed up a lesson from this experience in the national economic adjustments in 1962: Any works of socialist economic construction, be it plan making, economy managing, or material supplying, must put simple reproduction at the first place before undertaking expanded reproduction.

Because of this, in the capital construction plan of 1962, under the capital construction investment target, an investment quota for maintaining simple reproduction was specially set up. It provided that "production capacity was to be maintained, production content and investment volume should be itemized, and the fund for compensating the defunct production capacity in the investment for maintaining current production capacity should be specified." The central government also stipulated that when departments employed the expansion expenses of coal mining and forest harvesting and the oilfield maintenance costs in mine development and oilfield maintenance, they should make a capital construction plan by themselves. It should be said that the separation by the state of the simple reproduction investment in the excavating and logging industries from the capital construction investment during the economic adjustments in 1960s practically solved the leftist impact from the Great Leap Forward. This method of directly extracting funds for maintaining simple reproduction from the product sales revenue complied with the rule of production and was a supplement to the capital formation mechanism.

The development of fixed-asset depreciation funds was not as unsmooth as that of funds for simple reproduction. Despite repeatedly being blamed, the Ministry of Finance required enterprises to turn over depreciation funds to the state instead of keeping it for the update of fixed assets until 1969 (i.e. during the Cultural Revolution). But afterwards many grassroots enterprises still could not benefit from the changed policy, since some central departments and local governments continued to use all or parts of the depreciation funds in a centralized way. To leave the depreciation fund to enterprises was for the renewal of fixed assets, but many central departments and local governments concentrated on the fund themselves for expanded reproduction. The survey after the reform and opening up of 1978 discovered that the debts incurred by the update of fixed assets were worse than those of the early 1960s.

The situation of fixed-asset investment after the 1970s was different from that in the past when the depreciation fund was turned over to the financial department or diverted to other purposes, or that during the Great Leap Forward when the fund for expanded reproduction crowded out the investment for simple reproduction. For one thing, the State Planning Commission intended to devote the capital construction investment of billions to expanded reproduction projects while leaving small investment at the disposal of the finance department. For another, the Ministry of Finance was willing to set aside a portion of money for the innovation and renovation projects of local departments. In fact, the State Development Planning Commission and the Ministry of Finance left a large number of funds for enterprise innovations and created many capital channels for small projects and small economic measures. Competent departments and manufacturing enterprises welcomed these innovation funds. They are a supplement in the capital formation mechanism for small investment and innovation investment of enterprises under the circumstances of fixed-asset renewal fund being diverted to other purposes and funds for maintaining simple reproduction being not guaranteed.

In this way, many replacement investments were divorced from capital construction and there were roughly 5 categories:

1. Special appropriations directly from financial budgets, such as innovation, renovation, and reconstruction funds, subsidies to five types of small industrial enterprises (i.e., iron and steel plant, coal mine, chemical fertilizer plant, power station and machinery plant, later non-ferrous metals, agricultural machinery and cement plans were added to this category), mobilization subsidies for producing deficient products or manufacturing goods for civil use by military industrial enterprises, and investment allowance for specialization and collaboration.

2. Funds extracted or retained from costs (commerce circulation costs), such as small construction funds of simple sheds and warehouses for commercial use, food and trade departments, funds for the simple construction of retail outlets for the aforementioned departments, funds for small oil tanks.

3. Bank loans, such as small technical loans to industrial enterprises by the CCB and special loans for industrial exports to the manufacturing enterprises.

4. Local governments can impose certain fees on enterprises, for example, 49 municipal governments extracted urban construction and maintenance fees from industrial and commercial profits.

5. The foreign capital borrowed and repaid independently by enterprises could be excluded from the capital construction plan and state budget, namely, the so-called "second-front investment."

In this way, the fixed-asset investment is divided into two parts: One was capital construction investment; the second was the investment for innovation and transformation. But the investment scale of the innovation fund grew larger and larger over a long period and was similar to that of capital construction. Moreover, the State Planning Commission did not want to see a slight decrease in the planned capital investment and, as a result, the investment scale of fixed assets got out of control.

Great Debate on the Concept of Investment Triggered by Double Expansion of Investment

In 1979, when the reform and opening up policy was first announced, there was a debate on the concept of investment in capital construction and fixed assets in the economic sphere. On one side of the debate was the State Planning Commission, and on the other side was the CCB. The question being debated seemingly was whether innovation investment should be included in fixed-asset investment, but the real focus was on whether the investment scale of fixed assets was too large.

The origin of this controversy lied in the definition of capital construction investment in the early stages of New China. In 1952, China initiated the first five-year plan of massive economic construction. At that time, China undertook 156 major construction projects with the aid of the Soviet Union, and borrowed from the Soviets the concept of capital investment as a replacement for the commonly mentioned fixed-asset investment in economic life. So what is capital investment? According to the *Interim Measures for Capital Construction Works* promulgated by the Government Administration Council of China's Central People's Government in 1952, "whatever new construction, reconstruction, restoration projects of the expanded reproduction of fixed assets or the related projects should be considered as capital construction." The *Political Economy* (third edition), a textbook issued by the Economics Institute of the Academy of Sciences of the Union of Soviet Socialist Republics also gave a definition of capital construction: "Capital investments are the total outlays used over a particular period to create new productive and non-productive fixed funds and to reconstruct those already in existence."[13] Based on economic common sense, social reproduction always means expanded reproduction and the expanded reproduction is always carried out under the basis of simple reproduction, just as Marx has said: "As far as accumulation does take place, simple reproduction is always a part of it ... and is an actual factor of accumulation."[14] Therefore, there is no doubt that capital investment has to comprise both expanded reproduction and simple reproduction of fixed assets. During the socialist construction of New China, however, the aggressive leftist thinking always prevailed. People wondered that despite the fact that the economic development of European capitalism extended over 300 years, could the economic construction of a socialist society develop faster? So China put the pursuit of high speed and high growth of economic development above everything. The definition in the *Interim Measures for Capital Construction Works* provided an important basis for many economic departments equating capital construction with the expanded reproduction of fixed assets. This was also the reason why many economic departments diverted the capital investment allocated according to the state plan to the investment of expanded reproduction, which crowded out the funds for simple reproduction and caused debts in equipment replacement during the Great Leap Forward.

In the later period of the Cultural Revolution of the 1970s, the leftist thinking in economic life surged and people were eager to boost the economy. It was principally manifested in the fact that the planning department pursued a fast and high economic growth and intended to use large-scale capital investment to ensure the high target in the economic plan. It was because of this that the planning department extended the definition of expanded reproduction of fixed assets in the *Interim Measures for Capital Construction Works* to an unwritten definition: Capital investment is the state spending for changing the structure of the national economy, rationally allocating productive forces and increasing production capacity and project benefits. This unofficial definition, in fact, became a principle of investment allocation in real economic life for a long period of time. So the planning department regarded investment as capital construction for the expanded reproduction of the national economy and equated capital construction with accumulation and expanded reproduction. The department allocated the budget appropriations for capital investment to expanded reproduction projects, and the innovation projects of simple reproduction were excluded from the capital construction plan under a separate investment arrangement. Local governments and governmental departments were, however, frequently in need of innovation projects and had to ask the finance department to set aside a fund for this purpose. Since these innovation projects contributed a lot to the increase of fiscal revenue, the finance department was willing to help. In this way, the investment scale of fixed assets was expanded through two channels of capital construction and technical innovation, and thus the special situation of double expansion of investment came into being in this period.

In 1975, Deng Xiaoping took to the political stage again and emphasized overall economic improvements. In the middle of the same year, I returned to

Beijing from the May Seventh Cadre Schools of the Ministry of Finance, and the CCB, and I was transferred to the financial department for capital construction under the Ministry of Finance where I worked closely with the Capital Investment Bureau of the State Planning Commission. When I came back, the authorities of the CCB had designated me to research the investment scale of fixed assets, and I found that there was a large amount of innovation and renovation investment from the financial budget, government departments' funds, bank loans, and enterprises' production costs beyond the planned capital investment, which created a massive expansion of fixed-asset investment. I joined the "ghost hunting" activities led by Xu Yi in 1959 and studied the impact of runaway investment on the economy and finance during the Great Leap Forward. Later in 1962, I experienced the period when the CCB was asked by the finance department to fill the capital holes created by the local government and government departments which were attempting to double investment, and thus deeply understood the severe damage of excessive investment expansion on financial works. We had prepared a report about the double expansion of investment but it was not made public due to the political criticism of Deng Xiaoping.

Since the toppling of the Gang of Four in 1976, the national economy experienced a period of contraction and rectification. Vice Premier Hua Guofeng was anxious for success, so he demanded that we "aim high and go all out" and intended to construct 10 oilfields as large as Daqing Oilfield, 20 iron and steel plants as powerful as Angang Steel, 10 sizeable coal bases, and 22 imported projects. The construction scale was extremely huge. The root cause for the rush for quick results was the leftist thinking which pursued high speed and new advances. In September 1978, Li Xiannian made a calculation in the Theory-Discussing Meeting of the State Council. The planned investment in projects under construction was RMB280 billion while now the total amount increased to RMB360 billion. There were 12,000 unplanned projects under construction with an investment of RMB12 billion. If all these projects were to be completed, RMB160 billion more investment was probably needed. The investment amount was inflated once again.

The Third Plenary Session of the 11th Party Central Committee was convened in 1978. In early 1979, Deng Xiaoping and Chen Yun noticed the leftist thinking in the economic works, and proposed to adjust the economy by "pressing down accumulation and reducing capital construction." Against such a backdrop, the Vice President of the CCB, Liu Lixin, asked us to recalculate the investment scale. Based on the accounts of 1975, we continued to investigate the planned innovation and reformation projects beyond capital construction, and as a result, we got the five categories as stated in the previous section.

According to the calculation, the investment in capital construction within the state plan was no larger than RMB39.6 billion while the unplanned investment in simple reproduction and renovation projects was RMB36.4 billion. The total planned and unplanned investment amounted to RMB76 billion and was collectively called the "six battlefields." Of course, it was not parallel with the current annual fixed-asset investment of several trillion, but under the then national power, RMB 10 or 20 billion more investment would be enough to disrupt the whole economy.

What is the proper size of investment? The generally accepted standard was the "two, three, and four principle" suggested by Bo Yibo when he concluded the experience from the first five-year plan. The principle stipulated that accumulation should account for 20% of national income, fiscal revenue should account for 30% of national income, and capital construction expenditure should account for 40% of fiscal expenditure. Based on our previous calculation, the proportion of capital construction expenditure to fiscal expenditure was around 38%, which was within the proper size of 40%; however, if the innovation investment was also included (namely, all fixed-asset investment was counted in), the proportion would go up to 56%, much larger than the generally accepted ceiling and that of the first five-year plan but close to the percentage during the second five-year plan when the three-year Leap Forward gave rise to a huge investment expansion.

A larger problem was that although a large amount of money was allocated by the state to support those projects, there were no sufficient materials and even no corresponding material supply channels. This material shortage caused the retention of funds. According to statistics, the annual surplus in the innovation and renovation funds in industrial enterprises nationwide was around RMB12–13 billion, among which half was for materials and remaining construction, and the rest was bank deposits. The project duration was usually very long and among the 4,287 undergoing innovation and renovation projects above RMB1 million, 2,068 projects (48%) have been under construction for two years and are still not yet finished; 895 projects have been underway for three to five years, 307 projects for five to eight years, and 61 projects for over eight years.

Due to the double expansion of investment in capital construction and renovation, all fixed-asset investment was equal to 56% of the total sum of capital in and out of the budget. Liu Lixin, Vice President of the CCB, asked us to draft a report about the current investment to the central government. The Report of the

CCB said that the new situation of investment indicated that the term of capital investment could no longer truly reflect the construction investment scale and therefore "fixed-asset investment" comprising capital construction and technical transformation was a better choice for measuring construction investment scale. It was a sensitive question, however. The CCB officials dared not directly report to the central government. Liu Lixin decided to turn the report to the Central Leading Group on Financial and Economic Affairs of the Communist Party of China (CPC) and Chen Yun, and this created a great stir. The State Planning Commission criticized the CCB for "placing a heavy bomb" for the group, and wrote an article to rebut. The State Planning Commission said that the "depreciation fund is aimed to compensate the wear and tear of fixed assets instead of expanded reproduction," and "you cannot call the adding of a new motor in a manufacturing shop as a capital construction. The commission also questioned the CCB's definition of fixed-asset investment and thought that the definition "mixed up various funds of a different nature, purpose and objective" and thus the new definition could neither accurately indicate the scale of capital construction nor show the difference between capital construction and innovation projects, and between expanded reproduction and simple reproduction. CCB was also blamed for "not being serious and conscientious" and "fabricating questionable figures and confusing the concept.

Chen Yun was cautious. He said the figures of just one year could hardly disclose any problems and assigned the CCB to make a 30-year report by applying the same criteria. Later on, the Ministry of Finance and the CCB collectively sent a new report of fixed-asset expenditure in and out of budge for 30 years to the Central Leading Group on Financial and Economic Affairs and Chen Yun. Finally, Chen concluded that "economic adjustment is necessary." He explained: "The capital investment of the next year (namely, 1980) proposed by the State Planning Commission is RMB25 billion, and that by the finance department was RMB17 billion. Both figures are less than the investment in 1978 of RMB45.1 billion and that in 1979 of RMB36 billion. This actually proves that the investment in either 1978 or 1979 exceeded the state's financial and material capabilities." Chen Yun continued to emphasize that "the investment beyond national financial and material capabilities emerged after 1970, and that is why the duration of capital construction was very long." At that time, Chen Yun's words carried weight and confirmed the excessively long duration of capital construction after 1970, and therefore the State Planning Commission had to examine the planning work, especially the capital construction, of this period.

Since the State Planning Commission stated that the depreciation fund could only be used for simple reproduction rather than accumulation and expanded reproduction, Tian Chunsheng and other people from the CCB including me drafted a report and prepared some special quotations from Marx on expanded reproduction and simple reproduction as an appendix to the report. One of the quotations said that "The sinking fund, i.e., the fund for wear and tear of the fixed capital, is, in my opinion, at the same time a fund for accumulation." Li Xiannian attached great importance to this sentence and regarded it as an important discovery.

The State Planning Commission and our CCB team split on the definition of fixed-asset investment since the former insisted that innovation and renovation should not be counted in the expanded reproduction. At that time, Gu Mu was the Director of the State Planning Commission and he appointed Xue Baoding to take charge of the newly built Research Institution of Capital Construction. The institution was responsible for studying the concept of fixed-asset investment, and thereby a great debate on the concept of capital construction and fixed-asset investment was started in the theoretical circle. The report from the CCB for the first time formally adopted the term of "fixed-asset investment" and put forward that the investment sizes of its two components, namely capital construction and technical reform, should be limited to a total amount with the increase of one at the expense of the decrease of the other. On the contrary, the State Planning Commission held that only capital construction would realize the expanded production of the national economy and accused the CCB of confusing different concepts. The debate on the definition was just an appearance, the real issue was whether and how to control investment scale. In spite of the argument from the State Planning Commission, it was undeniable that the duration of capital construction was too long and the investment size was too large. Later, the Research Institution of Capital Construction specially wrote an article on this debate and admitted that capital construction was merely a concept of management rather than theory.

One of the important achievements of this debate was the confirmation of the concept of "fixed-asset investment." During The 4th Plenary Session of the 5th National People's Congress in August 1980, Zhao Ziyang substituted Hu Guofeng as Premier of the State Council. When Zhao Ziyang talked about the plan of 1981 on the Central Work Conference on December 16, 1980, he said: "How to reduce investment? We should first cut down the investment in capital construction. The capital construction investment within the state budget should be decreased from RMB24.1 billion of this year to RMB17 billion, a drop of RMB7.1 billion. The total scale, including the self-raised funds by the local government, government department and enterprises, bank loans, and investment in the installation of imported equipment, should be reduced from RMB50 billion this year to RMB30 billion." The total scale of investment in and out of the budget mentioned by his was in fact that of fixed-asset investment covering both capital construction and technical reform. The *Report on the Work of the Government* of 1981 decided that since 1982, the plan of fixed-asset investment prepared by the State Planning Commission should collectively arrange the distribution of the capital construction fund and the technical reform fund. From then on, the investments in fixed-asset renewal and that in innovation and reformation projects were collectively called "technological upgrading investment," which was listed in the fixed-asset investment plan together with capital construction investment. The technological upgrading investment got its rightful place in capital formation mechanism and the reproduction of fixed assets finally returned to its proper position in the reproduction theory of Marx.

Five Kinds of Moral Depreciation

There is another problem in the fixed-asset upgrading, that is, concerning the wear and tear of fixed assets, Chinese people for a long period of time focused only on material depreciation rather than moral depreciation and its proper compensation. China's financial system always practices a low depreciation rate and takes no account of moral wear and tear, and thus China is reluctant to adopt the accelerated depreciation. Marx once talked about two kinds of moral depreciation of fixed assets, and in fact many more kinds of new moral depreciation are added in real economic life since the upgrading of technology and technical equipment was really fast thanks to the rapid scientific and technological advances. In 1986, I made an analysis of five kinds of moral depreciation.

1. The drop of selling price of machines and equipment due to the improvement in labor productivity and the reduction in cost, or in other words, the loss caused by the devaluation of old equipment is called "moral depreciation 1." For instance, a factory buys two sets of C-type grinding machines when the machine first comes out at a price of RMB50,000 per set. One year later, the price of the grinder is decreased to RMB20,000 per set due to the increase in labor productivity, and thereby the C-type grinders bought at first depreciated RMB30,000.

2. The emergence of new machines with better quality, lower consumption, and higher efficiency would bring down the economic benefits of the original machines, and thus give rise to the advanced replacement of the old machines. The loss in efficiency of old equipment is called "moral depreciation 2." There are two examples: 1) The Model DG250/160 industrial pump with energy-saving effect could substitute for the Model DG270/140 pump. If such a substitution is made at an early date, the money saved on electricity bills in one year will be enough to buy a new pump. On the contrary, if the old pump continues to be used, more than 720,000 kilowatt-hours of electricity will be consumed each year, and the moral depreciation of RMB57,000 production cost will thus be created; 2) The medium and low-voltage power generation units will consume 500 grams of coal per kilowatt-hour of electricity they generate, while the high-voltage units only need 350 grams. Therefore, the power plant can choose to either bear the moral wear and tear and replace the medium and low-voltage power generation units with high-voltage ones in order to save 150 grams of coal per kilowatt-hour of electricity and reduce costs, or continue to use the old units and pay the production cost of consuming 150 grams more of coal per kilowatt-hour of electricity.

Moral depreciation 1 and 2 are the two types of wear and tear mentioned in Marx's works.

3. The loss caused by the advanced retirement of fixed assets due to the upgrade of products is called "moral depreciation 3." Different from the above two kinds, moral depreciation 3 is not a result of the change in the means of labor but that of the rapid development of science and technology. The significant breakthrough in science and technology brings about the upgrade of products and also calls for the adoption of new materials, new equipment, and new processes to produce multi-function and high-quality products. As a result, the subject of labor is changed and there is a need to transform factories, workshops, and production lines, which in turn causes the advanced retirement and upgrading of fixed assets even when their value and use value are in good condition and thus generating moral depreciation by redistributing productive forces.

The following are the examples of moral depreciation 3 which appeared during the upgrading of products.

Phosphate fertilizer products were produced in place of the products with normal superphosphate in order to lead to the production of the high-efficient ammonium phosphate fertilizers and heavy calcium carbonate fertilizers. Urea fertilizers and compound fertilizers were developed since ammonium bicarbonate is eliminated by nitrogen in fertilizer products. Consequently, a batch of equipment, production lines, workshops, and factories will be scrapped ahead of schedule and a number of qualified factories will be transformed and switched to the production of other things.

Since the low-efficiency and highly toxic pesticides with chlorine as the main ingredient are weeded out, the whole fixed assets of some pesticide plants need to be abandoned. Moreover, the caustic soda industry lost a big consumer of chlorine and demanded rearrangement.

Children's toys used to be made of iron and wood, but now they are made of plastic and electronic parts. Therefore, a loss is incurred by the advanced retirement of the original production lines of wood and iron; on the contrary, the production lines of plastics and integrated circuits as well as new assembly lines will be needed.

The product cycle of the electronic industry has accelerated the most significantly. China's first tube television was available in 1957 and before the tube TV was popularized, transistor black-and-white TV was developed in the 1970s, followed by the emergence of integrated circuit color TV in the 1980s. The development of the computer took the same path: The first generation computer used vacuum tubes, the second generation used transistor computers, the third were computers with integrated circuits, and the fourth were large scale integrated circuit computers. The products' development followed a trend of more miniaturized products, which apparently accelerated the advanced retirement and replacement of the original fixed assets.

The above upgrading of products created a new kind of moral wear and tear, totally different from the already existing two kinds of moral depreciation. The reproduction of fixed assets is now not predetermined by the physical properties of fixed assets but whether the fixed assets could adapt to the needs of new products. The advanced retirement of equipment or production lines is a result of the loss of works instead of the loss of the productive capacity or efficiency.

4. The loss created by the rearrangement of enterprises' fixed assets due to the socioeconomic adjustment is called "moral depreciation 4." The first three kinds of moral depreciation are viewed within the scope of an enterprise, while moral depreciation 4 is related to the rearrangement of fixed assets among different enterprises and the early retirement of fixed assets during the merger and acquisition of enterprises and urban renewal, namely, socio-economic

adjustment. This new moral depreciation is considered from the perspective of the whole society instead of one enterprise, and roughly includes the following situations:

a. The development of socialized mass production and specialization and collaboration pushes enterprises to undertake scale management and reduce costs, and thereby big and all-embracing plants built in the early period of industrial construction have to be reformed into specialized ones with specialized division of labor and collaboration between each other. To be more specific, the workshops of casting and forging, heat treatment, and plating process and the parts production line will be separated into specialized production factories which collaborate in various forms (such as separated contractual joint venture, integrated contractual joint venture, joint venture company) to serve for a larger product and, therefore, advanced renewal and retirement of fixed assets will be incurred due to the fact that some factories have to eliminate the workshops of casting and forging, heat treatment, and plating process and the parts production line in order to become specialized ones.

b. The Industrial restructuring causes the reorganization of productive forces among different enterprises and industries. The reorganization sometimes resulted from the emergence of new products, new technology, or new industry; and at other times it may have been an industrial reorganization since comprehensive utilization of raw materials facilitates the production of new products. For example, oil refineries, chemical plants, and chemical fiber plants, which all depend on oil as raw materials, originally belonged to three different industries of petroleum, chemicals, and textiles, but their production processes overlap with each other and some intermediate products discarded by one factory may be absolutely necessary for the production of others. The oil refineries cast away the highly processed products which are needed by the chemical and chemical fiber plants, while C4 abandoned by the chemical fiber plants is indispensable for the chemical plants. This causes a waste of materials. Later, learning from the overseas experience, China establishes the China Petrochemical Corporation which undertakes the extensive processing of crude oil under the integrated planning of oil refining, chemical processing, and chemical fiber production in order to develop more processed oil, chemicals, and chemical fiber products by making the most of crude oil, and, therefore, there is a need for the reorganization of fixed assets.

c. The pursuit of economies of scale in industrial development gives rise to the adjustment and early reformation of fixed assets among different enterprises. The most typical example is the small nitrogenous fertilizer plants. In the early 1960s, China built a group of small ammonia plants with an annual output of 3,000 tons. Due to the small size, these plants recorded a loss every year, so they were gradually transformed into plants with an annual output of 5,000 tons. However, the deficits were not eliminated until the plants expanded their annual output into 10,000 tons, and if the plants intend to be profitable, they have to produce at least 40,000 tons of ammonia per year and at the same time be engaged in the co-production of other products. This transformation towards economies of scale demands, of course, the adjustment of productivity among different enterprises and the early retirement of fixed assets.

d. Urban renewal will bring about industrial restructuring. For example, urban renewal planning will decide which industry should be developed, retained, or restricted according to the development direction of a city. A city may regulate the enterprises which generate liquid waste, waste residue, or waste gas in a centralized way and lead the high heat-consuming enterprises to replace dispersed heating with centralized heating, which will cause the reallocation of corporate fixed assets.

e. In the market-oriented reforms, enterprises undertake vertical or horizontal mergers and acquisitions as well as restructuring and practice technical transformation in order to adapt to the socialized mass production. For instance, petrochemical enterprises have to take into account the mergers and acquisitions of upstream and downstream product processing firms; machinery enterprises consider the common needs in manufacturing technique through mergers and acquisitions to prop up the development of casting center, heat treatment center, and electroplating center. The facilities equipped by each factory in the initial stage of industrialization, such as power, water, oxygen, gas, machine maintenance, warehouses, and transportation will develop towards a trend of socialization during the market-oriented reform, which will cause the early retirement and losses of a number of workshops and facilities.

f. The moral wear and tear of intangible property is categorized as "moral depreciation 5." Enterprises of Western countries take account of intangible properties, while China only records tangible properties without consideration of intangible properties. In fact, however, Socialist enterprises own intangible properties, such as imported technology, patents and know-how, and enterprises' inventions and creations, production techniques, specialized technology, product design, drawings, etc. Moreover, corporate trademarks and goodwill also belong to intangible properties. All of these are properties created by the enterprise staff through hard work. Similarly, intangible properties will also generate moral depreciation which results from the shortening of economic life and the early obsolescence of these properties with the rapid development of science and technology.

The problem is that the establishment of intangible property is just a one-time activity. Once a company buys and masters a technical patent or achieves know-how, the company can repeatedly use the patent within the patent's economic life. Before a more advanced patent or bit of know-how replaces the old one, the company will not bother to make another purchase. Therefore, the moral depreciation of intangible properties will be incurred when a more advanced technique or bit of know-how is created ahead of the termination of the expected economic life of the old ones. For example, in 1980, a computer factory introduced the S-model computer production line by investing RMB56 million, among which RMB10 million was used to purchase the S-model product design drawings and the production know-how. The factory originally conceived that after the construction of the factory, 400 sets of S-model computers would be produced every year with six years of the product lifecycle. However, when the factory was finally built in 1983, the technology was on the brink of elimination, so that among the 200 sets of S-model computers produced by the factory between 1983 and 1985, only 50 sets were sold. The factory, thus, had to update its production line and purchase new technical patents and know-how, and in this way, the factory simultaneously incurred moral depreciation 3 and 5.

I believe that when calculating the production costs of industrial products, people should admit and take into account this kind of moral depreciation of fixed assets and study the development trend and rule, and the key to this is to carry out accelerated depreciation.

China practiced a low depreciation rate during the planned economy and the early market-oriented reforms, and gave more attention to material depreciation than moral depreciation and compensation of fixed assets. Over the years, voices for increasing the depreciation rate and practicing accelerated depreciation were frequently heard, but none of these generated any results. One high-sounding reason was that the increase of the depreciation rate will impact fiscal revenue and 1% growth of the depreciation rate will deprive the government of several billions in revenue. In fact, it reflects a lack of knowledge towards the positive impact of moral depreciation on scientific and technological advances. In China's experience of financial works, people have long held a comparatively negative impression about moral wear and tear by regarding moral depreciation merely as a loss.

This view is one-sided. In reality, no matter which kind of moral depreciation of fixed assets, it is the small price to be paid during the tremendous progress in science and technology. Despite the fact that the advanced adoption of new technology and equipment and the early obsolescence of old ones will incur a part of economic loss, the enterprise and the whole society will thereby receive larger economic benefits as a reward than when keeping the old equipment and technology. Specifically, these economic benefits are reflected in four aspects: First, advanced means of labor reduces the consumption of raw materials and increases labor productivity, namely, reduces production costs; second, through replacing old products with new products in the market, enterprises will see a growth in both production and profits; third, the reallocation of productive forces and specialization and collaboration resulting from industrial restructuring, corporate mergers and acquisitions, and urban renewal, will create huge economic benefits; fourth, early upgrading of fixed assets and technical reform will create massive economic benefits for both individual enterprises and the society. In conclusion, the moral wear and tear of fixed assets is an inevitable outcome of the scientific and technological progress.

For example, according to our investigation in 1980s, there were 260,000 sets of outmoded draft fans in China's industrial and mining enterprises, which could consume 3 billion kilowatt-hours of electricity every year. Then, we suggested the fan factories accept the moral depreciation caused by the early upgrading of fan products and turn to the manufacturing of energy-saving fans while the industrial and mining enterprises substituted the old-fashioned fans ahead of schedule in an organized way. Although bearing the loss caused by advanced replacement, fan factories could make a profit by manufacturing energy-saving fans and industrial and mining enterprises could cut the cost of RMB240 million by consuming 3 billion kilowatt-hours less of electricity. More importantly, the society would save an investment of RMB780 million in power station construction, coal mining, and road building since the adoption of new fans was equal to increasing 600,000 kilowatts of power generating capacity, an annual output of 1.8 million tons of raw coal for generating electricity and the corresponding railway transportation power. Unfortunately, the government cannot make up its mind to update the policy and was reluctant to take out money to reform fan factories and replace over 200,000 sets of outmoded draft fans.

This makes two things explicit: First, moral depreciation of fixed assets is a natural outcome of scientific and technological advances. Only when we take a right attitude towards moral wear, and accept the achievements from scientific and technological development by eliminating early old products and equipment, can we transfer scientific and technological results into social productivity to push the advancement of society. Otherwise, we will hardly benefit from the scientific and technological achievements and be burdened with high-energy-consuming and low-efficiency outdated equipment.

Second, people only see moral depreciation in financial works but are blind to the huge economic benefits accompanying the moral depreciation. When replacing equipment and production lines, people usually judge the economic benefits of this replacement from the perspective of an individual company instead of considering the huge social economic benefits from the perspective of national economy. People often say because of the shortage of money that they do not upgrade their equipment; however, the opposite is true — people have no money, because they do not update the equipment. Therefore, whether we or not we hold a proper attitude towards moral depreciation has a direct bearing on the transfer of scientific and technological achievements into social productivity.

6 Chapter

Financial Leasing

Prologue: Financial Leasing during the Bus Upgrade Scheme in Hangzhou

When an enterprise intends to scale up its production, it can rely on financial leasing instead of capital increases and bank credit. The greatest merit of this method is that it performs the functions of both financing assets and raising funds, which will leave the company with ample own capital and a credit line for other development opportunities. The enterprises under a market economy enrich capital culture with a leasing culture.

Qu Yankai, Managing Vice President of the Leasing Business Committee of the China Association of Enterprises with Foreign Investment, told a story:

In 1999, Hangzhou City planned to upgrade its buses. The local source of finance, however, could not afford the upgrading of the buses and considered pursuing financial leasing after discussions with leasing companies. The advantage of this method was that industrial users could choose the equipment and supplier they wanted while leasing companies raised the funds to purchase the specified equipment before renting it to the users. Rather than increasing capital or arranging loans, the lessees would pay monthly rentals which were counted as costs.

The leasing company set out a condition: The public transit system had to be reformed and different bus routes must be contracted to different companies which would be charged operating expenses. Then, the leasing company placed a bus purchase contract with the automobile factory according to the bus company's requirements, and at the same time signed a lease contract with the bus company. The local financial department offered 1/3 of the total transformation costs, and the leasing company who possessed the ownership of the new buses bore the rest of the expenses. The contracts were mortgaged to a bank by the leasing company for bank loans and the bank opened a special account for the leasing company to collect rentals which were directly deducted from the daily income saved in the same bank by each contracted company of different bus routes. Since the reform of the public transit system would both enlarge cash flow and expand deposits, the bank was willing to grant loans to the leasing company.

This is a successful example of taking advantage of financial leasing to reform the urban public transit system.

Financial Leasing: Industrial Users Select an Asset While Leasing Companies Rent It to the Users

Financial leasing, also known as equipment leasing or modern leasing, is different from traditional operating leasing. Traditional leasing is a situation in which a finance company purchases an asset (such as a camera or an automobile), then leases that asset to a client for a specified amount of time. It is a trade and involves one lease contract and two contracting parties — the lessor and lessee. The operating leasing can only raise funds but not finance assets. In contrast, financial leasing can both finance assets and funds. In a financial leasing activity, industrial users can select which equipment and supplier they want, before leasing companies raise funds to buy the equipment for renting it to the industrial users. This activity involves one trade, two contracts, and three participants. The two contracts are: 1. A purchase contract in which the lessee chooses an asset that will be purchased by the lessor and the lessee bears the rights while the lessor shoulders the obligations; 2. A lease contract which specifies the rights of the lessor and the obligations of the lessee. These two contracts are inseparable from each other. Only when the lessee decides to use the equipment will the lessor buy the equipment; and as long as the lessor purchases the equipment, the lessee must rent the equipment. The three participants are lessor, supplier, and lessee. The leasing company is the buyer or lessor who will pay for the equipment specified by the lessee. Although it is the leasing company who makes the purchase, the supplier will deliver the equipment to and answer for the lessee instead of the lessor. Then, the leasing company charges a series of rentals from the lessee. The rights and obligations of the three participants are cross-performed in those two contracts. To put it simply, financial leasing collects lease fees based on the principle of accelerated depreciation and flexibly uses equipment as loan capital. This method is an innovation in the capital formation mechanism since it bypasses banks as intermediaries by regarding equipment as loan capital. Financial leasing, as an emerging industry, breaks the restrictions of traditional credit and financial institution systems, and injects new vigor into the reform of financial system. Now, financial leasing has become a major financing means for updating corporate equipment around the world and has thus been praised as a "sunrise industry." The rise of financial leasing adds a non-banking financial sector to the financial system and introduces a competition mechanism in China's financial industry. In addition, this method renders a new choice for the technological reform of enterprises in terms of the mode of both credit and trade.

The innovations of financial leasing in capital formation mechanism lie in:

1. The leasing company invests in certain leased equipment rather than the whole industry and seizes the ownership of the equipment. The company sporadically sells the use value of the equipment by way of leasing and gains compensation and added value through rental fees which are equal to accelerated depreciation plus average profit.
2. The industrial user does not need to make additional investment, but can acquire the usufruct of the latest technological equipment by way of leasing in order to produce competitive products and repay rentals from profits.
3. Equipment leasing is different from applying for loans. What the leasing company lends is not money capital but physical capital, and to be more precise, the usufruct of physical capital. It is because of this that the industrial user can wholly devote themselves to operation instead of worrying about repaying the principal of loans.

Meanwhile, equipment leasing, as a new investment industry independent from the banking industry, possesses a certain progressive significance.

1. It stimulates new investment demands and opens a vast new field for investment in the monetary market.
2. It is helpful for promoting the sales of equipment manufacturing firms by creating a new sales market.
3. It will speed up the transfer of scientific and technological achievements into social productivity by leasing the latest products. For the latest products which employ new technological achievements, equipment leasing will connect together scientific research, production, sales and application, and create an effective way for promoting the sales of new technology and new equipment.
4. It will enable industrial users to acquire new technical equipment by means of leasing and thus obtain larger marginal benefits. In fact, equipment manufacturing firms will directly participate in the creation and distribution of marginal benefit of the production enterprises (the users) by financial leasing. The government can also encourage such a method by tax cuts.
5. It renovates assets management mode. Financial leasing separates ownership from management right, which provides a space for the innovation of assets management. Now, some assets management companies take over from banks the troubled assets, among which the idle equipment, or even the whole

production line, factory, and shop is rent out. Some multinational corporations only have current assets in their accounts and all the fixed assets are leased from leasing firms, or gotten through the sale and leaseback. In the latter case, a company sells a property and then leases it back from the buyer, namely, the leasing firm who will record the depreciation expenses in the account and issue the rental invoice. On the account of the lessee, however, there are only working capital, rents, wages, expenses and income.

The History of Financial Leasing

Modern leasing is derived from the United States. After the Second World War, American producers adopted an installment plan in order to promote their products. Concerning the great risk in capital recovery, the ownership of equipment was left to the producers while the purchasers only enjoyed the usufruct and would not acquire the ownership until all the costs of the equipment were recouped by the producer. This mode of transaction is called "financial leasing." In 1952, the world's first financial leasing company was established in the United States. In the late 1950s, financial leasing was introduced to the rest of North America, in the 1960s to Western Europe and Asia, and in the 1970s to South America. As of now, there are more than 80 countries engaged in financial leasing business. Since Japan learned financial leasing from the United States, the leasing turnover annually grew by 91.4% before the rate slowed down to 20% after the 1980s, and thus financial leasing became the most vigorous emerging industry in Japan.

The rapid advances of science and technology accelerate the upgrading of equipment. Enterprises place more and more attention on the liquidity of assets in order to avoid the risk from obsolete equipment and improve their financial situations. In addition, the imbalance of regional development and the diversified demands of clients create a large space for the development of the leasing market. Under such a background, the modern leasing industry represented by financial leasing has developed rapidly in the international arena. In 2000, the turnover of global leasing transactions exceeded USD470 billion (excluding personal automobile leasing). The United States is the country where the leasing business has flourished the most, and the industry occupies over 40% of the world's transaction volume of leasing. The leasing transaction volume of European countries is USD140 billion, accounting for 30% of the world's leasing business. Asian countries record a leasing transaction volume of USD67.7 billion, 15.7% of the world's total. In the developed countries, such as the United States and Europe, the leasing of equipment, such as aircraft, information equipment, construction machinery, commercial vehicles, marine and medical equipment, takes up 50%–80% of the global leasing transactions, and the proportion of the cross-border leasing business expands year by year.

The business models are constantly innovated during the development of financial leasing and basically comprise the following three methods:

1. The most common and typical approach is the direct financial lease which allows users to select the supplier and equipment that will be purchased and rented to the users by a leasing company. China's mobile telecommunications is developed under such a kind of leasing model. In the past, the telecommunication projects in China were funded by the state appropriation or planned loans from China Construction Banks (CCB) allocated by the Planning Commission. In 1991, under the suggestion of leasing companies, the financial department promulgated a document which allowed several categories of telecommunication projects, such as computerized telephone, mobile phones, and satellite ground stations to try financial leasing, which paved the way for the business expansion of financial leasing joint ventures in the telecommunication leases.

Equipment leasing further develops from the direct leasing of single equipment to that of a whole project. This method demands less time but offers more benefits than build operate transfer (BOT).[1] The new approach is a great progress based on the BOT and also an advanced form of direct financial leasing.

2. Trust lease. Industrial enterprises can trust leasing companies with equipment, and investors or enterprises with ample capital can trust leasing companies with capital. Basically, the lessor will negotiate with the lessee about the equipment and its model, and then the leasing company will purchase the equipment according to the instruction of the lessor and at the same time bear the risks herein incurred. Trust lease creates a new investment channel for investors.

In a trust lease agreement, the leasing firm may take the initiative to make a leasing arrangement, and now the leasing firm acts as a lease arranger. For instance, in a financial lease of large equipment or a big airplane, the leasing firm has to apply for a bank loan since the money needed for this transaction is substantial. The bank demands 20% of the total purchase price as a guarantee from the leasing firm, and if the leasing firm does not own or want to offer such an amount of money, it can find an investor to join this trust lease. The investor will trust the leasing firm with capital to purchase the airplane whose ownership is held by the investor. Then, the leasing firm will use the 20% of the total cost from the investor as collateral to ask for a bank loan of 80% of total purchasing expense. Meanwhile, the leasing firm has to assure the investor of his investment by hiring an investment guarantee corporation. In addition, the ownership of the airplane, the rights to earnings in the lease contract, and the insurance beneficial right are all mortgaged to the bank. The leasing firm shares the income with the lessor. Of course, all of these can be negotiated in advance and specified in the lease contract.

For some Western countries, such as the United States, the biggest benefit of trust lease is tax avoidance, because the U.S. tax code stipulates that corporate investment can enjoy preferential income tax credit. In this kind of trust lease, the investor is the owner of the airplane and this investment is reflected on his balance sheet, thus he can enjoy the exemption of income tax according to the price of the airplane. So what the lessor is concerned about is not return on investment but tax benefits. The benefit is far larger than the return from investing 20% of the total purchasing expense of the aircraft. This is one of the reasons why aircraft and large equipment leasing businesses have leapt forward in Western countries. Statistics disclose that 60%–70% of the world's airplanes are purchased through leasing. A great number of aircraft in China's civil aviation industry were introduced into service through leasing contracts. It can be said that China's civil aviation took off on the wing of leasing. Without leasing, the scale of China's civil aviation would not be as large as it is today.

3. Sale-and-leaseback. Industrial enterprises may sometimes be in urgent need of money. When it is too late to ask for approval of state appropriation and the enterprises are reluctant to lend money, they can resort to going to leasing companies. An industrial enterprise can sell certain equipment (such as a rolling mill) which it owns to a leasing company in exchange for millions of dollars which are used to lease the equipment back by the industrial enterprise. In this way, the turnover of capital is quickened without hindering the industrial production, and the equipment can be repurchased at any time if the enterprise has sufficient money.

In addition, there is leveraged leasing, joint leasing, and sub-leasing, among other forms.

The organizational forms of enterprises in the financial leasing industry are of a great variety. Some leasing firms are funded solely or controlled by commercial banks. Since industrial users prefer leasing rather than bank loans, the leasing firms set up by commercial banks which have advantages in capital and cost create a new investment channel of surplus capital to satisfy the needs of clients. Some leasing firms are established by industrial enterprises or the circulation sector through relying on manufacturers, which aim to promote the sales of industrial products or provide specialized services. Some are independent leasing companies which can offer a large range of comprehensive services. There are also strategic financial leasing firms whose shareholders are mainly government, insurance companies, brokerage firms, investment banks, and other investment institutions. Their targets are infrastructure projects relating to civil aviation, shipping, energy, etc. They pursue a new kind of investment portfolio and investment method to secure safe and reliable long-term investment returns.

I was commissioned by the CCB to join the talks with Japan's Nomura Securities about the establishment of a joint venture called International Union Leasing Corporation in 1988. The meeting was hosted by the first general manager of the Japanese party, and I was invited as a consultant. The Japanese partner was told that when doing leasing business in China, the only choice is the middle- and small-sized enterprises which can withstand market competition while large enterprises which are under the state planning sector will absorb investment without repaying the debts. Later, I led the Japanese manager to visit Shougang Group, China Second Auto Works (now Dongfeng Motor Corporation), Wuhan Iron and Steel Group, and other large state-owned enterprises which were listed in the top 500 domestic large enterprises, which made him change his attitude towards China's large companies. This manager was very enterprising and immediately decided to conduct financial leasing business with large enterprises. During the two years when he assumed General Manager of the International Union Leasing Corporation, the business developed quickly without rent arrears. In fact, the reason why Nomura Securities participated in the financial leasing joint venture is not to undertake leasing business but to build a good relationship with large enterprises, which paves the way for its future listing recommendation business of large enterprises.

Since the 1990s, electronic commerce has been booming. It has enabled lessors to break the traditional concepts of management and service and create brand-new operation modes, such as network leasing providers, self-leasing business, cell phone rental business, and information service centers, in order to achieve a client-oriented, all-embracing, personalized, and international service mode. The operation model of leasing enterprises develops towards virtualization and intelligentization, the transaction cost is significantly reduced, and the market competition rules are restructured. Currently, the trends of the global leasing industry are displayed in the following aspects:

Specialization (the leasing proportion of specific products is substantially increased), business convergence (the boundaries between various kinds of leases are increasingly blurred), chain operation (rental chains will emerge), regionalization (leasing business shows certain regional characteristics) and popularization (small-scale community leasing networks grow in number, and personal leasing networks, online leasing agents and internet intermediaries will be developed). Network Information has eliminated the information asymmetry in the leasing business to the largest extent and greatly increased the proportion of matching or automatic pairing businesses with a significant reduction of transaction costs.

Policy Support

Europe and the United States put the leasing industry at a significant place in the national economy, and have attached great importance to the industry in legislation, taxation, insurance, and other areas by giving preferential policies of investment tax credit and accelerated depreciation, among others.

There are two lessons that are worth learning from the U.S. leasing industry: 1. The government formulates a sound regulatory system which provides a legal guarantee for the development of the rental market and effectively regulates trading activities; 2. There is a complete security system which guarantees the simplification of leasing procedure and the expansion of leasing scale and varieties. In America, leasing firms can check the credibility of enterprises or individuals at any time through banks, tax departments, and other relevant government authorities. Credit card payment reduces the risk of rent arrears that may be entailed on the leasing firms, and multiple types of services offered by insurance companies also lowers the risks to the leasing firms during the use of the leased items.

Japan is the most typical country concerning the policy support. The measures that the Japanese government takes to encourage the leasing industry include: Policy-based loans will be given to certain industries or undertakings which the government encourages or protects when they are doing leasing projects, that is 50% of total investment will be funded by the Development Bank of Japan; rental subsidies will be granted to the enterprises of government-supported industries by relevant administrative departments; compulsory credit insurance in leasing is applied to all leasing businesses and once a lessee company goes bankrupt, policy-oriented insurance companies will pay 50% of the rental loss; investment tax credit will be given to the small and medium-sized enterprises according to a certain percentage of the rental fee when they import special mechanical equipment by way of leasing.

The Development of China's Financial Leasing

China introduced financial leasing at the initial stage of the reform and opening up. At first, financial leasing was developed as a way to utilize foreign capital by the Ministry of Foreign Trade (now the Department of Foreign Trade under the Ministry of Commerce), which was solely responsible for approving and managing leasing projects. The Ministry of Foreign Trade only focused on leasing transactions and evaded financing issues. But the leasing business could hardly develop without financing activities. Later, owing to the fact that many departments got involved in the management of financial leasing and there was no special financial support or favorable policies, the leasing industry developed at a slow speed. The progress of domestic-funded leasing firms was not very smooth as well. In the latter half of 2004, the Ministry of Commerce and State Administration of Taxation collectively launched a pilot project of operating financial leasing businesses in domestic-funded enterprises. Some 24 firms from 14 provinces or cities, such as Beijing, Shanghai, and Zhejiang, jointed the pilot and enjoyed relevant preferential policies in taxation. In the following two years, the pilot enterprises made use of their advantages and actively searched for new profit growth points and risk reduction approaches. In 2006, the value of newly signed financial leasing contracts reached RMB6.57 billion with a profit of RMB135 million and a tax payment of RMB62.05 million. In the new contracts, there were not only currently mature operation models such as direct leasing, leaseback, trust lease, but also some more flexible and market-oriented models. For example, Shanghai Ronglian Finance Leasing Share Corporation signed a medical equipment leasing contract which distributed profits according to the participants' investment and connected among the lending bank, the lessee, and the lessor of three different places. This contract provided a successful experience for supporting the off-site leasing projects by banks. Beijing Zoomlion Xinxing Construction Machinery Leasing Corporation drew in insurance companies in the leasing business in order to reduce the operation risk. Changjiang Leasing Company purchased 10 aircraft via bank loans for leasing and broke the large-term monopoly of foreign enterprises in China's aviation leasing market.

Can banks get involved in leasing? Before the 1990s, banks were allowed to carry out financial leasing business, but most operations were illicit and usually engaged in the investment in the stock and real estate markets, thus accumulating high risks. Under the shock of the Asian financial crisis in 1997, the non-performing loan ratio shot up. With the hope of evading the financial tsunami, the Chinese government ordered banks to exit the financial leasing field. By then, China's financial leasing business fell to the bottom. Afterwards, regulatory authority once allowed private capital to participate in the leasing transactions in order to revive the financial leasing. In 2001, private capital dominated the financial leasing companies, but within less than two years, serious illegal operations emerged in those companies owing to mixed motives. Many leasing companies misappropriated money under the guise of financial leasing. As a result of this, the financial leasing industry which had been expecting a revival was hit with another crisis. Up until the end of 2006, there were just 12 financial leasing firms under the China Banking Regulatory Commission (CBRC). Among these enterprises, six continued operation and recorded a total net after-tax profit of RMB130 million in that year, two declared bankruptcy, two were closed for internal rectification, and two suspended business operations. From 2000 when financial leasing firms started reorganization and rectification to 2006, the CBRC has not approved any new financial leasing company.

In 2008, the CBRC promulgated the *Measures for the Administration of Finance Leasing Companies*, which was a milestone in the development of China's financial leasing industry. Prior to this, banking financial leasing was banned. In fact, there was a huge demand for financial leasing service in economic life. China's Minsheng Banking Corporation cooperated with a financial leasing company to launch a banking-leasing win-win plan through bypassing the existing regulations, which spurred an increase in the assets of leasing business to RMB10 billion. This plan was a great innovation in rejuvenating the financial leasing industry in an indirect way. After the *Measures for the Administration of Finance Leasing Companies* was announced, the bank-affiliated financial leasing business switched into the fast lane.

In 2007, the first group of banking firms, including the Industrial and Commercial Bank of China, China Construction Bank, Bank of Communications, China Minsheng Banking Corporation, China Merchants Bank, and China Development Bank, were successively approved to set up financial leasing firms. After the absence from the financial leasing market for 10 years, the banking sector resumed the responsibility of reviving the financial leasing industry. But undertakings usually develop intermittently in China. After the icebreaking action, the approval for the financial leasing firms stalled due to prudential supervision. In May 2009, the State Council gave permission to expand the pilot scope of bank-based financial leasing companies. A dozen joint-stock banks, such as Huaxia Bank, Shanghai Pudong Development Bank, Industrial Bank, and China Everbright Bank, applied to join the pilot project and the list of approved banks was not released until early 2010. According to the *China Financial Leasing Industry Report 2006–2010* from the ResearchInChina website, during the 11th Five-Year Guideline period, China's financial leasing industry witnessed exponential growth, and the total leasing fund increased by 86-fold from RMB8 billion in 2006 to RMB700 billion in 2010. In 2010, the investment in financial leasing in China exceeded RMB20 billion, the operating income registered RMB15 billion, total profit RMB4.7 billion, and net income RMB3.6 billion. Financial leasing will no doubt develop into an important service provided by banks.

At present, China's financial leasing firms face two kinds of difficulties:

First, the business staff of bank-affiliated financial leasing companies mostly come from banks, therefore the financial leasing does not develop in a specialized way since the staff can hardly get rid of their mindset of bank credit. As a matter of fact, the real professional financial leasing should focus on the leased items, understand the production process, and know the industrial value. Financial leasing separates the ownership from the use of the equipment by first letting the lessee obtain the use of the product at the expense of regular rental payments or installments and then allowing the lessee to acquire the ownership at a low price (typically the residual value) at the end of the lease term. It enables enterprises to produce with leased equipment without suffering from the pressure from the one-off capital payment. The rental business, however, is essentially a kind of financial service, and its profitability comes from the knowledge towards the industry and the leased items. If there is no professional staff, or specialized knowledge of the industry and equipment, the profitability will be limited once the clients own the upmost decision power in selecting the leased products.

Second, the leasing business is harassed by high taxes. For instance, if a domestic leasing company plans to buy an aircraft from overseas for renting to a domestic airline, the leasing company has to make a one-time payment of import tax of around 24%. For a similar business, foreign leasing companies may enjoy a very low or even zero tariff. This kind of tax makes domestic leasing companies less competitive in rental quotes.

According to the report of "Expansion of Financial Leasing" in *Caijing Magazine* (Issue No. 10, 2010), the CBRC has to approve the establishment of project companies by the financial leasing firms under the Industrial and Commercial Bank of China, China Construction Bank, and China Minsheng Banking Corporation in bonded areas as the finance and taxation departments were reluctant to lower tariffs. This is a flexible method which indirectly solves the high taxes by amortizing the originally one-off taxes and dues over the whole lease term when the leasing firms import large pieces of equipment like aircraft. In foreign countries, investment banks avail themselves of loopholes in the laws and regulations to create marginal benefit. In China, however, it is the government departments which handicap the development of the leasing industry, so the CBRC has to take the lead to exploit the legal loopholes in taxation. It is really a creative step taken by the Chinese people in expanding the financial leasing business.

7

Chapter

Reorganization and Debt-For-Equity Swaps of Distressed Enterprises

Prologue: A Pair of Ice Skates

In 1996, Professor Wang Weiguo from China University of Political Science and Law told us a story:

On the lake of a small town in Pennsylvania, a little boy called Hans was skating in a pair of beautiful new skates. Suddenly, the boy skated on thin ice and fell into the water. Another little boy who was there with Hans immediately jumped into the water to rescue Hans. The local town mayor praised the boy for his bravery and sacrifice. The boy bluntly answered back: "I do not understand why you are talking about courage; the truth is that I had to save Hans simply because he was wearing my new designer ice skates!"

Professor Wang recounted this story in a meeting about corporate bankruptcy and reorganization in Tianjin. Then, he introduced the idea that Western countries had bankruptcy laws, but corporate bankruptcies and instances of insolvency would generate social repercussions and this was not good for creditors. As a result, corporate bankruptcy law underwent a revolution in the United States in the 1970s, and one of the core concepts was the balancing of the interests of creditors and debtors.

It was during the United States congressional hearings on the reform of bankruptcy law that Peter Coogan advocated the participation of creditors in the restructuring of distressed companies, and then he told the above story. Coogan explained that he and all the other creditors were like the brave boy who had to save debtors in order to save his loans, because the debtors were "wearing the ice skates" of the creditors!

In 1996, I represented China Construction Bank (CCB) in formulating a bankruptcy reconciliation and reorganization plan for Xinghuo Pulp Mill in Shanghai. When Hua Jianming, then Vice Mayor of Shanghai, asked me why the CCB undertook the bankruptcy reconciliation and reorganization of Xinhuo, I told him the same story and concluded my answer by saying "Because Xinhuo Pulp Mill was wearing my ice skates!"

In fact, the bankruptcy and reorganization of distressed enterprises should be a part of capital culture.

The Revolution in Bankruptcy Law in Western Countries: Finding A Way Out from Reorganization

In the market economy, it is right that when capitalists do business, they make use of own capital to make profits and repay debts after borrowing others' money. If the enterprise cannot pay off its debts and is trapped in insolvency, it has to go bankrupt and be put into liquidation. Therefore, Western countries have long established bankruptcy laws to regulate the bankruptcy liquidation of distressed enterprises.

Bankruptcy liquidation, however, is a backward concept in Western countries. Although it can compensate creditors for a portion of interests, the aftereffects of bankruptcy such as unemployment of staff will entail high social costs and social unrests. Besides, these aftereffects which usually last for a long time will also create huge losses to creditors. Consequently, since the 1970s, Western countries launched a revolution in bankruptcy law and intended to search for a solution from reorganization.

The United States set about studying the bankruptcy law after 1970 and released the famous Brookings Report[1] in 1971. The government enacted the new *Bankruptcy Code* in 1978, and the newly added Chapter 11 of corporate reorganization stipulated that after an insolvent enterprise files its petition in the bankruptcy court, the enterprises can develop a plan of reorganization to be approved by the court under the permission of creditors. Thereafter, the trend of corporate reorganization swept Europe and America. In 1986, the United Kingdom formulated the *Insolvency Act* which provided that the *Company Directors Disqualification Act* and *The Insolvency Rules* were no longer applicable to enterprises on the verge of bankruptcy, and these enterprises had to adopt reorganization schemes. This act impacted the Commonwealth countries of Australia, Canada, and Ireland who had successively amended and enacted their bankruptcy laws or corporate laws in the 1990s. France is a country which has undergone a thorough reform of bankruptcy law. In 1985, France enacted *Relative Au Redressement Et À La Liquidation Judiciaires Des Entreprises* (Judicial Reorganization and Liquidation of Enterprises) and also set up alert procedures and reconciliation and liquidation procedures. Some people argued that France stood in front of all other countries in the bankruptcy law reform by representing a comparatively progressive legal concept.

There are theoretical bases for implementing corporate reorganization rather than bankruptcy liquidation for distressed enterprises:

1. Going-concern value theory. The theory admits that the value of an on-going business is higher than that of a liquidated company. If the enterprise operates well through reorganization, it will be sold at a better price than through bankruptcy liquidation. That is to say, it is wiser to make money by raising a horse to draw wagons than killing it and selling the horsemeat.

2. Theory of common interests between creditors and debtors. Only when creditors assist debtors in corporate restructuring, the enterprises of the debtors can be sold at a good price, and thus the debt repayment rate will be raised. Just as the aforementioned story has shown, the other little boy had to save the life of Hans because Hans was wearing the other boy's ice stakes!
3. Social interest theory. Corporate reorganization will reduce the asset loss, the number of laid-off workers and the chain bankruptcy of related companies, thus causing less social repercussions. Judging rationally from the perspective of overall social benefit, reorganization is beneficial to the conservation and effective use of resources of the whole society.

The advocacy of reorganization by Western countries in their bankruptcy laws is in essence full recognition of creditors' interests. One of the important measures in corporate reorganization is to allow bank creditors to carry out debt-for-equity swaps in struggling companies. A debt-for-equity swap is different from corporate bankruptcy in that creditors prefer to recoup losses by acting as shareholders than passively bear the risk of bad debt losses. This is a flexible exchange between debt and equity. The debt-for-equity swap has reshaped the capital formation mechanism and is unique in the following aspects: First, creditors are transferred into being the owners of enterprises; second, unpayable debts are changed into the capital of enterprises; third, once depressed enterprises own this converted capital, they are transformed from insolvent debtors into active operators with corresponding debt-bearing capacity and new financial power, and are thus able to borrow new loans from banks.

Credit Loans as Equity Shares

Similarly, banks in Western European countries such as France, promote "share loans," which redeem credit loans as equity shares. The operation mode of this kind of loan resembles that of preferred stocks, that is, the injection of capital into distressed companies and then the cultivation of marginal benefits from the revival of the enterprises. In 1981 when doing research in France, I learned that when some small-sized enterprises got trapped in financial difficulties, they welcomed the loans as shares and were unwilling to be taken over and reorganized. The characteristics of share loans were as follows:

1. The share loans are regarded as shares and once the borrowing enterprises file for bankruptcy, the loans will be settled before the shareholders' equity but after all the outstanding debts.

2. It is in nature a loan rather than a real share, because it has to be repaid at the end.
3. With share loans, the borrowing enterprises will increase their debt-bearing capacity and thus regain loan eligibility.
4. The interest rate of share loans is different from that of other loans. At first, the rate is very low or even zero and when the operation of the borrowing enterprise picks up, higher marginal benefits will be given to the bank as a special reward for bearing the risk.

Thanks to these merits, share loans may well be a way to rescue the heavily indebted non-public or listed companies.

Bankruptcy Boom: The Frustration in Helping Out Distressed State-Owned Enterprises

China has implemented a planned economy for a long time, and the state-owned enterprises are funded by the state. Therefore, once these enterprises are established, they should never be afraid of going bankrupt. Due to the long-term avoidance of talking about capital, and the lack of a capital culture, China is also absent from the culture of corporate bankruptcy and restructuring. During China's economic transition to a market-oriented economy in the 1990s, local governments allowed their local state-enterprises to repudiate the debts in a creative way in consideration of local interests. There was a prevailing trend of bankruptcy and debt repudiation in China roughly between 1993 and 1995, which was a shock to the economy then, especially to the relationship between banks and enterprises.

At first, a large general knitting factory in southwest China got into a predicament of excessive debts in 1993 and thus the factory had to announce bankruptcy by advocating "public tendering, conditional auction" in order to repudiate its debts to banks and leasing companies. Some people learned a lesson from this practice and realized that bankruptcy was the best way to disown debts. Consequently, a large number of bankrupt companies emerged in many cities. Since then, bankruptcy became the prevailing practice, for instance, there was the partial transformation of Liaoyuan Woolen Mill in Liaoning Province, the fraudulent bankruptcy of Yuncheng Detergent Factory in Shanxi Province, and the avoidance of debts by leasing of Qianxi County Fertilizer Plant in Guizhou Province. For a time, bankruptcy was widespread and was, in reality, a strategy for troubled state-owned enterprises to dodge debts. The most typical practice was partial transformation, that is, to detach the departments of profitable products from the rest of the enterprises to form one or several individual new legal entities which will be transferred, rented, contracted to others or even independent in order to fend off the debts of the original enterprise. On the other hand, the original enterprise continued operation with the rest of the departments and assumed the outstanding bank debts. It seems that the indebted enterprises try to survive without evading their debts while banks permit the enterprises' partial transformation without writing off the debts, but in reality the debts will never be repaid. This partial transformation is also called an "escape-by-crafty-scheme" strategy or an "unshelling operation."

"Partial transformation" or an "unshelling operation" are pleasant terms for this process but the sad truth is that this practice allows distressed enterprises to repudiate their debts or loans at the expense of banks. The climax of the bankruptcies was the case reported by *Financial News* in the headline on December 14, 1995 — "The bankruptcy of Wuhan Native Produce Company caused a loan loss of RMB80 million to Bank of China." Afterwards, foreign trade enterprises poured into Wuhan from other areas in the hopes of emulating that success, and thus bankruptcy and debt defaults reached a peak. At that time, several state-owned large banks discussed the countermeasures and decided to implement financial sanctions on Wuhan by declaring it a "high risk" city. The relationship between banks and enterprises became very tense. *Financial News* published a signed article named "The bankruptcy of foreign trade enterprises should slow down," but in fact, the foreign trade industry was not the only industry that should decelerate the speed of bankruptcy. At last, this unhealthy trend of bankruptcy was curbed as higher government authorities intervened by encouraging mergers, standardizing bankruptcy procedures, and clarifying the guidelines of "more mergers and less bankruptcies."

The root cause for the bankruptcies in China's state-owned enterprises was due to capital, rather than property rights. More importantly, after the replacement of state appropriation by bank loans in the 1980s, the policies of acquiring all circulating funds through credit loans and financing through fiscal credit were also implemented, and in this way, several budgetary allocations were changed into repayable loans. Accordingly, when local governments ran new projects or established new companies, the state took out no or little money. Since the debt-to-equity ratio can be as high as 98%, enterprises would hardly withstand risks. The negative result is: When setting up a new enterprise, local governments will risk the money of banks; when the enterprise runs into difficulties in operation, the local governments will allow the troubled enterprise to default on debts through bankruptcy. The emergence of the bankruptcy boom is a serious outcome of a series of systematic defects. The significant restrictive function of the corporate capital fund system here can be seen. If the state does not explicitly demand state-owned enterprises to refill their capital within a fixed period but allows the absurd practice of operating without equity and the resulting bankruptcies to continue, the ultimate result will be bank failures.

Meanwhile, this bankruptcy boom burdened the state-owned banks with the policy-based historical debts left over from the planned economic system, including foreign trade policy-related longstanding debts, old debts from decision-making mistakes of capital construction and technical reform, and the old accounts of loans for national stability and unity, which ought to be borne by local finance or shared among central and local governments. It is actually to let the commercial banks under the socialist market economy pay the bills of the past planned economy.

The bankruptcy boom reflects a failure in China's corporate reform and will have a serious impact on the relationship between banks and companies. This trend occurs when local enterprises try to repudiate their debts owed to the state banks, and it is essentially a twisted reflection of local finance directing financial pressure to central finance under the old economic system.

The rise of this bankruptcy boom occurred for the following four reasons:

1. Severely inadequate capital of state-owned enterprises. In Western countries, the proportion of own capital in industrial enterprises usually accounts for around 30% of total operating capital and the own capital will be increased along with the development of business to maintain the average debt ratio at 50%–60%. After the founding of new China, state-owned enterprises, despite avoiding talking about capital, had plenty of capital from the 1950s until the mid-1980s. In 1980, the average debt ratio of enterprises was just 18% and own capital occupied 82% of the total working capital, namely the ratio of equity to debt was roughly 8:2. In 1988, the Chinese government carried out its trial *Bankruptcy Law* which was formulated based on the fact that enterprises owned sufficient capital. However, when the policy of the replacement of state appropriation by repayable loans was fully implemented in 1985, newly-built state-owned enterprises suffered a severe shortage of capital with a high debt-to-equity ratio. Things were worse for local enterprises. Especially after the replacement of appropriations by loan, local governments contributed no or little capital to project construction or enterprise operation, and thus these local enterprises lost their risk resistance capacity. Local governments risked the

banks' money to fund new projects of enterprises and allowed these distressed enterprises to default on debts by filing for bankruptcy. These were the serious consequences of the systematic deficits in the policies of the replacement of state appropriation by loans in capital construction, the acquisition of all circulating funds through credits, and the implementation of fiscal credit. From here, we can see the important restrictive role of the corporate capital fund. (The reasons why China's state-owned enterprises got into financial troubles will be detailed in the next section.)

2. The *Bankruptcy Law* (refers to the trial *Bankruptcy Law* enacted in 1988) left some loopholes to be exploited later on. The socialist market economy, same as all the other market economies of socialized mass production, should expose enterprises to market competitions. It is impossible to only start new businesses without shutting down uncompetitive ones. To allow the bankruptcy of some insolvent company is evitable in a market economy, so it does not need to be worried about. But the question is who will bear the loss? Bankruptcy, by definition, is the state in which the shareholders' capital cannot pay off the enterprise's debts and the purpose of going bankrupt is to repay debts. However, the reality is that the policies of replacing appropriation with loans in capital construction and acquiring all circulating funds through credits and the trend of substituting credit loans for local financial allocation enables some state-owned enterprises to operate on borrowings under the circumstances of insufficient capital or even zero own capital. As a result, bankruptcy at that time means to redirect the loss to creditors (i.e. banks), which is unfair. The *Bankruptcy Law* stipulates that the bearers of decision-making mistakes and the competent authorities of shareholders are included in the bankruptcy liquidation group while banks as creditors are excluded from the group. The fact that the *Bankruptcy Law* lacks both effective protection for creditors and terms allowing creditors to perform receivership or trusteeship of the insolvent enterprises leaves loopholes for some local authorities and enterprises to take advantage of. Besides, if the investment of a new project exceeds RMB200 million, the project in general should seek for approval from the State Council; so how could the bankruptcy of a large enterprise with a liability of RMB800 million be permitted by the local Industrial Development Bureau of a big city instead of the state? Is this not unreasonable?

The causes for enterprises going bankrupt are various: The bankruptcy of some enterprises is owed to wrong decisions and investment failures, that is to say, as soon as the wrongly-decided project is put into production, losses will be created; some bankruptcies are the results of the rash decisions of bureaucrats, such as to demand that the entire textile industry be equipped with more than 10 million spindles; some bankruptcies are subject to market changes which may cause a short-term investment to become a long-term one; some enterprises suffer from belated technical reforms and since backward technology and products give rise to long-term loss, these enterprises become insolvent; others declare bankruptcy also because of poor management. Above all, the high debt-to-equity ratio after the replacement of state appropriation by bank loans makes enterprises become more vulnerable to bankruptcy. If this situation continues and the state-owned enterprises still do not replenish their own capital, the ultimate result will be the bankruptcy of banks.

3. There is, however, an absence of due respect to bank creditors in the *Bankruptcy Law*. The members of the bankruptcy liquidation group could include, according to the *Bankruptcy Law*, competent authorities of the bankrupt enterprise, representatives from financial departments and other supervisors of the planned economy with bank creditors being left out. It indicates that the formulation of laws and regulations is still strongly influenced by the old ideas of the planned economic system. Since all these members are either shareholders of the insolvent enterprises or bearers of decision-making mistakes, how would we ensure that the insolvency process was objective, reasonable, and fair if these people take charge of liquidation, appraisal, and the disposition and distribution of bankruptcy property? How could we expect them to not harm the interests of banks, the largest creditors?

Why does not the *Bankruptcy Law* protect creditors in its terms? A compiler of the *Bankruptcy Law* said: "We think bankruptcy is, naturally, to force debtors to repay the money of creditors, and how could we know that debtors should divert their losses to banks by taking advantage of the *Bankruptcy Law*? Foreign enterprises find loopholes in laws to evade taxes while China's local governments use legal loopholes to repudiate the debts to state banks. Who says Chinese people are not creative?"

4. Bankruptcy which should be a market behavior now becomes an administrative act of local governments. Some cities point out that the whole process of bankruptcy from the drawing up of the list of distressed enterprises, formulation of bankruptcy plans, property liquidations, to auction and assets restructuring is solely decided by local government departments (Economic Commission, or Restructuring Commission). The process is, thus, by no means

transparent, and there is no involvement of intermediary organizations, which will give rise to a lot of unjust losses. Some local governments monopolize the development of bankruptcy plans by excluding banks and creditors. Certain local governments even request banks in advance to neither question the decisions of bankruptcy courts nor affix legal liabilities on guarantors. Some courts yield to the power of local governments by declaring that "this decision is final," which means the decision cannot be overturned. It is actually a conspiracy between courts and local governments against banks.

In 1993, a large knitting factory in southwest China declared bankruptcy and was sold at a low price to an overseas company through the so-called "public tendering, conditional auction." Later, a scandal was reported that the Deputy Mayor who was in charge of this bankruptcy had accepted bribes. Is that a coincidence? Certainly not in this case. Since corporate bankruptcy is regarded as a mere government behavior and there is no transparency in the bankruptcy process, it is hard to prevent some people from reaping some profits through illegal deals. Thus, if the bankruptcy process remains opaque and banks as the largest creditors still have no right to file a petition with the bankruptcy court for the reorganization, trusteeship, and takeover of the insolvent enterprises, how could the interests of creditors be protected? And how would the socialist market economy be developed?

The Over-Indebtedness of State-Owned Enterprises Rooted in the Misallocation between Equity and Debt

Why did Chinese enterprises get into deep debt during the seventh and eighth five-year plans?

The over-indebtedness of state-owned enterprises is mainly reflected in the insufficient capital and the over-reliance on banking lending of enterprises. In essence, it is the result of a new systematic capital misallocation and deficiency created after the replacement of state appropriation by repayable loans. It reverses the places of borrowed capital and own capital in the capital formation mechanism. To understand this problem, I have made special investigations in the 1990s and found that this systematic capital misallocation and deficiency resulting from the excessive debts of enterprises has two major features.

1. The misallocation between capital and loans, namely, the money which should be allocated for capital funds is lent out as bank loans. There are roughly four

kinds of enterprises which suffer from capital shortage: First, enterprises whose state funding for capital construction is replaced by repayable loans; second, enterprises which are established based on bank loans; third, enterprises which are involved in foreign-financed projects, namely, utilizing foreign government loans or export credits; fourth, enterprises which are set up on the basis of financial credit. These four kinds of companies, due to a lack of capital funds, operate on borrowings and are short of stable operating funds that can be occupied for a long time without being repaid. Consequently, as soon as projects are completed and put into production, the enterprises are trapped in long-term debt. The debt tension will never be gotten rid of, if the capital fund is not refilled. This systematic capital misallocation and deficiency actually reflects the reversed relationships between equity and debts in the capital formation mechanism, which is an inborn defect in the mechanism.

2. There are a series of funding gaps which have occupied the capital borrowed or diverted from other sources in state-owned enterprises, and these gaps are also known as "capital deficiencies." According to my investigations, there are mainly 10 causes of capital deficiencies: 1. Local governments use their self-financed funds to attract projects but these funds are hardly put into place; 2. Investment omissions in the project plan will lead to capital gaps; 3. The costs of construction exceed the budget; 4. The planned investment takes no account of the interest incurred during construction; 5. The fluctuations of exchange rates, especially the strong appreciation of the Yen, cause the Yen-denominated debts and other foreign currency-denominated debts to create a severe deficiency in capital; 6. More money is needed to repay loans when the repayment of loans before tax is changed into after-tax loan repayment; 7. The cost of trial production is omitted or underestimated in the budget; 8. The credit quota is not allocated for working capital; 9. Construction rework will also increase the demand for capital; 10. Poor management brings about cost overruns.

Additionally, capital deficiencies may also result from the increase of production costs due to the rising price of raw materials and a lack of credit quota for working capital loans, among other things. In addition to the above factors, decision failures and market changes also drag many enterprises into financial plight in terms of capital turnover.

Overall, the capital tension of enterprises at that time is an outcome of systematic capital misallocation and deficiency. The capital which should be appropriated by the government can only be obtained through bank loans, while other capital which ought to be received from loans has to be raised through other financing channels. Although the money is spent, it is not used for its original purposes, so it is necessary to correct the capital misallocation and deficiency in capital reserves.

The systematic capital shortage will bring about four serious consequences.

1. Enterprises lack stable operating capital and thus are vulnerable to risks.
2. There are a great many funding gaps which will be compensated by diverting the money earmarked for other purposes, and therefore chain debts will be generated. In a considerable number of enterprises, the financial deficit accounts for 15%–20% of the total operating fund. This phenomenon exists, more or less, in almost all the enterprises which rely on the state to grant loans for project construction, so it reflects a flaw in the system. The root problem does not lie in the financial gaps, but the fact that no one promises to expand financing channels. Enterprises dare not ask for more money from higher authorities although the money is necessary for production and construction. Consequently, these enterprises have to resort to makeshift solutions: To use the money for trial production to compensate for construction overruns; apply for working capital loans to eliminate exchange-rate spreads; and delay the repayment of loans for raw materials and semi-manufactured goods to pay back bank interest. In this way, those enterprises are trapped in endless chain debts. People often criticize the slack rules of debt settlement. In reality, since there are some unfilled substantial financing gaps, the lax rules of settlement ferment and amplify these gaps into chain debts after many arrears. And the above-mentioned unpromised funding gaps are the real cause for the financial strain of enterprises. Imagine if a normal enterprise from the very beginning of corporate system design lacked stable operating funds, which accounted for 20%–30% of total working capital and can be occupied for a long time without being repaid, and an unpromised funding gap of 15%–20% of total capital once the enterprise was put into production. It has to repay its debts and divert money earmarked for other purposes to fill this financing gap. So how could the enterprise avoid chain debts?
3. Enterprises operate with insufficient own capital and possess no debt paying ability owing to an extremely high debt-to-equity ratio.
4. Once enterprises suffer from financial losses or fail to repay debts in a timely way, banks will stop lending money to the enterprises, which will in turn

generate a credit crisis. It should also be mentioned that the relationship between enterprises and banks is twisted in the case of over-indebtedness. Knowing that an enterprise fails to make debt repayments, the bank intentionally avoids the enterprise in case it will borrow new loans. The enterprise also feels embarrassed about being unable to repay the loans of the bank, so it has to turn away from the bank and resort to other banks to raise loans. Since similar situations will repeatedly happen, enterprises and banks are increasingly alienated from each other.

We call it systematic capital misallocation and deficiency because the government agreed to allow enterprises to use pre-tax profits to repay loans at the initial stage of the replacement of state appropriation by repayable loans. Later, when banks issued loans and financial credit on the basis of savings, they followed the regulations of the policy to require pre-tax repayment. The financial department, however, changed the regulations by replacing pre-tax repayment with after-tax repayment in 1992 in view of the heavy losses of fiscal revenue caused by the pre-tax repayment. This change aggregated the financial burden of state-owned enterprises which fell into an inextricable systematic pitfall.

In 2004, Zhou Xiaochuan, President of the People's Bank of China, made an analysis about the reasons for huge non-performing assets of China's banks. He believed that nearly 30% of the non-performing assets were created by poor decisions of local governments who left over massive toxic assets when pushing forward economic development; another 30% was owing to poor management of state-owned enterprises; 20% was attributed to banks' own factors; the remaining 20% was caused by defects in laws and regulations and economic restructuring.

Debt-For-Equity Swap: An Innovation in China's Capital Formation Mechanism

The systematic defect of the misplacement between debt and equity in the capital formation mechanism after the replacement of appropriation by loans makes state-owned enterprises fall into over-indebtedness, and the fundamental solution is to swap debt for equity. The debt-for-equity swap in China is a good example of the innovation in capital formation mechanism.

In 1995, 18 industrial cities participated in the pilot project of the optimization of capital structure. At that time, due to the long-term implementation of replacing state appropriation with bank loans, the ratio of equity to debt in state-owned enterprises was 16.7:83.3 (lower than 2:8), which signified a full-blown crisis of over-indebtedness. It was estimated that to lower the debt ratio by 20%, another RMB950 billion state capital would be needed.

Soon afterwards, the pilot of optimizing capital structure was expanded to over 100 industrial cities. The Chinese government issued some official documents to help the distressed enterprises to overcome difficulties by encouraging mergers and acquisitions, standardizing bankruptcy procedures, suspending repayment of loans and interest or reducing overdue interest, but a debt-for-equity swap was not mentioned. Besides, various misunderstandings caused senior government officials to adopt a bitterly critical and prohibitive attitude towards several pilot cases of debt-for-equity swaps in banks.

In September 1995, China International Capital Corporation Limited (CICC) was established. At that time, Wang Qishan was both President of CCB and Chairman of CICC, and Edwin Lin and Harrison Young were the first and the second presidents of the company. As the company's Senior Consultant, I was invited to work with the two vice-presidents, Fang Fenglei and Bi Mingjian, on the investigation of the over-indebted Xinhuo Pulp Mill in Shanghai. We prepared a plan of bankruptcy, reconciliation, and restructuring, and tried to help the company through a substitution of bankruptcy liquidation with debt-for-equity swaps. This was proposed namely by asking the creditor bank to entrust the CICC to temporarily hold shares of the distressed company. This was an innovation which won the attention and support from the State Economic and Trade Commission, the Central Bank, the Shanghai Municipal Government, and other authorities. We had placed high expectations on the popularization of "Xinhuo restructuring mode," but since high-level government officials were keen on encouraging mergers and standardizing bankruptcy, this pilot program (which could serve as a supplement to the mergers and bankruptcies in the state-owned enterprises reform) came under heavy criticism and exclusion, and was prohibited from being imitated and promoted.

However, the government documents of encouraging mergers and standardizing bankruptcies, as well as other relief measures, were not that effective. The over-indebtedness was not fundamentally changed due to the fact that a large number of enterprises with high debt-to-equity ratios failed to replenish their own capital. Until 1998, under the pressures from the impact of the Asian financial crisis and the severe over-indebtedness of domestic state-owned enterprises, the state government set a time limit of three years to overcome the difficulties of large- and medium-sized state-owned enterprises and made an important decision to fundamentally solve the excessive debts. The government decided to establish four asset management companies in the second half of 1999 and applied debt-for-equity swaps to a certain portion of large- and medium-sized state-owned enterprises which defaulted on loans of state-owned commercial banks. It was encouraging that the government policy of a debt-for-equity swap basically accepted the experience and the major principles of the "Xinhuo restructuring scheme."

The greatest merit of a debt-for-equity swap was to end the 15-year long over-indebtedness of state-owned enterprises and correct the reversed roles of debt and equity since the implementation of replacing state allocation with bank loans. It was, in fact, the complete denial and final settlement of China's 40-year avoidance of capital.

Through this debt-for-equity swap, the overdue bank loans (i.e., non-performing loans) of RMB460 billion by state-owned enterprises were converted into these enterprises' shares held by the assets management companies. The greatest innovation of the debt-for-equity swap was to transfer the bad loans into the equity of the indebted enterprises. After the swap, the rights of creditors were transferred into stock rights and the enterprises reduced their debts while increasing their capital. The more magic function of the debt-for-equity swap was to not only solve the excessive debts of enterprises but also optimize the capital structure of the enterprises. As a consequence, those financially distressed enterprises gained a debt-paying ability of RMB460 billion, and this method became an effective means to boost bank loans and ease inflation at that time.

The case of a debt-for-equity swap vividly illustrates that if you put the same amount of money into equity instead of debt, its contributions to economy and finance will be totally different. This is an impressive lesson of capital culture for a large number of government officials, business men, as well as economic and financial professionals.

If the practice of debt-for-equity swap has any deficiency it is that this practice ought to be a vigorous measure for investment banks to dilute non-performing loans instead of a stiff administrative act promoted by issuing official documents by the government departments. People know more about the subservient bureaucratic style of work rather than the customer-tailored intelligence service and financial innovation provided by investment bankers. It was rumored that on each flight to Beijing, there would be at least one passenger asking for approval from the central government ministries for a debt-for-equity swap, and this might not be just hyperbole.

Besides, the policy of debt-for-equity swap came out four years after the policy of mergers and bankruptcy in state-owned enterprises reform. As a result, the financial power of some competitive enterprises without affluent capital was reduced once they increased their debt-to-equity ratios by annexing disadvantaged enterprises. If the pilot scheme of Shanghai Xinhuo Pulp Mill had been promoted in 1996 (which would have brought forward the implementation of a debt-for-equity swap by four or five years) the achievements of state-owned enterprises reform would now be more significant with mergers as the supporting measure. Still, the implementation of the debt-for-equity swap policy was a great achievement overall and, in 2001, Prime Minister Zhu Rongji rightly declared a victory in the three-year relief plan for state-owned enterprises in the *Report on the Work of the Government*.

Notes

Preface

1. Marx, "Inquiry into How It Is Possible for the Annual Profit and Wages to Buy the Annual Commodities, Which Besides Profit and Wages Also Contain Constant Capital," Chap. 3 in *Theories of Surplus Value,* Vol.4 of *Das Kapital.*
2. Engels, *Anti-Dühring,* Vol. 3 of *Marx and Engels Collected Works.*
3. Jiang Zemin, *16th Party Congress Report.*
4. Hu Jintao, *17th Party Congress Report.*
5. Marx, "The Expansion of the Market Does Not Keep in Step with the Expansion of Production. The Ricardian Conception That an Unlimited Expansion of Consumption and of the Internal Market Is Possible," Section 13 in "Ricardo's Theory of Accumulation and a Critique of it," Chap. 17 in *Theories of Surplus Value,* Vol.4 of *Das Kapital.*
6. Marx, "Credit and Fictitious Capital," Chap. 25 in *The Process of Capitalist Production as a Whole,* Vol. 3 of *Das Kapital.*
7. Marx, "Letter from Marx to Nikolai Danielson in St. Petersburg (April 10, 1879)," *Marx and Engels Correspondence 1879.*
8. Marx, "The Role of Credit in Capitalist Production," Chap 27 in *The Process of Capitalist Production as a Whole,* Vol. 3 in *Das Kapital.*
9. In preparation of next year's expenditure budget, the previous year's actual expenditure is regarded as a premise or base, and by taking into account the possible growth factors of the next year, the government would calculate the budget of the next year.
10. Chen Yun, "Construction Scale Should Comply With National Power."
11. Zhao Xiao, "What Kind of Macroeconomic Control Does China Need."
12. Qian Yingyi, Bai Chongen, and Xie Changtai, "The Return to Capital in China," 61–102.
13. Sheng Songcheng, "The Implication and Practical Significance of Aggregate Social Financing."
14. Property income refers to the capital gains from bank deposits, securities, real estate, automobiles and collection.
15. Jones, "Obama Talks about Financial Regulations."
16. Associated Press, "Wall Street Will Play Less Dominant Role."
17. Dow Jones Newswires, "Greenspan Repeats His Opposition to More Regulation of Derivatives."
18. Ibid.
19. Greenspan, "We Need a Better Cushion against Risk."
20. Zuckerman, "Greenspan Shocked at Failure of Free Markets."
21. Greenspan, "We Need a Better Cushion against Risk."
22. China Securities News, "Liu Mingkang Talked about Financial Innovation and Warned Banks with Three 'Resolute Oppositions'."
23. Three-anti refers to: To combat corruption, waste, and bureaucratism; Five-anti refers to: To fight bribery, tax evasion, cheating in labor or materials, theft of government property, and stealing of state economic intelligence.

24. Socialist industrialization and socialist transformation of agriculture, handicrafts and capitalist industry.
25. To achieve socialism, the government adopted a policy of redemption by steps in nationalizing means of production privately owned by the bourgeoisie. After the conversion of private enterprises into joint state-private management by whole trades, redemption has taken the form of payment of a fixed rate of interest, i.e., for a certain period the state pays through the special companies for whole trades, a fixed rate of interest on their investment to the capitalists. (Liu Shaoqi, *The Political Report of the Central Committee of the CPC to the Eighth National Congress of the CPC*, September 15, 1956, http://www.marxists.org/subject/china/documents/cpc/8th_congress.htm)
26. Deng Xiaoping, "We Shall Draw on Historical Experience."
27. Deng Xiaoping, "We Shall Concentrate on Economic Development."
28. Deng Xiaoping, "We Shall Draw on Historical Experience."
29. Deng Xiaoping, "We Are Taking an Entirely New Endeavor."
30. Marx, "Position of the Communists in Relation to the Various Existing Opposition Parties," Chap. 4 in *Manifesto of the Communist Party*.

Chapter 1

1. Marx, "The Expansion of the Market Does Not Keep in Step with the Expansion of Production. The Ricardian Conception That an Unlimited Expansion of Consumption and of the Internal Market Is Possible," Section 13 in "Ricardo's Theory of Accumulation and a Critique of it," Chap. 17 in *Theories of Surplus Value*, Vol.4 of *Das Kapital*.
2. Marx, "Pre-Capitalist Relationships," Chap. 36 in *The Process of Capitalist Production as a Whole*, Vol.3 of *Das Kapital*.
3. Marx mentioned that the sinking fund is also a fund for accumulation in Part 3, Chapter 19, Section 12 in *Theories of Surplus Value*. He also discussed the issue in letters to Engels dated August 20, 1862, and August 24, 1867.

Chapter 2

1. Marx, "Contradictions in the General Formula of Capital," Chap.5 in *The Process of Circulation of Capital*, Vol. 1 of *Das Kapital*.
2. Marx, "Interest-Bearing Capital," Chap. 21 in *The Process of Capitalist Production as a Whole*, Vol.3 of *Das Kapital*.
3. Marx and Engels, "Bourgeois and Proletarians," Chap. 1 in *The Communist Manifesto*.
4. Engels, preface to *The Process of Circulation of Capital*, Vol. 2 of *Das Kapital*.
5. Marx, "Inquiry into How It Is Possible for the Annual Profit and Wages to Buy the Annual Commodities, Which Besides Profit and Wages Also Contain Constant Capital," Chap. 3 in *Theories of Surplus Value*, Vol.4 of *Das Kapital*.
6. Marx, "Genesis of the Industrial Capitalist," Chap. 31 in *The Process of Production of Capital*, Vol. 1 of *Das Kapital*.
7. Marx and Engels, "Bourgeois and Proletarians," Chap. 1 in *The Communist Manifesto*.
8. Zhou Youguang, "Looking Back on the Capitalist Age," 23–31.
9. Marx, *Critique of the Gotha Program*, 9.
10. Engels, *Anti-Dühring*, 350, 340, 341.
11. Marx, "The Role of Credit in Capitalist Production," Chap. 27 in *The Process of Capitalist Production as a Whole*, Vol.3 of *Das Kapital*, 497–498.

Chapter 3

1. Marx, "The General Law of Capitalist Accumulation," Chap. 25 in *The Process of Production of Capital,* Vol. 1 of *Das Kapital.*
2. Marx, "Letter from Marx to Nikolai Danielson in St. Petersburg (April 10, 1879)," *Marx and Engels Correspondence 1879.*
3. Marx, "Credit and Fictitious Capital," Chap. 25 in *The Process of Capitalist Production as a Whole,* Vol. 3 of *Das Kapital.*
4. Deng Xiaoping, *Selected Works of Deng Xiaoping,* Vol.3, 373.
5. Mao Zedong, "Refute Right Deviationist Views That Depart from the General Line," *Selected Works of Mao Tse-tung,* Vol. 5.
6. Marx, "The Role of Credit in Capitalist Production," Chap. 27 in *The Process of Capitalist Production as a Whole,* Vol.3 of *Das Kapital.*
7. Marx, "Circulation Costs," in "Section Two: The Circulation Process of Capital, The Chapter On Capital," *The Grundrisse;*
   Vitaly Vygodsky, "How 'Capital' took shape," Chap. 8 in *The Story of a Great Discovery;*
8. Marx, "The Role of Credit in Capitalist Production," Chap. 27 in *The Process of Capitalist Production as a Whole,* Vol.3 of *Das Kapital.*
   Editor's notes: "Society" and "Social," in the original German are "Gesellschaft" and "Gesellschaftlich," which also mean "Company" and "Company's."
9. Marx, "The General Law of Capitalist Accumulation," Chap. 25 in *The Process of Production of Capital,* Vol. 1 of *Das Kapital.*
10. Marx, "Circulation Costs," in "Section Two: The Circulation Process of Capital, The Chapter on Capital," *The Grundrisse.*
11. Marx, "The General Law of Capitalist Accumulation," Chap. 25 in *The Process of Production of Capital,* Vol. 1 of *Das Kapital.*
12. Marx, "Letter from Marx to Nikolai Danielson in St. Petersburg (April 10, 1879)," *Marx and Engels Correspondence 1879.*
13. Marx, "Circulation Costs," in "Section Two: The Circulation Process of Capital, The Chapter on Capital," *The Grundrisse.*
14. Marx, "The Time of Production," Chap. 13 in *The Process of Circulation of Capital,* Vol. 2 of *Das Kapital.*
15. Marx, "Co-operation," Chap. 13 in *The Process of Production of Capital,* Vol. 1 of *Das Kapital.*
16. Marx, "Competition (continued)," in "Section Two: The Circulation Process of Capital, The Chapter on Capital," *The Grundrisse.*
17. Marx, "The Role of Credit in Capitalist Production," Chap. 27 in *The Process of Capitalist Production as a Whole,* Vol. 3 of *Das Kapital.*
18. Ibid.
19. Engels, "Introduction," *Supplement by Frederick Engels,* Vol. 3 of *Das Kapital.*
20. Marx, "The Role of Credit in Capitalist Production," Chap. 27 in *The Process of Capitalist Production as a Whole,* Vol. 3 of *Das Kapital.*
21. Ibid.
22. Ibid.
23. Marx, "Competition (continued)," in "Section Two: The Circulation Process of Capital, The Chapter on Capital," *The Grundrisse.*
24. Marx, "Interest and Profit of Enterprise," Chap. 23 in *The Process of Capitalist Production as a Whole,* Vol. 3 of *Das Kapital.*

25. Marx, "The Role of Credit in Capitalist Production," Chap. 27 in *The Process of Capitalist Production as a Whole*, Vol. 3 of *Das Kapital*.
26. Ibid.
27. Marx, "Historical Tendency of Capitalist Accumulation," Chap. 32 in *The Process of Capitalist Production as a Whole*, Vol. 1 of *Das Kapital*.
28. Marx, "Commodities," Chap. 1 in *The Process of Capitalist Production as a Whole*, Vol. 1 of *Das Kapital*.
29. Marx, "Letter from Marx to Engels on April 2, 1858," *Marx-Engels Correspondence 1858*.
30. Marx, "The Role of Credit in Capitalist Production," Chap. 27 in *The Process of Capitalist Production as a Whole*, Vol. 3 of *Das Kapital*.
31. Ibid.
32. Shares in companies based in mainland China that trade on either the Shanghai or Shenzhen stock exchanges. B Shares are eligible for foreign investment provided the investment account is in the proper currency (Shanghai B shares trade in U.S. dollars, while Shenzhen B-shares trade in Hong Kong dollars).

Chapter 4

1. Lenin, "The Immediate Tasks of the Soviet Government," *Lenin's Collected Works*, Vol. 27.
2. Lenin, "The Economic Basis of the Withering Away of the State," Chap. 5 in *The State and Revolution*, *Lenin's Collected Works*, Vol. 25;

   Lenin, "Supplementary Explanations by Engels," Chap. 4 in *The State and Revolution*, *Lenin's Collected Works*, Vol. 25.
3. Stalin, "Industrialization of the country and the Right Deviation in the CPSU (B.)," Works, Vol. 11, 255–302.
4. Stalin, "2. Commodity Production under Socialism," *Economic Problems of the USSR*.
5. Ibid.
6. Mao Zedong, "Critique of Stalin's Economic Problems of Socialism in the USSR," *Selected Works of Mao Tse-tung*, Vol. 8.
7. Stalin, "2. Commodity Production under Socialism," *Economic Problems of the USSR*.
8. Mao Zedong, "Critique of Stalin's Economic Problems of Socialism in the USSR," *Selected Works of Mao Tse-tung*, Vol. 8.
9. Hoover, Inaugural Addresses.
10. Mao Zedong, "On the Draft Constitution of the People's Republic of China," *Selected Works of Mao Tse-tung*, Vol. 5.
11. Xiang Huaicheng, *Fifty Years of China's Finance*.
12. At that time, the planning department left out the following 10 projects from the fixed-asset investment: 1. equipment rebuilding; 2. housing renovation and relocation; 3. water conservancy projects and the refurbishment of embankments and reservoirs; 4. oilfield maintenance; 5. expansion projects of the extractive and logging industry; 6. municipal engineering maintenance; 7. railway overhaul and water damage repair; 8. fairway, road, and bridge maintenance; 9. the construction of simple warehouse sheds by commercial, food, and supply and marketing departments with simple construction funds; 10. the construction or purchase of a single piece of equipment or an individual project of fixed assets below RMB50,000.
13. The 5 exclusions include: 1. The construction of elementary and secondary schools by the stand-by financial resources of local governments and enterprises or extra-budgetary funds; 2. the construction of hospitals, health centers, cultural centers, sports centers, libraries, and museums of or below the county level by the stand-by financial resources of county governments or extra-budgetary funds; 3. Highway expansion with the toll for highway maintenance; 4. the construction or expansion of urban highways and

the purchase of new public transportation vehicles with the city maintenance and construction funds; 5. the arrangement of the employee dormitory by long-established enterprises by their own funds.

14. Namely, a secure job, stable pay, and a guaranteed leading post.
15. Jiang Zemin, *15th Party Congress Report.*
16. "Three attributes": Safety, principle, and efficiency. "Four-self": Self-management, self-financing, risk self-retention, and self-balancing.

Chapter 5

1. Marx, "Introduction," Chap. 18 in *The Process of Circulation of Capital,* Vol. 2 of *Das Kapital.*
2. Marx, "The Turnover of Variable Capital," Chap. 16 in *The Process of Circulation of Capital,* Vol. 2 of *Das Kapital.*
3. Marx, "Letter from Marx to Engels on August 20, 1862," *Marx-Engels Correspondence 1862.*
4. Engels, "Letter from Engels to Marx on September 9, 1862," *Marx-Engels Correspondence 1862.*
5. Marx, "Letter from Marx to Engels on August 24, 1867," *Marx-Engels Correspondence 1867.*
6. Engels, "Letter from Engels to Marx on August 26, 1867," *Marx-Engels Correspondence 1867.*
7. Engels, "Letter from Engels to Marx on August 27, 1867," *Marx-Engels Correspondence 1867.*
8. Marx, "12. The Social Essence of Malthus's Polemic against Ricardo. Malthus's Distortion of Sismondi's Views on the Contradictions in Bourgeois Production," in "Thomas Robert Malthus," Chap. 19 in *Theories of Surplus Value,* Vol. 4 of *Das Kapital.*
9. Marx, "15. Malthus's Principles Expounded in the Anonymous 'Outlines of Political Economy'," in "Thomas Robert Malthus," Chap. 19 in *Theories of Surplus Value,* Vol. 4 of *Das Kapital.*
10. Ibid.
11. Marx, "3. Necessary Conditions for the Accumulation of Capital. Amortization of Fixed Capital and Its Role in the Process of Accumulation," in "Ricardo's Theory of Accumulation and a Critique of it," Chap. 17 in *Theories of Surplus Value,* Vol. 4 of *Das Kapital.*
12. Marx, "4. The Connection between Different Branches of Production in the Process of Accumulation. The Direct Transformation of a Part of Surplus-Value into Constant Capital — a Characteristic Peculiar to Accumulation in Agriculture and the Machine-building Industry," in "Ricardo's Theory of Accumulation and a Critique of it," Chap. 17 in *Theories of Surplus Value,* Vol. 4 of *Das Kapital.*
13. Economics Institute of the Academy of Sciences of the U.S.S.R.,"Socialist Accumulation. Accumulation and Consumption in Socialist Society," in "Socialist Reproduction," Chap. 39 in *Political Economy.*
14. Marx, "Simple Reproduction," Chap. 20 in *The Process of Circulation of Capital,* Vol. 2 of *Das Kapital.*

Chapter 6

1. Build–operate–transfer (BOT) is a form of project financing, wherein government and contractors cooperate to undertake infrastructure projects. The operation mode is specifically as follows: A government grants the concession of an infrastructure project, such as the construction of roads, bridges, and quays, to a contractor (usually an international consortium). The contractor is responsible for the project design, financing, construction, and operation during the concession period. At the same time, the contractor also has to recover the costs, repay loans, and earn a profit. The infrastructure project will be transferred to the government at the end of the concession period.

Chapter 7

1. Stanley and Girth, *Bankruptcy: Problem, Process, Reform.*

References

Preface

English materials:

Associated Press. "Wall Street will play less dominant role." *The Economic Times*, May 3, 2009. http://articles.economictimes.indiatimes.com/2009-05-03/news/27638276_1_financial-sector-risk-taking-president-barack-obama.

Dow Jones Newswires. "Greenspan Repeats His Opposition to More Regulation of Derivatives." Berkman Center for Internet and Society of Harvard University, March 19, 1999. http://cyber.law.harvard.edu/rfi/press/opposition.htm.

Engels, Friedrich. *Anti-Dühring*. Vol. 3 of *Marx and Engels Collected Works*. Beijing: People's Publishing House, 1972.

Jones, Athena. "Obama talks about financial regulations." *NBC News*, February 25, 2009. http://firstread.nbcnews.com/_news/2009/02/25/4432813-obama-talks-about-financial-regulations?lite.

Marx, Karl. *Manifesto of the Communist Party*. Moscow: Progress Publishers, 1848. http://www.marxists.org/archive/marx/works/1848/communist-manifesto/ (accessed April 15, 2013).

———. *Marx and Engels Correspondence 1879*. New York: International Publishers, 1968. http://www.marxists.org/archive/marx/works/1879/letters/.

———. *The Process of Capitalist Production as a Whole*. Vol. 3 of *Das Kapital*. New York: International Publishers, 1894. http://www.marxists.org/archive/marx/works/1894-c3/.

———. *Theories of Surplus Value*. Vol.4 of *Das Kapital*. Moscow: Progress Publishers, 1863. http://www.marxists.org/archive/marx/works/1863/theories-surplus-value/.

Qian Yingyi, Bai Chongen, and Xie Changtai. "The Return to Capital in China." *Brookings Papers on Economic Activity*, Economic Studies Program, The Brookings Institution, vol. 37, 2 (2006).

Zuckerman, Sam. "Greenspan Shocked at Failure of Free Markets." *San Francisco Chronicle*, October 24, 2008. http://www.sfgate.com/business/article/Greenspan-shocked-at-failure-of-free-markets-3188694.php#ixzz2Q2plvoiO (accessed April 10, 2013).

References

Chinese materials:

Chen Yun 陳雲. "Jianshe guimo yao he guoli xiang shiying" 建設規模要和國力相適應 (Construction Scale Should Comply With National Power). *Xinhua Net*, January 18, 1957. http://news.xinhuanet.com/ziliao/2005-01/05/content_2418623.htm (accessed April 22, 2013.

China Securities News. "Liu Mingkang tan jinrong chuangxin, gaojie yinhang tichu sange 'jianjue fandui' " 劉明康談金融創新 告誡銀行提出三個"堅決反對" (Liu Mingkang Talked about Financial Innovation and Warned Banks with Three "Resolute Oppositions"). *Xinhua Net*, April 24, 2009. http://news.xinhuanet.com/fortune/2009-04/24/content_11246764.htm (accessed April 10, 2013).

Sheng Songcheng 盛松成. "Shehui rongzi zongliang de neihan ji shijian yiyi" 社會融資總量的內涵及實踐意義 (The Implication and Practical Significance of Aggregate Social Financing). Website of the People's Bank of China, February 17, 2011. http://www.pbc.gov.cn/publish/diaochatongjisi/866/2011/20110217180043605992604/20110217180043605992604_.html.

Zhao Xiao 趙曉. "Dangqian Zhongguo xuyao shenmeyang de hongguan tiaokong" 當前中國需要什麼樣的巨集觀調控 (What Kind of Macroeconomic Control Does China Need). *Zhao Xiao Sohu Blog*. http://zhaoxiao.i.sohu.com/blog/view/37415865.htm.

Translated materials:

Deng Xiaoping 鄧小平. "Women gan de shiye shi quanxin de shiye" 我們干的事業是全新的事業 (We Are Taking an Entirely New Endeavor), October 13, 1987. *Deng Xiaoping wenxuan* 鄧小平文選 (Selected Works of Deng Xiaoping), Vol.3. Website of *People's Daily*. http://english.peopledaily.com.cn/dengxp/vol3/text/c1810.html (accessed April 15, 2013).

———. "Yixinyiyi gao jianshe" 一心一意搞建設 (We Shall Concentrate on Economic Development), September 18, 1982. *Deng Xiaoping wenxuan* 鄧小平文選 (Selected Works of Deng Xiaoping), Vol.3. Website of *People's Daily*. http://english.peopledaily.com.cn/dengxp/vol3/text/c1030.html (accessed April 15, 2013).

———. "Xiqu lishi jingyan, fangzhi cuowu qingxiang" 吸取歷史經驗 防止錯誤傾向 (We Shall Draw on Historical Experience), April 30, 1987. *Deng Xiaoping wenxuan* 鄧小平文選 (Selected Works of Deng Xiaoping), Vol.3. Website of *People's Daily*. http://english.peopledaily.com.cn/dengxp/vol3/text/c1730.html (accessed April 15, 2013).

Greenspan, Alan. "We Need a Better Cushion against Risk." *Financial Times*, March 26, 2009.
http://www.ft.com/intl/cms/s/0/9c158a92-1a3c-11de-9f91-0000779fd2ac.html#axzz2Q28EBxP9 (accessed April 10, 2013).

Hu Jintao 胡錦濤. "*Zhongguo gongchandang Shiqi ci quanguo daibiao dahui baogao*" 中國共產黨十七次全國代表大會報告 (17th Party Congress Report). Report presented at the 17th National Congress of the Communist Party of China, October 24, 2007.
http://news.xinhuanet.com/english/2007-10/24/content_6938749_7.htm.

Jiang Zemin 江澤民. "*Zhongguo gongchandang Shiliu ci quanguo daibiao dahui baogao*" 中國共產黨十六次全國代表大會報告 (16th Party Congress Report). Report presented at the 16th National Congress of the Communist Party of China, July 10, 2007.
http://www.chinadaily.com.cn/china/2007-07/10/content_6142007.htm.

Introduction

English materials:

Greenspan, Alan. "Equities Show Us the Way to Recovery." *Financial Times*. March 29, 2009.

———. "We Need a Better Cushion Against Risk." *Financial Times*. March 26, 2009.

Marx, Karl. *Shengyu jiazhi lilun* 剩餘價值理論 (Theories of Surplus Value). Trans. and eds. Central Compilation and Translation Bureau for Works of Marx, Engels, Lenin, and Stalin. Beijing: People's Publishing House, 1975.

———. *Ziben lun* 資本論 (Das Kapital). Trans. and eds. Central Compilation and Translation Bureau for Works of Marx, Engels, Lenin and Stalin. Beijing: People's Publishing House, 2004.

Chinese materials:

Ba Shusong 巴曙松. "Cidai weiji de genyuan" 次貸危機的根源 (The Root Causes of the Subprime Crisis). *China Macroeconomic Information Network*, April 10, 2009.

Bai Chongen 白重恩, Xiechang Tai 謝長泰, and Qian Yingyi 錢穎一. *Zhongguo de ziben huibaolü* 中國的資本回報率 (Return on Capital in China). Beijing: CITIC Publishing House, 2007.

Cao Erjie 曹爾階. "Rang laodongzhe chengwei youchanzhe" 讓勞動者成為有產者 (Turn Workers into Men of Property). *Guoji hangkong bao* 國際航空報 (International Aviation News), April 17, 2000.

Chen Huai 陳淮. "Fangdi chanye fazhan yu zhongguo guoqing" 房地產業發展與中國國情 (Real Estate Development and China's National Conditions). *Zhongguo Jingji shibao* 中國經濟時報 (China Economic Times), February 23, 2009.

Deng Xiaoping 鄧小平. *Deng Xiaoping wenxuan* 鄧小平文選 (Selected Works of Deng Xiaoping). Beijing: People's Publishing House, 1993.

Fan Gang 樊綱. "Weiji jiuzai nail, ni zenme keneng bu shou yingxiang?" 危機就在那裡 你怎麼可能不受影響 (Crisis Is Right There, How Could You Not Be Affected?). Speeches made in the International Convention Center of National Accounting Institute, April 11, 2009.

———. "Zhongguo yao dali fazhan zhonghua gongye" 中國要大力發展重化工業 (China Should Vigorously Develop the Heavy and Chemical Industries). *21 shiji jingji baodao* 21世紀經濟報導 (21st Century Business Herald), August 27, 2005.

Research Group of the Subprime Mortgage Crisis. *Cidai fengbo qishilu* 次貸風波啟示錄 (Revelation of Subprime Mortgage Crisis). Beijing: China Financial Publishing House, 2008.

Sheng Songcheng 盛松成. "Shehui rongzi zongliang de neihan ji shijian yiyi" 社會融資總量的內涵及實踐意義 (The Implication and Practical Significance of Aggregate Social Financing). Website of People's Bank of China, February 17, 2011.

Song Guoqing 宋國青. "Zhongguo touzilü taidi" 中國投資率太低 (China's Investment Rate Is Too Low). *21 shiji jingji baodao* 21世紀經濟報導 (21st Century Business Herald), August 29, 2006.

Song Hongbing 宋鴻兵. *Huobi zhanzheng* 貨幣戰爭 (Currency War). Beijing: CITIC Publishing House, 2007.

Tang Shisheng 湯世生. "Cong Meiguo ciji zhai wenti kan Zhongguo jinrong chuangxin zhi lu" 從美國次級債問題看中國金融創新之路 (To Find a Road for China's Financial Innovation by Learning from the U.S. Subprime Debt Crisis). *Dangdai jinrongjia* 當代金融家 (Modern Bankers), (3) (2008).

The Chinese Academy of Social Sciences. *Chengshi lanpishu: Zhongguo chengshi fazhan baogao* 城市藍皮書:中國城市發展報告 (Blue Book of Cities in China: Annual Report on Urban Development of China). Beijing: Social Sciences Academic Press, 2009.

Wang Jian 王建. "Lun zouchu digu de weiyi daolu shi chengshihua" 論走出低谷的唯一道路是城市化 (The Only Way Out of China's Economic Downturn Is Urbanization). *China Macroeconomic Information Network*, April 16, 2009.

"Woguo gengdi zongshu jiejin 18 yi mu hongxian, kongzhi mianji chaoguo 1 yi mu" 我國耕地總數接近18億畝紅線 空置面積超1億畝 (The Total Arable Land in China Is Close to the Warning Line of 1.8 Billion *Mu*, and Idle Rural Land Has Surpassed 100 Million *Mu*). *Banyuetan* 半月談 (China Comment), February 17, 2011.

Xin Qiaoli 辛喬利, and Sun Zhaodong 孫兆東. *Cidai weiji* 次貸危機 (Subprime Crisis). Beijing: China Economic Publishing House, 2008.

Xu Xiaonian 許小年. "Jinrong gaige he touzi yinhang de fazhan" 金融改革和投資銀行的發展 (Financial Reform and the Development of Investment Banks). Website of Renmin University of China News, April 9, 2003.

Zhang Weiying 張維迎. "Lijie he hanwei shichang jingji" 理解和捍衛市場經濟 (Understand and Defend the Market Economy). *China Economic Net*, December 23, 2007.

Zhaobing Xian 趙炳賢. *Ziben yunying lun* 資本運營論 (Theory of Capital Operation). Beijing: Enterprise Management Publishing House, 1997.

Zheng Xinli 鄭新立. "Wu da xiaofei redian jiang tuidong weilai Zhongguo jingji" 五大消費熱點將推動未來中國經濟 (Five Growth Points in Consumption Will Drive Forward China's Economy). *Sina News*, August 26, 2003. http://news.sina.com.cn/c/2003-08-26/0349636034s.shtml (accessed March 26, 2013).

Zhong Wei 鐘偉. "Cong cidai weiji kan jinrong lilun he shijian de kunhuo" 從次貸危機看金融理論和實踐的困惑 (The Confusions in Financial Theories and Practice Judging from the Subprime Mortgage Crisis). *Nanfang zhoumo* 南方週末 (Southern Weekly), April 27, 2009.

Zhu Xiaohuang 朱小黃. "Cidai weiji: Huoqi ganggan shikong" 次貸危機:禍起杠杆失控 (Subprime Mortgage Crisis: Result from Out-of-Control Leverage). *Fengxian guanli cankao* 風險管理參考 (Risk Management Reference), (10) (2008).

Translated materials:

Roach, Stephen. "Meiguo shiheng yu zhongguo wuguan" 美國失衡與中國無關 (America's Inflated Asset Prices Must Fall). *FT Chinese Website*, January 15, 2008.

Chapter 1

English materials:

Marx, Karl and Engels, Frederick. *Letters of Karl Marx and Frederick Engels for the 1860s*. http://www.marxists.org/archive/marx/letters/date/1860s.htm.

Marx, Karl. *The Process of Capitalist Production as a Whole*. Vol. 3 of *Das Kapital*. New York: International Publishers, 1894. http://www.marxists.org/archive/marx/works/1894-c3/.

———. *Theories of Surplus Value*. Vol.4 of *Das Kapital*. Moscow: Progress Publishers, 1863. http://www.marxists.org/archive/marx/works/1863/theories-surplus-value/.

Chinese materials:

Cao Erjie 曹爾階. "Tuokuan ziben xingcheng jizhi chuangxin de huodong kongjian" 拓寬資本形成創新的活動空間 (Enlarging the Space for Capital Formation and Innovation). *Financial Times*, May 2006.

Translated materials:

Adda, Jacques. *Jingji quan quanqiuhu* 經濟全球化 (The Globalization of Economy). Trans. He Jing and Zhou Xiaoxing. Beijing: Central Compilation & Translation Press, 2001.

Chesnais, François. *Jinrong quanqiuhua* 金融全球化 (The Globalization of Finance). Trans. Qi Jianhua and Hu Zhenliang. Beijing: Central Compilation and Translation Press, 2006.

———. *Ziben quanqiuhua* 資本全球化 (The Globalization of Capital). Trans. Qi Jianhua. Beijing: Central Compilation & Translation Press, 2001.

Martin, Peter N. and Hollnagel, Bruno. *Zhiben zhanzheng* 資本戰爭 (Capital War / Die großen Spekulationen der Weltgeschichte). Trans. Wang Yinhao. Tianjin: Tianjin Education Press, 2008.

Marx, Karl. *Ziben lun*資本論 (Das Kapital). Beijing: People's Publishing House, 2004.

Mishkin, Frederick. *Xia yi lun weida de quanqiuhu*下一輪偉大的全球化 (The Next Great Globalization). Trans. Jian Shiming. Beijing: CITIC Publishing House, 2007.

Sachs, Jeffery. *Pinqiong de zhongjie* 貧窮的終結 (The End of Poverty). Shanghai: Shanghai People's Publishing House, 2007.

Chapter 2

English materials:

Engels, Friedrich. *Anti-Dühring*. Vol. 3 of *Marx and Engels Collected Works*. Beijing: People's Publishing House, 1972.

———. Preface to *The Process of Circulation of Capital*. Vol. 2 of *Das Kapital*. Moscow: Progress Publishers, 1885. http://www.marxists.org/archive/marx/works/1885-c2/index.htm.

Marx, Karl and Engels, Frederick. "Bourgeois and Proletarians." Chap 1 in *The Communist Manifesto*. Moscow: Progress Publishers, 1848. http://www.marxists.org/archive/marx/letters/date/1860s.htm.

Marx, Karl. *Critique of the Gotha Program*. Vol. 3 of *Marx and Engels Collected Works*. Beijing: People's Publishing House, 1972.

———. *The Process of Capitalist Production as a Whole*. Vol. 3 of *Das Kapital*. New York: International Publishers, 1894. http://www.marxists.org/archive/marx/works/1894-c3/.

———. *The Process of Circulation of Capital*. Vol. 1 of *Das Kapital*. Moscow: Progress Publishers, 1887. http://www.marxists.org/archive/marx/works/1867-c1/index.htm.

———. *Theories of Surplus Value*. Vol.4 of *Das Kapital*. Moscow: Progress Publishers, 1863. http://www.marxists.org/archive/marx/works/1863/theories-surplus-value/.

Chinese materials:

Cao Erjie 曹爾階. "Ziben wenti yiersan" 資本問題一二三 (One Two Three: Questions on Capital). *Touzi yanjiu* 投資研究 (Investment Studies), (2) (1998).

Feng Zibiao 馮子標 et al. *"Shehui zhuyi ziben" huigu yu yanjiu* "社會主義資本"回顧與研究 (Review and Research of Socialist Capital). Beijing: Economic Science Press, 2000.

Mao Yushi 茅於軾. *Guofu guoqiong: Zhidu he zhongguo de jingji gaige* 國富國窮:制度和中國的經濟改革 (The Wealth and Poverty of Nations: System and China's Economic Reform). Website of TECN, January 7, 2008.

Zeng Kanglin 曾康霖. *Zijin lun* 資金論 (On Capital). Beijing: China Financial Publishing House, 1990.

Zhang Duan 張端. "Shehui ziben" chulun 社會資本初論 (Preliminary Discussion on Social Capital). *Touzi yanjiu* 投資研究 (Investment Research), (7) (1995).

Zhou Youguang 周有光. "Huigu ziben zhuyi shiqi" 回顧資本主義時期 (Looking Back on the Capitalist Age). *Zhou Youguang banshui xingao* 周有光百歲新稿 (New Writings of a Hundred Year-Old Man).Beijing: People's Publishing House, 2005.

Translated materials:

Marx, Karl. *Ziben lun* 資本論 (Das Kapital). Trans. Central Compilation and Translation Bureau for Works of Marx, Engels, Lenin and Stalin. Beijing: People's Publishing House, 2004.

Chapter 3

English materials:

Engels, Frederick. *Supplement by Frederick Engels*. Vol. 3 of *Das Kapital*. New York: International Publishers, 1894. http://www.marxists.org/archive/marx/works/1894-c3/supp.htm#intro.

———. *The Process of Circulation of Capital*. Vol. 2 of *Das Kapital*. Moscow: Progress Publishers, 1885. http://www.marxists.org/archive/marx/works/1885-c2/index.htm.

Marx, Karl and Engels, Friedrich. *Marx-Engels Correspondence 1858*. http://www.marxists.org/archive/marx/works/1858/letters/.

Marx, Karl. *Letter from Marx to Nikolai Danielson in St. Petersburg (April 10, 1879)*. *Marx and Engels Correspondence*. New York: International Publishers, 1968. http://www.marxists.org/archive/marx/works/1879/letters/79_04_10.htm.

———. *The Grundrisse*. http://www.marxists.org/archive/marx/works/1857/grundrisse/ch10.htm;

———. *The Process of Capitalist Production as a Whole*. Vol. 3 of *Das Kapital*. New York: International Publishers, 1894. http://www.marxists.org/archive/marx/works/1894-c3/.

———. *The Process of Circulation of Capital*. Vol. 1 of *Das Kapital*. Moscow: Progress Publishers, 1887. http://www.marxists.org/archive/marx/works/1867-c1/index.htm.

Vygodsky, Vitaly. *The Story of a Great Discovery*, 1965. http://www.marxists.org/archive/vygodsky/1965/ch8.htm.

Chinese materials:

Cao Erjie 曹爾階. *Zhongguo zhengquan shichang yanjiu yu zhanwang* 中國證券市場研究與展望 (The Research and Outlook of China's Securities Market). Beijing: China Financial and Economic Publishing House, 1993.

Cao Fengqi 曹鳳岐. *Zhongguo qiye gufenzhi de lilun yu shijian* 中國企業股份制的理論與實踐 (Theory and Practice of the Sharing System in China). Beijing: Enterprise Management Publishing House, 1989.

Liu Hongru 劉鴻儒. "Guanyu woguo shixing gufenzhi de jige wenti" 關於我國試行股份制的幾個問題 (Several Questions on the Pilots of a Joint-Stock System). *People's Daily*, June 23, 1992.

Translated materials:

Deng Xiaoping 鄧小平. *Deng Xiaoping wenxuan* 鄧小平文選 (Selected Works of Deng Xiaoping), Vol. 3. Website of University of Mississippi, http://www.olemiss.edu/courses/pol324/dengxp92.htm (accessed April 26, 2013).

Mao Zedong 毛澤東. "Pipan likai zong luxian de youqin guandian" 批判離開總路線的右傾觀點 (Refute Right Deviationist Views That Depart from the General Line). Speech delivered on June 15, 1953. *Mao Zedong xuanji* 毛澤東選集 (Selected Works of Mao Tse-tung), Vol. 5. http://www.marxists.org/reference/archive/mao/selected-works/volume-5/mswv5_28.htm.

Marx, Karl. *Ziben lun* 資本論 (Das Kapital). Trans. and eds. Central Compilation and Translation Bureau for Works of Marx, Engels, Lenin and Stalin. Beijing: People's Publishing House, 2004.

Chapter 4

English materials:

Hoover, Herbert. Inaugural Addresses, delivered on March 4, 1929. http://www.bartleby.com/124/pres48.html.

Lenin, V. I. *Lenin's Collected Works*. http://www.marxists.org/archive/lenin/works/cw/index.htm

Stalin, J. V. "Industrialization of the country and the Right Deviation in the CPSU (B.)." Speech delivered at the Plenum of the C.P.S.U.(B.) on November 19, 1928. *Works*, Vol. 11. Moscow: Foreign Languages Publishing House, 1954. http://www.marx2mao.com/Stalin/ICRD28.html.

Stalin, J. V. *Economic Problems of the USSR*. Beijing: Foreign Language Press, 1972. http://www.marxists.org/reference/archive/stalin/works/1951/economic-problems/ch03.htm.

Chinese materials:

Bai Hejin, et al. 白和金 等. *Jingji Zhongguo* 經濟中國 (China's Economy). Beijing: China Financial and Economic Publishing House, 1998.

Bian Hongdeng 卞洪登. *Ziben yunyin fanglue* 資本運營方略 (Capital Operation Strategy). Beijing: China Reform Publishing House, 1997.

Bo Yibo 薄一波. *Ruogan zhongda juece yu shijian de huigui* 若干重大決策與事件的回顧 (Reviews on Several Major Decisions and Events). Beijing: CPC Central

Party School Publishing House, 1991.

Cao Erjie, et al. 曹爾階 等. *Xin Zhongguo touzi shigang* 新中國投資史綱 (Investment History of New China). Beijing: China Financial and Economic Publishing House, 1992.

Ding Bing 丁冰. "Xin Zhongguo gongye jianshe, liushi nian zhujiu huihuang" 新中國工業建設 六十年鑄就輝煌 (Industrial Construction of New China Obtains Splendid Achievements in Sixty Years). *Hongqi Wengao* 紅旗文稿 (Red Flag Manuscripts), October 27, 2009.

Fang Ning 房寧. *Shehui zhuyi shi yizhong hexie* 社會主義是一種和諧 (Socialism Is a Kind of Harmony). Beijing: China Social Science Press, 2007.

Jia Kang 賈康. "Zhongguo caizheng gaige sanshi nian de lujing yu mailuo" 中國財政改革30年的路徑與脈絡 (Thirty-Year Reform of China's Finance). *Jingji yanjiu cankao* 經濟研究參考 (Review of Economic Research), February 6, 2009.

Jiang Yiwei 蔣一葦. *Wo de jingji gaige guan* 我的經濟改革觀 (My Ideas on Economic Reform). Beijing: Economy and Management Publishing House, 1993.

Li Rongrong 李榮融. "Guoyou qiye gaige zai xin de qidian shang wen bu tuijin" 國有企業改革在新的起點上穩步推進 (To Steadily Promote the State-Owned Enterprises Reform on a New Start). *Qiushi* 求是 (Seeking Truth), August 2007.

Li Rui 李銳. *Mao Zedong de zaonian yu wannian* 毛澤東的早年與晚年 (Mao Zedong in His Early and Later Years). Guiyang: Guizhou People's Publishing House, 1992.

Liu Xuyi 劉緒貽 and Yang Shengmao 楊生茂. *Fu lan ke lin D. luo sifu shidai* 佛蘭克林·D·羅斯福時代 (The Age of Franklin D. Roosevelt [1929–1945]). Beijing: People's Publishing House, 1994.

Lü Zongsu 呂宗恕. "Chu Shijian shoushen" 褚時健受審 (The Trial of Chu Shijian). *Xin Jingbao* 新京報 (The Beijing News), January 3, 2009.

Peng Jianguo 彭建國. "Zhongguo qiye gaige sanshi nian huishou" 中國企業改革三十年回首 (Thirty-Year Review of China's Corporate Reform). *Zhongguo xiangzhen qiye* 中國鄉鎮企業 (China Township Enterprises), (12) (2008).

Qin Hui 秦暉. "Zhongguo qiji de xingcheng yu weilai, gaige sanshi nian zhi wo jian" 中國奇跡的形成與未來 改革三十年之我見 (The Formation and Future of the China Miracle, My Views on the 30-Year Reform). *Nanfang zhoumo* 南方週末 (Southern Weekly), February 21, 2008.

Sun Yefang 孫冶方. *Shehui zhuyi jingji de ruogan lilun wenti* 社會主義經濟的若干理論問題 (Several Theoretical Problems on Socialist Economy). Beijing: People's Publishing House, 1982.

Wu Jinglian 吳敬璉. *Lun jingzheng xing shichang tizhi* 論競爭性市場體制 (On Competitive Market System). Beijing: China Financial and Economic Publishing House, 1991.

Xiang Huaicheng 項懷誠. *Zhongguo caizheng wushi nian* 中國財政50年 (Fifty Years of China's Finance). Beijing: China Financial and Economic Publishing House, 1999.

Xue Muqiao 薛暮橋. *Lun jingji tizhi gaige* 論經濟體制改革 (On Economic Reform). Beijing: People's Publishing House, 1990.

———. *Zhongguo shehui zhuyi jingji wenti yanjiu* 中國社會主義經濟問題研究 (Research on China's Socialist Economic Issues). Beijing: People's Publishing House, 1979.

Yang Jishen 楊繼繩. Deng Xiaoping shidai 鄧小平時代 (The Era of Deng Xiaoping). Beijing: Central Compilation and Translation Press, 1998.

Zhang Dicheng 章迪誠. "Guoqi gaige sanshi nian, shishi zhua da fang xiao zhanlue" 國企改革三十年 實施抓大放小戰略 (Thirty-Year Reform of State-Owned Enterprises, Implementation of the Policy of Invigorate Large Enterprises While Relaxing Control Over Small Ones). *China Industry News Net*, November 26, 2008.

Zhang Weiying 張維迎. *Zhongguo gaige sanshi nian* 中國改革30年 (Thirty Years of China's Reform). Shanghai: Shanghai People's Publishing House, 2008.

Zhang Zuoyuan 張卓元. "Cong Bainian ji ruo dao jingji daguo de kuayue" 從百年積弱到經濟大國的跨越 (Development from a Weak Country to an Economic Superpower). *Guangming ribao* 光明日報 (Guangming Daily), August 27, 2009.

Translated materials:

Jiang Zemin 江澤民. "*Zhongguo gongchandang Shiwu ci quanguo daibiao dahui baogao*" 中國共產黨十五次全國代表大會報告 (15th Party Congress Report). Report presented at the 15th National Congress of the Communist Party of China, September 12, 1997. http://www.fas.org/news/china/1997/970912-prc.htm.

Keynes, John Maynard. *Jiuye lixi he huobi tonglun* 就業利息和貨幣通論 (The General Theory of Employment, Interest, and Money). Trans. Shang Hongye 商鴻業. Beijing: Commercial Press, 1963.

Krugman, Paul R. *Meiguo zenme le*? 美國怎麼了 (The Conscience of a Liberal). Trans. Liu Bo. Beijing: CITIC Publishing House, 2008.

Mao Zedong 毛澤東. "Du sidalin 'sulian shehui zhuyi jingji wenti' pizhu" 讀史達林 蘇聯社會主義經濟問題 批註 (Critique of Stalin's Economic Problems of

Socialism in the USSR). *Mao Zedong xuanji* 毛澤東選集 (Selected Works of Mao Tse-tung), Vol.8. http://www.marxists.org/reference/archive/mao/selected-works/volume-8/mswv8_66.htm.

Mao Zedong 毛澤東. "Guanyu Zhonghua renmin gongheguo xianfa caoan" 關於中華人民共和國憲法草案 (On the Draft Constitution of the People's Republic of China). *Mao Zedong xuanji* 毛澤東選集 (Selected Works of Mao Tse-tung), Vol. 5. http://www.marxists.org/reference/archive/mao/selected-works/volume-5/mswv5_37.htm

Ohmae Kenichi. *M xin shehui* M型社會 (M-Shape Society). Trans. Liu Jinxiu 劉錦秀 and Jiang Yuzhen 江裕真. Beijing: CITIC Publishing House, 2007.

Chapter 5

English materials:

Economics Institute of the Academy of Sciences of the U.S.S.R. *Political Economy*. London: Lawrence and Wishart, 1957.

Marx, Karl and Engels, Friedrich. *Marx-Engels Correspondence 1862*. http://www.marxists.org/archive/marx/works/1862/letters/.

———. *Marx-Engels Correspondence 1867*. http://www.marxists.org/archive/marx/works/1867/letters/

Marx, Karl. *The Process of Circulation of Capital*. Vol. 2 of *Das Kapital*. Moscow: Progress Publishers, 1956. http://www.marxists.org/archive/marx/works/1885-c2/index.htm.

———. *Theories of Surplus Value*. Vol. 4 of *Das Kapital*. http://www.marxists.org/archive/marx/works/1863/theories-surplus-value/

Chinese materials:

Cao Erjie 曹爾階. "Chanpin gengxin huandai yu guding zichan zai shengchan" 產品更新換代與固定資產再生產 (Product Updates and Reproduction of Fixed-Assets). *Jingji yanjiu* 經濟研究 (Economic Research Journal), (10) (1984).

———. "Guding zichan zai shengchan he xin de wuxing sunhao" 固定資產再生產和新的無形損耗 (Reproduction of Fixed-Assets and New Moral Depreciation). *Caizheng yanjiu* 財政研究 (Public Finance Research), (5) (1986).

Liu Guoguang 劉國光. *Shehui zhuyi zaishengchan wenti* 社會主義再生產問題 (Socialist Reproduction). Beijing: Joint Publishing, 1980.

Tian Chunsheng 田椿生 and Liu Huiyong 劉慧勇. *Lun zhejiu* 論折舊 (On Depreciation). Beijing: China Financial and Economic Publishing House, 1986.

Translated materials:

Davidson, Sidney. *Xiandai kuaiji shouce* 現代會計手冊 (Handbook of Modern Accounting). Trans. Yang jiwan et al. 楊紀婉 等. Beijing: China Financial and Economic Publishing House, 1982.

Marx, Karl. *Shengyu jiazhi lilun* 剩餘價值理論 (Theories of Surplus Value). Trans. and eds. Central Compilation and Translation Bureau for Works of Marx, Engels, Lenin and Stalin. Beijing: People's Publishing House, 1975.

Chapter 6

Chinese materials:

Dong Yuxiao 董欲曉, and Zhang Man 張曼. Jinrong zulin zai kuorong 金融租賃再擴容 (Re-expansion of Financial Leasing). *Caijing* 財經 (Finance), (10) (2010).

Qu Yankai 屈延凱. "Rongzi zulin zai ziben shichang zhong de yingyong" 融資租賃在資本市場中的應用 (The Application of Financial Leasing in the Capital Market). Xiang cai zhengquan gaoji luntan 湘財證券高級論壇 (Xiangcai Securities High-Level Forum), July 2000.

ResearchInChina. "2010–2011 nian Zhongguo rongzi zulin hangye yanjiu" 2010–2011年中國融資租賃行業研究 (Research on China's Financial Leasing Industry 2010–2011). http://wenku.baidu.com/view/5d638246852458fb770b56ba.html (accessed July 31, 2013).

"2006 nian Zhongguo rongzi zulin hangye fenxi" 2006年中國融資租賃行業分析 (Research on China's Financial Leasing Industry 2006). *Baogao zaixian* 報告在線 (Report on line), March 23, 2007.

Chapter 7

English materials:

1. Stanley, David T., and Girth, Marjorie. *Bankruptcy: Problem, Process, Reform.* Washington, D.C.: Brookings Institution Press, 1971.

Chinese materials:

Cao Erjie 曹爾階. " 'Zhai zhuan gu' de teshu gongxian" "債轉股"的特殊貢獻 (Special Contribution of Debt-For-Equity Swaps). *Jingrong shibao* 金融時報 (Financial News), November 13, 1999.

Cao Erjie 曹爾階. " 'Zhai zhuan gu' gongbukemo" "債轉股"功不可沒 (The Important Role of Debt-For-Equity Swaps). *Beijing jingji bao* 北京經濟報 (Beijing Economic Daily), September 18, 2000.

Cao Erjie 曹爾階. " 'Zhai zhuan gu' yu jinrong zichan guanli gongsi de gongneng dingwei" "債轉股"與金融資產管理公司的功能定位 (Functions of Debt-For-Equity Swaps and Financial Assets Management Companies). *Shanghai touzi* 上海投資 (Shanghai Investment), (1) (2000).

Cao Erjie 曹爾階. " 'Zhai zhuan gu': Zhongguo chongxin renshi ziben" "債轉股": 中國重新認識資本 (Debt-For-Equity Swaps: To Rethink Capital). *Guoji hangkong bao* 國際航空報 (International Aviation News), August 23, 1999.

Cao Erjie 曹爾階. "Mo dao bu wu kan chai gong" 磨刀不誤砍柴工 (A beard well lathered is half shaved). *Beijing jingji bao* 北京經濟報 (Beijing Economic Daily), February 9, 2001.

Cao Erjie 曹爾階. "Zai tan 'zhai zhuan gu' de teshu gongxian" 再談"債轉股"的特殊貢獻 (Special Contribution of Debt-For-Equity Swaps Two). *Jingrong shibao* 金融時報 (Financial News), March 11, 2000.

Cao Erjie 曹爾階. "Zhai zhuan gu: Fei gong jingji de jinru jiyu" 債轉股:非公經濟的進入機遇 (Debt-For-Equity Swaps: Opportunities for Non-Public Economies). *Beijing jingji bao* 北京經濟報 (Beijing Economic Daily), December 12, 1999.

Cao Erjie 曹爾階. "Zican chongzu de xin jiyu" 資產重組的新機遇 (New Opportunities for Asset Restructuring). *Jingji ribao* 經濟日報 (Economic Daily News), February 19, 2001.

Wang Weiguo 王衛國. "Lun chongzheng zhidu" 論重整制度 (On Corporate Restructuring). *Faxue yanjiu* 法學研究 (Chinese Journal of Law), (1) (1996).

Zhou Xiaochuan 周小川. *Chongjian yu zaisheng* 重建與再生 (Restructuring and Rebirth). Beijing: China Financial Publishing House, 1999.

Zhou Xiaochuan 周小川. "Tan yinhang buliang zichan" 談銀行不良資產 (On Toxic Assets of Banks). Speeches presented at the Chinese Economists 50 Forum. *Zhengquan zhixin* 證券之星 (Securities Star), December 7, 2004.

Index

Index